Under the Literary Microscope

AnthropoScene
THE SLSA BOOK SERIES

Lucinda Cole and Robert Markley, General Editors

Advisory Board:
Stacy Alaimo (University of Texas at Arlington)
Ron Broglio (Arizona State University)
Carol Colatrella (Georgia Institute of Technology)
Heidi Hutner (Stony Brook University)
Stephanie LeMenager (University of Oregon)
Christopher Morris (University of Texas at Arlington)
Laura Otis (Emory University)
Will Potter (Washington, DC)
Ronald Schleifer (University of Oklahoma)
Susan Squier (Pennsylvania State University)
Rajani Sudan (Southern Methodist University)
Kari Weil (Wesleyan University)

Published in collaboration with the Society for Literature, Science, and the Arts, AnthropoScene presents books that examine relationships and points of intersection among the natural, biological, and applied sciences and the literary, visual, and performing arts. Books in the series promote new kinds of cross-disciplinary thinking arising from the idea that humans are changing the planet and its environments in radical and irreversible ways.

Under the Literary Microscope

Science and Society in the Contemporary Novel

Edited by
Sina Farzin,
Susan M. Gaines,
and Roslynn D. Haynes

The Pennsylvania
State University Press
University Park,
Pennsylvania

Library of Congress Cataloging-in-Publication Data

Names: Farzin, Sina, editor. | Gaines, Susan M., editor. | Haynes, Roslynn D. (Roslynn Doris), 1940– editor.
Title: Under the literary microscope : science and society in the contemporary novel / edited by Sina Farzin, Susan M. Gaines, and Roslynn D. Haynes.
Other titles: AnthropoScene.
Description: University Park, Pennsylvania : The Pennsylvania State University Press, [2021] | Series: AnthropoScene: the SLSA book series | Includes bibliographical references and index.
Summary: "A collection of essays examining literary discussions of the role of science, focusing on the interactions between processes of knowledge formation and the socioeconomic and political spheres"— Provided by publisher.
Identifiers: LCCN 2021001806 | ISBN 9780271089782 (cloth)
Subjects: LCSH: Science in literature. | Science in literature—Social aspects. | Science fiction—History and criticism. | LCGFT: Essays.
Classification: LCC PN3352.S34 U53 2021 | DDC 809.3/936—dc23
LC record available at https://lccn.loc.gov/2021001806

Copyright © 2021 The Pennsylvania State University
All rights reserved
Printed in the United States of America
Published by The Pennsylvania State University Press,
University Park, PA 16802-1003

The Pennsylvania State University Press is a member of the Association of University Presses.

It is the policy of The Pennsylvania State University Press to use acid-free paper. Publications on uncoated stock satisfy the minimum requirements of American National Standard for Information Sciences—Permanence of Paper for Printed Library Material, ANSI Z39.48–1992.

Contents

Acknowledgments | vii

Introduction: Science Under
the Literary Microscope | 1
Susan M. Gaines, Sina Farzin,
and Roslynn D. Haynes

Part 1 | Background and Context

1. Science and Society in Recent Fiction | 21
   Natalie Roxburgh and Jay Clayton

2. From Individual to Collective Knowledge
   Production: A Brief Nonfiction History | 37
   Peter Weingart and Luz María Hernández Nieto

3. Between Mad and Mundane:
   Mixed Stereotypical and Realistic Portrayals of
   Science in Contemporary Fiction Media | 54
   Luz María Hernández Nieto and Peter Weingart

Part 2 | Embedded Science: Societal Impacts
on Scientific Work and Knowledge

4. Scientists at Risk | 77
   Roslynn D. Haynes and Raymond Haynes

5. Speculative Fiction and the Significance
   of Plausibility: Dystopian Science in the
   Critical Response to Margaret Atwood's
   Oryx and Crake | 101
   Anna Auguscik, Sina Farzin, Emanuel Herold,
   and Anton Kirchhofer

6   When the Scientist Is a Woman:
    Novels and Feminist Science Studies | 126
    Carol Colatrella

7   Economization of Science:
    Insights from Science Novels | 148
    Uwe Schimank

    Part 3 | Cause and Effect?
    Science and Its Societal Outcomes

8   The Science Fiction of Technological
    Modernity: Images of Science
    in Recent Science Fiction | 175
    Sherryl Vint

9   Unruly Creatures, Obstinate Things: Bio-
    Objects and Scientific Knowledge Production
    in Contemporary Science Fiction | 198
    Karin Hoepker and Antje Kley

10 A Fictional Risk Narrative and Its Potential
    for Social Resonance: Reception of
    Barbara Kingsolver's *Flight Behavior*
    in Reviews and Reading Groups | 218
    Sonja Fücker, Anna Auguscik, Anton Kirchhofer,
    and Uwe Schimank

List of Contributors | 249

Index | 253

Acknowledgments

The editors are grateful to the Volkswagen Foundation, the University of Bremen, the University of Oldenburg, and the Hanse-Wissenschaftskolleg (Institute for Advanced Study, HWK) for their support of the Fiction Meets Science program. Particular thanks to Dr. Dorothe Poggel and the staff of the HWK for their graciousness and flexibility in hosting the Fiction Meets Science workshops and, in particular, Roslynn and Raymond Haynes's research stays.

Introduction
Science Under the Literary Microscope

Susan M. Gaines,
Sina Farzin, and
Roslynn D. Haynes

Over the course of the twentieth century, scientific literacy and public engagement with science became increasingly critical to socioeconomic development and democratic governance. Nearly every sphere of society in the industrialized world came to depend on scientific knowledge and technology. In democratic societies, this meant that scientific practice and knowledge production were accompanied by new forms of public awareness and debate. Media coverage of science intensified, school science curricula expanded, and scientific institutions dedicated more and more attention to science communication. In the cultural realm, nonfiction popular-science books, magazines, and TV programs flourished, as did the imaginative extrapolations of technological innovation that gave rise to the publishing category known as science fiction, or SF. In the last decade of the century, we also began to see a proliferation of novels with explicit, in-depth depictions and explorations of actual scientific research practices—both contemporary and historical—and of the lives and work-worlds of scientist characters. Ian McEwan, Richard Powers, Barbara Kingsolver, Ann Patchett, A. S. Byatt, Simon Mawer, Allegra Goodman, Joyce Carol Oates, Anthony Doerr, and Jonathan Franzen are just a few of the more well-known authors of literary fiction who have focused on scientific subjects in their novels since the 1990s.

The rising turn-of-the-millennium tide of novels *about* science opened a creative space in which the novel-reading public—including cultural commentators and their audiences, working scientists, and general readers—can experience and think critically about the ways that scientific knowledge is generated and used. In *Under the Literary Microscope*, we examine the public discourse taking place in and around this creative space, focusing on novels that explore the complex social institutions and practices of modern science as well as the labyrinth of economic, political, educational, and moral factors that impact those practices and the knowledge produced. Before we delve into this distinctly contemporary discourse—which should interest not only literary and cultural-studies scholars and sociologists of science but also educators and practitioners of science communication—we take a quick gallop through time to review its antecedents in the novel's long history of engagement with public discourse about science.[1]

The Novel and the Rise of Modern Science

Over its long history, the novel has explored nearly every domain of human experience and relationships, from love, sex, family, and friendship to hate, violence, and death. It has participated in the major social discourses of its time, with stories that engaged with history, politics, economics, religion, philosophy, psychology, sociology, and the sciences. In recent decades, as humanities scholars have turned their attention to the study of literature and science, the coevolution of modern science and modern literary forms has become ever more apparent (see, for example, Secord 2014; Sleigh 2010; Rogers 2014). Even before the rise of the European novel, Johannes Kepler and Francis Bacon used a form of fictional narrative to develop and promote their thought experiments—Kepler on astronomy in *Somnium* (1634) and Bacon on scientific method and institutional structures in *New Atlantis* ([1627] 1909) (Chen-Morris 2005; Kelly 2016)—while Francis Godwin's speculative utopian fiction, *The Man in the Moone* (1638), was inspired by the new Copernican astronomy (Martin 2016). In Britain, debates in the newly founded Royal Society about experimental methods and about the relative merits of pure and applied knowledge—what Bacon called the "light" and "fruit" of science, respectively—circulated among the educated classes and made their way into fictional forms. Margaret Cavendish paired her publication of *Observations upon Experimental Philosophy* with publication of *The Descrip-*

tion of a New World, Called the Blazing World (1668), a satirical fantasy that mocked the Society for its obsession with new scientific instruments, which she thought interfered with natural vision and commonsense observation. Thomas Shadwell's popular play, *The Virtuoso* (1676), ridiculed the amateur scientific dabblers, or "virtuosi," as gullible fools who were out of touch with the real world, and Jonathan Swift's trenchant social satire, *Gulliver's Travels* (1726), exposed the squandering of resources in the pursuit of useless and potentially destructive scientific experiments.[2] But Robert Paltock's later *Life and Adventures of Peter Wilkins* (1751)—the story of a castaway whose survival depends on logical experimentation with his natural environment—celebrated the practical potential of the new forms of empiricism.

By the nineteenth century, the social and economic promises of scientific knowledge—and the power it engendered—had begun to spark the imaginations of creative writers and spawn new kinds of fictional speculation and experimentation. Mary Shelley's *Frankenstein* (1818) explored the presumed implications of early experiments with "animal electricity" in a cautionary tale about an overly optimistic attempt to transcend human limitations. In some of his early novels, H. G. Wells, who had a university science degree, engaged with the ongoing debates about vivisection and evolution, writing about the abuse of knowledge by arrogant, ethically deficient scientists. In *The Mudfog Papers* (1837–38), Charles Dickens satirized science enthusiasts' mental prowess, "obsession with detail," and generally "exaggerated sense of importance," which he saw reflected in the early attempts to institutionalize the practice of science (Zerbe 2016, 218, 219). Jules Verne, however, reacted to the new knowledge with unconditional wonder, producing a popular series of adventure stories that attempted "to sum up all the geographical, geological, physical, and astronomical knowledge amassed by modern science" ([1866] 2005, 320). The writer Émile Zola responded directly to the new epistemology as such, rather than to its products. Claiming that "if the experimental method leads to the knowledge of physical life, it should also lead to knowledge of the passionate and intellectual life," he set out to design a "literature governed on science," adapting the experimental method to the writing of his novels ([1880] 1893, 1–2).

With the rise of literary realism, novelists in the late nineteenth century began employing more rounded, fully realized characters while continuing to engage in debates about the changing social status of science and emerging scientific concepts: evolution and biological classification in Elisabeth Gaskell's *Wives and Daughters* (1866), the use of scientific methods in medicine and agriculture in George Eliot's *Middlemarch* (1871), new discoveries in astronomy in Thomas Hardy's *Two on a Tower* (1882), and debates over vivisection in Wilkie Collins's *Heart and Science* (1883). These novels and others of the time—including George Gissing's *Born in Exile* (1892) and H. G. Wells's *Love and Mr Lewisham* (1900), *Ann Veronica* (1909a), and *Tono-Bungay* (1909b)—recounted the struggles of young people who were trying to enter the new professions in a society that was not yet ready to adopt scientific values.[3]

While nineteenth-century novelists were responding imaginatively to new scientific methods and discoveries, scientists were utilizing the familiar narrative techniques of literature in their scientific reports and public presentations. The chemist Humphry Davy employed dialogue and made "visionary use of fact" to address the philosophical implications of new ideas about the geological history of the earth and the nature of time; Charles Lyell's *Principles of Geology* (1830–33) was embellished with rhetorical deftness and peppered with references to respected literary figures; and Charles Darwin's *On the Origin of Species* (1859) reads like a nineteenth-century novel, building a grand plot and larger meaning from the sequential first-person accounting of small observations and experiments (see Secord 2014, 157–62; Nieto-Galan 2016, 41–51). Scientific literature—both scientists' narrative accounts of their research and popularizations of science—was immensely popular, produced in mass and circulated not only in educated upper-class circles but also among the middle class and newly literate sectors of the working class (Nieto-Galan 2016, 38–41). The practice of science itself was gradually becoming professionalized, but there was still a continuum between the production of scientific knowledge and its integration in the wider society, where science was regarded as a practical and entertaining extension of common sense (Bensaude-Vincent 2001). Public interest in science coincided with and was fueled by new ideas about educating the masses and—with the invention of the steam-powered printing press—by mass-market publishing, as exemplified by the Society for the Diffusion of Useful Knowledge, with its *Penny Magazine* and "Library of Useful Knowledge" (Secord 2014, 16–17, 108–9). Along with professionals who practiced and taught science in universities, a new class of amateur and professional science writers emerged to interpret the new knowledge for lay audiences (see Nieto-Galan 2016, 38–41).[4]

The Knowledge Divide

By the end of the nineteenth century, the professionalization and formalization of science along with the explosion of knowledge, proliferation of disciplines, and separation of classical and scientific education systems had begun to generate a distinct knowledge gap between scientists and other members of the educated populace. The activities and institutional settings of scientific research disappeared from direct public view, and the knowledge produced was assessed by an exclusive scientific elite. Increasingly, reports of new scientific findings were published in dedicated scientific journals and written in a style and a technical language that were inaccessible not only to general readers but even to scientists from different disciplines. A distinct divide thus emerged between the specialized journals that scientists used in developing and verifying knowledge, and the popular scientific publications read by the general public. The professional scientific journals became the gatekeepers of knowledge, and the popular-science publications, which had engaged a wide cross section of amateur and professional scientists, ceased to play a role in the process of knowledge production and legitimation. Instead, scientists began to view popular-science publications and reports on scientific developments in the general media as tools for simplifying concepts and informing the public.[5]

Early twentieth-century discoveries in theoretical physics that seemed contrary to common sense and intuition contributed to a pervasive sense that scientists lived in a different world from ordinary citizens, and the media typically depicted them as high priests and "wizards" with special powers (LaFollette 1990). A wave of science popularization efforts after World War I had the counterproductive effect of portraying scientific knowledge as something that could be comprehended by the general public only if it was oversimplified and spoon-fed to them, either by scientists or by carefully selected science writers (Bensaude-Vincent 2001, 106–8). Understanding science became, in effect, a passive activity, and the lively public discussion that had accompanied the early development of modern science was replaced by a one-way flow of information. The technological "fruits" of science were contributing to what was seen as social and economic progress—the industrialization of production, new medicines and vaccines, transport and communication networks—and, more ambiguously, to national defense. But the basic scientific knowledge that made such technologies and applications possible—

Bacon's "light"—was now hidden from public view in what seemed to be a closed, unapproachable, and generally incomprehensible scientific culture. Scientists, as well as the public at large, regarded scientific practice and the knowledge it generated as being beyond the average citizen's purview—not just incomprehensible but also exempt from public scrutiny or responsibility.

The direct engagement with emerging scientific methods, ideas, and institutions—whether satirical, celebratory, emulative, or purely descriptive—that was so central to nineteenth-century literature and culture receded to the sidelines in the twentieth century. Although scholars of literature and science have documented interactions between the sciences and the arts throughout history,[6] they have also noted that reciprocity between these two cultural realms was much more apparent in the eighteenth and nineteenth centuries, before contemporary structures of institutional and professional science were fully consolidated, than it was during most of the twentieth century (Shuttleworth 2017, 46; Dillon 2018, 315). The restructuring of education systems at the turn of the century generated debates about the societal roles of science and the humanities that reverberated through academic communities for many decades and left their mark on literary production (e.g., Huxley 1901, 187–205; Arnold 1885; Collini 1998). In the Anglophone world, influential literary figures who had no scientific education or direct contact with science—D. H. Lawrence, Joseph Conrad, Henry James, and James Joyce, for example—tended to be hostile to its instrumentalization and skeptical of whether it was an appropriate or even accessible subject for serious literature. At the same time, they were exposed to science through popular-science writing in journals and books, and while lampooning scientific methods to expose the limitations of science and challenge narratives of scientific progress, they also appropriated scientific terminology and concepts for metaphors and for their experiments with form and character.[7] Virginia Woolf, who was less skeptical of scientific progress than many of her peers, went further, making a concerted effort to educate herself in the natural sciences and attempting to assimilate and explore the philosophical implications of scientific understandings of physics, geologic time, evolution, and biology in her fiction (Henry 2012; Livingstone 2018).

In the 1920s and 1930s a handful of British novelists who had trained as scientists wrote about the practices and everyday "business" of doing science,[8] but these works had relatively little enduring impact in the literary world (Russell 2010, 289–90). Most fiction writers with a more than passing interest in scientific discoveries followed the lead of Jules Verne's futuristic scientific adventure stories and H. G. Wells's immensely popular scientific romances. They used their novels to speculate about future technological innovations, focusing their attention on world-building rather than on the intersubjective social relations of bourgeois society, inward reflection, psychology, and aesthetic experimentation that dominated twentieth-century literary fashions and set the standard for mainstream publishing. The result was that the realm of literary production itself began to bifurcate, mirroring ever-more-pronounced disciplinary divisions in the wider culture—divisions that the physical chemist turned novelist C. P. Snow would later remonstrate against with his controversial but infectious catchphrase "two cultures" of sciences and arts, whose adherents, he claimed, were divided by a "gulf of mutual incomprehension" ([1959] 1998, 4).

When the American pulp-magazine industry appropriated and developed science fiction (SF) as a commercial publishing genre in the 1920s and 1930s, it emphasized mass production and required authors to follow certain formulas, earning the genre a reputation as low-grade escapist entertainment whose space wars, aliens, and distant future worlds were not taken seriously either as literature or as reflections on contemporary scientific practice and its repercussions. Many works transcended these specifications—successful midcentury SF writers such as Isaac Asimov, Arthur C. Clarke, Ursula Le Guin, J. G. Ballard, and Octavia Butler were certainly responding knowledgeably to developments in space exploration, artificial intelligence, telecommunications, nuclear physics, astronomy, and ecology, offering profound speculations about their social implications (Rees and Morus 2019).[9] Nevertheless, most early and midcentury SF was concerned with the effects and repercussions—whether social or material—of new technologies rather than with the processes and instrumentalization of scientific knowledge production that had generated them. In a 1968 essay, Arthur C. Clarke emphasized the imaginative limitations of science, noting that "any sufficiently advanced technology is indistinguishable from magic" when viewed from the past (255), and indeed, this is how the futuristic technologies of SF were usually portrayed, with little explication of the scientific, social, economic, and political processes that produced them. The actual practice of science in the twentieth century was increasingly collaborative, institution-based, and socially and politically contingent. But in literature and film, if the practice of scientific research was portrayed at all, it tended to be constrained by seventeenth-

and eighteenth-century stereotypes in which scientific knowledge and its consequences were determined by the bad or good intentions of obsessed villains or socially naive geniuses working in isolation (see Haynes 2017; Weingart, Muhl, and Pansegrau 2003).

Changing Societal Constellations and the New Scientific Literacy

In the 1960s, scientific, cultural, and socioeconomic developments again began to alter the relationship between science and the public, paving the way for the reengagement of literature and science that we see today. Developments in the life sciences and information sciences were giving rise to commercial research laboratories in fast-growing new industries that depended more on the acquisition and processing of science-based knowledge than on material resources. Such industries required new instruments of social, political, and economic monitoring, which in turn gave rise to service industries based on expertise in new math- and science-based disciplines such as computer programming, cybernetics, behavioral economics, and development planning. Sociologists began predicting the emergence of a "post-industrial society" in which highly educated workforces would replace production labor as the main motor for an economy that would be driven by knowledge and new ideas (Touraine 1969; Bell 1973). At the same time, the emphasis on individual equality and empowerment during the 1960s and the expansion of higher education over the following decades massively increased the proportion of the public that was privy to basic scientific knowledge and had a predisposition to critical thinking (Schofer and Meyer 2005).

As scientific principles and methodologies moved to the center of economic growth and became integrated into the fabric of society, the idea that rational, scientific planning was the key to solving the problems of the modern world became entrenched at all levels of society. But there was also a growing post–World War II disquiet among scientists about the uses and abuses of scientific knowledge. Physicists began to publicize their concerns about developing nuclear technologies, and in so doing they laid open to public scrutiny the disputes and uncertainties that had been playing out within the scientific community since before the war. Debates between experts became a public affair and had a feedback effect of creating a demand for yet more expertise and counterexpertise, which in turn drew more public attention (Agar 2008).

The publication of Rachel Carson's critically acclaimed and bestselling *The Sea Around Us* (1951) and *Silent Spring* (1962), with their careful research and eloquent prose, not only reopened the conversation between science and the public but also made a case for staging it in literature. Carson's lyrical writing brought decades of oceanographic research alive for an increasingly well-educated and interested public. And her detailed explanation of the ecological fallout of DDT made it clear that the fruits of science were not only contributing to social and economic progress but also generating unintended, delocalized, and unpredictable consequences. "If we are going to live," Carson wrote, "so intimately with these chemicals—eating and drinking them, taking them into the very marrow of our bones—we had better know something about their nature and their power" ([1962] 2002, 17). At a time when questioning established knowledge was becoming the norm, the highly visible scientific and political debates generated by *Silent Spring* revealed the inner workings of the hitherto closed and opaque scientific sphere.[10]

The new penchant for questioning the social outcomes of scientific research led to a heightened interest in both scrutinizing and promoting the activities of the scientific sphere. The 1970s and 1980s saw enhanced media coverage of scientific developments, renewed public outreach by scientific research institutions, the introduction of more science content into school curricula, and the emergence of science and technology studies as a discipline in Western universities. In the United States and Britain, popular-science publications in the form of scientific memoirs and books about new discoveries rose in popularity throughout the 1970s and 1980s, contributing to what Bruce Lewenstein, adopting the French term for the integration of science into a wider cultural matrix, considers the beginning of a new *"culture scientifique"* (2009, 347) and what Jay Clayton, considering the growing scientific literacy apparent in works of fiction at the end of the millennium, calls an "undisciplined culture"—a culture in which the exponentially bifurcating disciplines and forms of knowledge of the past century were beginning to mix and converge (2002).[11] The books that made the newspaper culture pages and hit bestseller lists were written by scientists as well as journalists, and they ranged from complex accounts of the latest research on the origin of the universe, chaos theory, and the extraordinary fossils in the Burgess Shale to exposés on socially and politically sensitive scientific issues such as evolution and climate change. Television documentary science series like *The Ascent of Man* (1973) and *Cosmos* (1980) became immensely popular, and scientists who interacted with the public or engaged with literature—Carl Sagan, David Attenborough, Richard Feynman, Oliver Sacks, and Stephen Jay Gould, among others—took on the character of public intellectuals or even celebrities.

New scientific understandings of the natural world and increased public interest in scientific discovery were accompanied by a growing awareness—among both scientists and the wider public—of the ambiguities of interpreting scientific observations and of the global-scale risks associated with technological progress. Observing the social contingencies of scientific research and the complex cultural and natural factors that determined technological development and its outcomes, social science scholars began to question modernity's mantra that a rational, formalized scientific culture could control nature and minimize risk and uncertainty (see Latour and Woolgar 1979; Douglas and Wildavsky 1982).

By the 1990s, the anticipation of risk had permeated the structure of Western societies to such an extent that sociologists coined the term "risk society" to describe the process of societal modernization (Giddens 1999; Beck 1992).[12] Scientists and their institutions were required to defend their knowledge in the public arena and to foresee the uses it might be put to and the risks it might incur as it rippled out into different social, economic, and political contexts. Deliberation on the fallouts of scientific discovery and technological progress—nuclear catastrophe, chemical pollution, loss of biodiversity, climate change, and the unforeseen consequences of geoengineering and genetic engineering—now takes place on the public stage, where scientists are called on to voice opinions and to enter into debate with economists and social scientists, representatives of citizens' social movements, ethicists, policy-makers, politicians, and one another. The debates and uncertainties inherent in the processes of establishing scientific facts are also played out and exploited in the political arena, where they may be invoked as grounds for action or inaction in political decision- and policy-making. The dynamic nature of the scientific process may even be cited as de facto grounds for ignoring scientific evidence, as we have seen in the treatment of climate change science and pandemic evidence in the United States.

Perhaps, then, it is no wonder that, with the Anthropocene epoch becoming apparent in the geologic record, the novel's place in this societal cacophony should begin to expand and transmute. The relationship between technological innovation and social risk has long been a topic of SF. In the mid-twentieth century, pivotal works of what is often described as postmodern fiction parodied Western society's mass consumption of new technologies and drew metaphors and analogies from the physical and biological sciences (Cordle 1999; McHale [1987] 2004).[13] And in the past few decades, scientifically literate novelists have begun writing about science *directly*, taking scientific issues and knowledge as their subjects and creating works that go even further toward blurring the boundaries of literary fiction and SF with their themes, approaches, and readerships. The SF worlds are moving closer to home—or home is moving closer to them—and we are seeing more stories about credible, near-future worlds and the scientific, economic, and social circumstances that produce them (see chapter 8). More remarkable after the long hiatus of attention is the rising tide of mainstream realist novels *about* science that began in the 1990s. Novels such as Barbara Kingsolver's *Flight Behavior* (2012), Ann Patchett's *State of Wonder* (2011), Allegra Goodman's *Intuition* (2006), Eileen Pollack's *Perfect Life* (2016), Simon Mawer's *Mendel's Dwarf* (1999), and Karen Joy Fowler's *We Are All Completely Beside Ourselves* (2013) have been taking science seriously in new ways (see chapter 1). They incorporate scientific understandings of the natural world, probe the institutions and practices of science, and rely on processes of scientific discovery for their plots. Often based on extensive background research in the scientific literature, these new works delve into the minds of scientist characters, carefully negotiating the interplay between fact, plausibility, realism, and imagination to render scientific knowledge, processes, applications, and technologies in great detail (Haynes 2016; Kirchhofer and Roxburgh 2016).[14]

Writers, critics, and pundits have alternately disregarded and celebrated this recent turn in the way that fiction is dealing with science and technology, providing labels such as "science in fiction," "geek novels," "lab lit," "mundane science fiction," and, simply, "science novels" (e.g., Gaines 2001; Clayton 2002; Rohn 2010; Bouton 2012; Schaffeld 2016). Whatever we call them, these science novels capture the attention of literary *and* scientific readerships, not least because of the ways they dramatize and humanize both the work of science and its potential repercussions (Kirchhofer and Auguscik 2017). In a culture dominated by the instant and often thoughtless exchange of out-of-context three-line messages and by floods of undigested information—of facts and not-facts, news and false news, anecdotes and gossip without context—we find an expanding fictional space for slow, contemplative, nuanced thinking about the socially and economically contingent power of science to both illuminate and transform nature and to both mitigate and generate social change and risk.

From a sociological perspective, the novel is exceptionally well suited to such a discourse, as it offers a narrative frame and a focusing mechanism for ambivalent and pluralistic perspectives on complex issues as well as a platform in the public sphere. In his influential discussion of Flaubert's realistic novels, sociologist Pierre Bourdieu emphasized this ability "to concentrate and condense in the concrete singularity of a sensitive figure . . . all the complexity of a structure and a history which scientific analysis must laboriously unfold and deploy" (1992, 24). This focusing mechanism and dependence on the singularity of character and perspective *in interaction with* others, combined with aesthetic devices that generate empathy with such characters and perspectives, allows us "a view of particular societies from the inside: we come to know something of what it feels like to be inside a particular habitus, to experience a world as self-evident" (Felski 2008, 92). Novels, of course, are neither mere representations or translations of social dynamics nor, for our purposes, purely works of art to be considered for their aesthetic qualities alone or without reference to the individual and social contexts and developments of their creation and reception. The interdisciplinary mix of literary and sociological expertise we have assembled for this volume, rather, allows us to consider these works of fiction from both within and beyond their texts.

The chapters in part 1 provide a literary and a sociological entrée to those that follow: In chapter 1, two literary scholars give an overview of the turn-of-the-millennium wave of literary fiction about science, with examples of the innovations in form, style, and character development that have been brought to bear on several of the most prominent scientific issues. In chapter 2, two sociologists review the institutional prehistory and history of science that still informs many cultural representations; and in chapter 3, they reexamine the sociological functions of stereotypes and investigate how old, entrenched stereotypes of scientists are used, adapted, or incorporated into the complex, differentiated representations of science found in recent fiction geared to different audiences.

Each of the chapters in parts 2 and 3 focuses on a different aspect of the practice and social context of science, as mediated by varied—though by no means exhaustive—and strategically overlapping selections of science novels.[15] Part 2 concentrates on how external societal factors impact scientific work and knowledge. In chapter 4, a literary scholar and an astronomer team up to explore how character-driven novels provide insight and elicit reader understanding of the risks inherent to work in scientific professions that are not typically viewed as dangerous to their practitioners but are often regarded as the source of new dangers and risks for society at large. Chapter 5 merges sociological approaches with those from cultural and literary studies to examine how a work of speculative fiction by the prominent novelist Margaret Atwood contributes to debates on the roles of science in society. Chapter 6 turns a feminist lens on the portrayal of science in novels featuring women scientists as main characters. Chapter 7, the pivotal final chapter of part 2, illustrates and dissects the sociological components and ramifications of the economization of science, as revealed by a cross section of contemporary novels about science.

The essays in part 3 focus on discussions of the societal outcomes of science. In chapter 8, a scholar of SF reviews the genre's historical development and takes a close look at its most recent preoccupations and its convergence with the new mainstream fiction about science. Chapter 9 looks at how top-selling SF novels are challenging the notion that science can contain and control its creations, and in chapter 10 another team of cultural studies scholars and sociologists makes a bold attempt to investigate the social resonance of Barbara Kingsolver's 2012 climate change novel, *Flight Behavior*. Taken together, the essays in *Under the Literary Microscope* reveal some of the ways that the contemporary novel may help us understand and come to grips with our science-based societies in the Anthropocene.

Notes

1. Since the 1970s, humanities scholars have generated a wide range of interdisciplinary research on the relationships, influences, and analogies between literary and scientific or technological developments. This research has deepened our understanding of the cultural embeddedness of scientific knowledge production and diffusion, and it has challenged overly simplistic and often Eurocentric narratives of rationalization and progress. There are many fine surveys of that literature, and it is not our goal to duplicate them here. Instead, this brief introduction offers a summary of the historical context of the contemporary science novel for our interdisciplinary readership.

For more comprehensive surveys of literature and science scholarship, see, for example, Markley 2018; Willis 2014; Clarke and Rossini 2011; and Gossin 2002.

2. On eighteenth-century satires of emerging scientific methodologies, see Lund 1998.

3. There are innumerable studies of the influence of science on nineteenth-century novels, such as Shuttleworth's now classic study of how scientific developments influenced George Eliot's work (1984). Otis (2002) provides a good introduction to this literature and an annotated collection of readings that exemplify nineteenth-century literature's engagement with science, and Willis (2006) discusses the science in nineteenth-century science fiction novels and what it reveals about the contemporaneous culture of science.

4. For detailed accounts of the nineteenth-century growth of popular-science periodicals and books and of their relationship to the creation of scientific knowledge, see also Lightman 2016; Shuttleworth and Cantor 2004; and Broks 2006, chaps. 1 and 2.

5. For accounts of the historic development of science writing and publishing and of their relationship to scientific knowledge production, the public, and the professionalization of science, see Broks 2006; and Henson et al. 2004.

6. Examples include Beer ([1983] 2009) on Darwin, Squier (1996) on early twentieth-century embryology, and Bruce Clarke (2001) on late nineteenth-century physics.

7. Whitworth (2010) reviews modernist novelists' ambivalent treatments of science in the early to mid-twentieth century; Morrisson (2017) synthesizes decades of what he calls "new modernism" and literature and science studies to trace the relationships between developments in early twentieth-century science, print media, and literary arts.

8. Examples include A. J. Cronin, E. C. Large, Nigel Balchin, C. P. Snow, and William Cooper (pseudonym of Harry Summerfield Hoff).

9. The marginalization of the science fiction genre became apparent not just in the publishing industry but also in the academic study of literature, where science fiction studies emerged as a separate subfield from literature and science studies (Dihal 2017).

10. For an account of how environmental literature has dealt with scientific ambiguities since Carson, see Heise 2015.

11. Clayton notes some similarities (and differences) between the turn-of-the-millennium intellectual traffic in science, engineering, and the arts, and cultural and intellectual transactions in the "pre-disciplinary" nineteenth century; Shuttleworth (2017) likewise sees such an analogy in the development of "citizen science" movements, and we might also note it in Milburn's examination of the ways that technology research enterprises have started consciously "using" or drawing on science fiction imaginaries to jumpstart innovation (2010).

12. For discussions of the concept of the risk society as manifest and generated by narrative representation, particularly in late twentieth-century and early twenty-first-century novels, see Mayer and von Mossner 2014; and Heise 2008.

13. In his discussion of postmodern writers' engagement with developments in the sciences of cybernetics, Porush (1992) credits Thomas Pynchon's "dialogue with various sciences" in *V.* (1963), *The Crying of Lot 49* (1967), and *Gravity's Rainbow* (1973) and his use of metaphor as a "weapon in his literary arsenal against cybernetic determinism" with "leading American literary critics into an engagement with contemporary scientific ideas" (214). McHale describes how writers such as William Burroughs, Kurt Vonnegut, Italo Calvino, and Pynchon were following parallel tracks with science fiction writers and "absorb[ing] motifs and topoi from science fiction writing, mining science fiction for its raw materials" (2004, 65). Vanderbeke (2011) discusses allusions and mentions of quantum physics in novels from the mid- and late twentieth century, and Cordle (2008) describes how writers from the pe-

riod were responding to the uncertainties of nuclear technologies.

14. In a broader literary context, the realism we see in these science novels may exemplify what Peter Boxall, in his bid to distinguish the characteristics of an emerging twenty-first-century novel, identified as "the attempt, in the contemporary novel, to grasp the texture of the contemporary real . . . a strikingly new attention to the nature of our reality—its materiality, its relation to touch, to narrative and to visuality" (2013, 10).

15. The wave of contemporary novels about science has been most prominent in British and American literature, which comprises the majority of this volume's corpus. To date, we find little mention of similar trends in other national literatures, though we can identify a handful of novels from Canada and Australia: Margaret Atwood's speculative *Oryx and Crake* (2003), Colin McAdam's *A Beautiful Truth* (2013), Andrew Westoll's *The Jungle South of the Mountain* (2016), and Esi Edugyan's historical novel *Washington Black* (2018) in Canada; and Graeme Simsion's *The Rosie Project* (2013), Janette Turner Hospital's *Charades* (1987), and Amanda Niehaus's *The Breeding Season* (2019) in Australia. In the German-language literature we find a dozen or so science novels—several by biologist turned novelist Bernhard Kegel as well as Thea Dorn's *Die Unglückseligen*, Franz Schätzing's *Der Schwarm*, and a number of historical science novels such as Jo Lendle's *Alles Land*, Martin Kluger's *Die Gehilfin*, and Daniel Kehlmann's *Die Vermessung der Welt*.

References

Agar, Jon. 2008. "What Happened in the Sixties?" *British Journal for the History of Science* 41 (4): 567–600. https://doi.org/10.1017/S0007087408001179.

Arnold, Matthew. 1885. "Literature and Science." In *Discourses in America*, 72–137. London: Macmillan.

Bacon, Francis. (1627) 1909. *The New Atlantis*. New York: P. F. Collier and Son.

Beck, Ulrich. 1992. *Risk Society: Towards a New Modernity*. Thousand Oaks, CA: Sage.

Beer, Gillian. (1983) 2009. *Darwin's Plots: Evolutionary Narrative in Darwin, George Eliot and Nineteenth-Century Fiction*. Cambridge, UK: Cambridge University Press.

Bell, Daniel. 1973. *The Coming of Post-Industrial Society: A Venture in Social Forecasting*. New York: Basic Books.

Bensaude-Vincent, Bernadette. 2001. "A Genealogy of the Increasing Gap Between Science and the Public." *Public Understanding of Science* 10 (1): 99–113. https://doi.org/10.1088/0963-6625/10/1/307.

Bourdieu, Pierre. 1992. *The Rules of Art*. Stanford, CA: Stanford University Press.

Bouton, Katharine. 2012. "In Lab Lit, Fiction Meets Science of the Real World." *New York Times*, December 4, 2012. http://www.nytimes.com/2012/12/04/science/in-lab-lit-fiction-meets-science-of-the-real-world.html.

Boxall, Peter. 2013. *Twenty-First-Century Fiction*. Cambridge, UK: Cambridge University Press.

Broks, Peter. 2006. *Understanding Popular Science*. Maidenhead, UK: Open University Press.

Carson, Rachel. (1962) 2002. *Silent Spring*. New York: Houghton Mifflin.

Chen-Morris, Raz. 2005. "Shadows of Instruction: Optics and Classical Authorities in Kepler's Somnium." *Journal of the History of Ideas* 66 (2): 223–43.

Clarke, Arthur C. 1968. "Clarke's Third Law on UFO's." *Science* 159 (3812): 255.

Clarke, Bruce. 2001. *Energy Forms: Allegory and Science in the Era of Classical Ther-*

modynamics. Ann Arbor: University of Michigan Press.

Clarke, Bruce, and Manuela Rossini, eds. 2011. *The Routledge Companion to Literature and Science*. Abingdon, UK: Routledge.

Clayton, Jay. 2002. *Charles Dickens in Cyberspace: The Afterlife of the Nineteenth Century in Postmodern Culture*. Oxford, UK: Oxford University Press.

Collini, Stefan. 1998. Introduction to *The Two Cultures*, by C. P. Snow, vii–lxxii. Cambridge, UK: Cambridge University Press.

Cordle, Daniel. 1999. *Postmodern Postures: Literature, Science and the Two Cultures Debate*. Aldershot, UK: Ashgate.

———. 2008. *States of Suspense: The Nuclear Age, Postmodernism and United States Fiction and Prose*. Manchester, UK: Manchester University Press.

Dihal, Kanta. 2017. "On Science Fiction as a Separate Field." *Journal of Literature and Science* 10 (1): 32–36.

Dillon, Sarah. 2018. "On the Influence of Literature on Science." *Configurations* 26 (3): 311–16.

Douglas, Mary, and Aaron Wildavsky. 1982. *Risk and Culture: An Essay on the Selection of Technical and Environmental Dangers*. Berkeley: University of California Press.

Felski, Rita. 2008. *Uses of Literature*. Oxford, UK: Blackwell.

Gaines, Susan. 2001. "Sex, Love, and Science." *Nature* 413 (6853): 255.

Giddens, Anthony. 1999. "Risk and Responsibility." *Modern Law Review* 62 (1): 1–10.

Gossin, Pamela, ed. 2002. *Encyclopedia of Literature and Science*. Westport, CT: Greenwood Press.

———. 2003. "Literature and the Modern Physical Sciences." In *The Cambridge History of Science*, vol. 5, *The Modern Physical and Mathematical Sciences*, edited by Mary Jo Nye, 91–109. Cambridge, UK: Cambridge University Press.

Haynes, Roslynn D. 2016. "Bringing Science into Fiction." *Zeitschrift für Anglistik und Amerikanistik* 64 (2): 127–48.

———. 2017. *From Madman to Crime Fighter: The Scientist in Western Culture*. Baltimore: Johns Hopkins University Press.

Heise, Ursula K. 2008. *Sense of Place and Sense of Planet: The Environmental Imagination of the Global*. Oxford, UK: Oxford University Press.

———. 2015. "Environmental Literature and the Ambiguities of Science." *Anglia* 133 (1): 22–36.

Henry, Holly. 2012. "Science and Technology." In *Virginia Woolf in Context*, edited by Bryony Randall and Jane Goldman, 254–66. Cambridge, UK: Cambridge University Press.

Henson, Louise, Geoffrey Cantor, Gowan Dawson, Richard Noakes, Sally Shuttleworth, and Jonathan R. Topham, eds. 2004. *Culture and Science in the Nineteenth-Century Media*. New York: Ashgate.

Huxley, Thomas H. 1901. *Science and Education: Essays*. New York: Appleton.

Kelly, Erin Kathleen. 2016. "'Experience Has Not Yet Learned Her Letters': Narrative and Information in the Works of Francis Bacon." *Configurations* 24 (2): 145–71.

Kirchhofer, Anton, and Anna Auguscik. 2017. "Triangulating the Two Cultures Entanglement: The Sciences and the Humanities in the Public Sphere." *Journal of Literature and Science* 10 (2): 26–37.

Kirchhofer, Anton, and Natalie Roxburgh. 2016. "The Scientist as 'Problematic Individual' in Contemporary Anglophone Fiction." *Zeitschrift für Anglistik und Amerikanistik* 64 (2): 148–68.

LaFollette, Marcel C. 1990. *Making Science Our Own: Public Images of Science, 1910–1955*. Chicago: University of Chicago Press.

Latour, Bruno, and Steve Woolgar. 1979. *Laboratory Life: The Construction of Scientific Facts*. Beverly Hills, CA: Sage.

Lewenstein, Bruce. 2009. "Science Books Since World War II." In *A History of the Book in America*, vol. 5, *The Enduring Book: Print Culture in Postwar America*, edited by David Paul Nord, Joan Shelley Rubin, and Michael Schudson, 347–60. Chapel Hill: University of North Carolina Press.

Lightman, Bernard. 2016. "Popularizers, Participation and the Transformations of Nineteenth-Century Publishing: From the 1860s to the 1880s." *Notes and Records: The Royal Society Journal of the History of Science* 70 (4): 343–59.

Livingstone, Catriona. 2018. "Experimental Identities: Quantum Physics in Popular Science Writing and Virginia Woolf's *The Waves*." *Journal of Literature and Science* 11 (1): 66–81.

Lund, Roger D. 1998. "The Eel of Science: Index Learning, Scriblerian Satire, and the Rise of Information Culture." *Eighteenth-Century Life* 22 (2): 18–42.

Markley, Robert. 2018. "As If: The Alternative Histories of Literature and Science." *Configurations* 26 (3): 259–68.

Martin, Catherine. 2016. "Sailing to the Moon: Francis Bacon, Francis Godwin and the First Science Fiction." In *Literature in the Age of Celestial Discovery: From Copernicus to Flamsteed*, edited by Judy A. Hayden, 109–32. New York: Palgrave Macmillan.

Mayer, Sylvia, and Alexa Weik von Mossner. 2014. *The Anticipation of Catastrophe: Environmental Risk in North American Literature and Culture*. Heidelberg, DE: Winter.

McHale, Brian. (1987) 2004. *Postmodernist Fiction*. London: Routledge.

Milburn, Colin. 2010. "Modifiable Futures: Science Fiction at the Bench." *Isis* 101 (3): 560–69.

Morrisson, Mark S. 2017. *Modernism, Science, and Technology*. New Modernisms. London: Bloomsbury Academic. Kindle.

Nieto-Galan, Agusti. 2016. *Science in the Public Sphere: A History of Lay Knowledge and Expertise*. New York: Routledge.

Otis, Laura. 2002. *Literature and Science in the Nineteenth Century: An Anthology*. Oxford, UK: Oxford University Press.

Porush, David. 1992. "Unfurrowing the Mind's Plowshare: Fiction in a Cybernetic Age." In *American Literature and Science*, edited by Robert J. Scholnick, 209–28. Lexington: University Press of Kentucky.

Rees, Amanda, and Iwan Rhys Morus. 2019. "Presenting Futures Past: Science Fiction and the History of Science." *Osiris* 34 (1): 1–15.

Rogers, Janine. 2014. *Unified Fields: Science and Literary Form*. Montreal: McGill-Queens University Press.

Rohn, Jennifer. 2010. "More Lab in the Library." *Nature* 465 (7298): 552.

Russell, Nicholas. 2010. *Communicating Science: Professional, Popular, Literary*. Cambridge, UK: Cambridge University Press.

Schaffeld, Norbert. 2016. "Aspects of the Science Novel." *Zeitschrift für Anglistik und Amerikanistik* 64 (2): 121–25.

Schofer, Evan, and John W. Meyer. 2005. "The Worldwide Expansion of Higher Education in the Twentieth Century." *American Sociological Review* 70 (6): 898–920.

Secord, James. 2014. *Visions of Science: Books and Readers at the Dawn of the Victorian Age*. Chicago: University of Chicago Press.

Shuttleworth, Sally. 1984. *George Eliot and Nineteenth Century Science: The Make-Believe of a Beginning*. Cambridge, UK: Cambridge University Press.

———. 2017. "Life in the Zooniverse: Working with Citizen Science." *Journal of Literature and Science* 10 (1): 46–51.

Shuttleworth, Sally, and Geoffrey Cantor. 2004. Introduction to *Science Serialized: Representations of Science in Nineteenth-Century Periodicals*, edited by Geoffrey Cantor and Sally Shuttleworth, 1–16. Cambridge, MA: MIT Press.

Sleigh, Charlotte. 2010. *Literature and Science*. Basingstoke, UK: Palgrave Macmillan.

Snow, C. P. (1959) 1998. *The Two Cultures*. Cambridge, UK: Cambridge University Press.

Squier, Susan. 1996. "Embryologies of Modernism." *Modernism/Modernity* 3 (3): 145–53.

Touraine, Alain. 1969. *La société post-industrielle*. Paris: Denoël.

Vanderbeke, Dirk. 2011. "Physics." In *The Routledge Companion to Literature and Science*, edited by Bruce Clarke and Manuela Rossini, 192–202. Abingdon, UK: Routledge.

Verne, Jules. (1866) 2005. *The Adventures of Captain Hatteras*. Translated by William Butcher. Oxford, UK: Oxford University Press.

Weingart, Peter, Claudia Muhl, and Petra Pansegrau. 2003. "Of Power Maniacs and Unethical Geniuses: Science and Scientists in Fiction Film." *Public Understanding of Science* 12 (3): 279–87.

Whitworth, Michael. 2010. "Science in the Age of Modernism." In *The Oxford Handbook of Modernisms*, edited by Peter Brooker, Andrzej Gasiorek, Deborah Longworth, and Andrew Thacker, 445–60. Oxford, UK: Oxford University Press. https://doi.org/10.1093/oxfordhb/9780199545445.013.0026.

Willis, Martin. 2006. *Mesmerists, Monsters, and Machines: Science Fiction and the Cultures of Science in the Nineteenth Century*. Kent, OH: Kent State University Press.

———. 2014. *Literature and Science*. Readers' Guides to Essential Criticism. Basingstoke, UK: Palgrave.

Zerbe, Michael J. 2016. "Satire of Science in Charles Dickens's *Mudfog Papers*: The Institutionalization of Science and the Importance of Rhetorical Diversity to Scientific Literacy." *Configurations* 24 (2): 197–227.

Zola, Émile. (1880) 1893. *The Experimental Novel and Other Essays*. Translated by Belle M. Sherman. London: Cassel.

Part 1
Background and Context

1.
Science and Society in Recent Fiction

Natalie Roxburgh
and Jay Clayton

In Richard Powers's *The Gold Bug Variations* (1991), a geneticist and computer programmer named Stuart Ressler opens his heart to a young acquaintance about his feelings for science: "Science is not about control. It is about cultivating a perpetual condition of wonder in the face of something that forever grows one step richer and subtler than our latest theory about it. It is about reverence, not mastery" (411). Powers's long, polyphonic novel contains some of the richest accounts of genetics research in all of literature, and these accounts are beautifully interwoven with meditations on language, computer codes, and musical form. The story of this scientist's quest to understand the genetic code illuminates his research with sympathy and striking realism. The novel depicts Ressler's tentative theories, the failures and occasional triumphs of experimental work, rivalry with colleagues, conflicts with a mentor, an illicit love affair in the department, university politics, the pressure of grant deadlines, and, perhaps most surprising of all, a fascinating account of the state of genetic knowledge at the time. One of the achievements of *The Gold Bug Variations* is to have brought to life the story of a scientist engaged in science.

Sympathetic attention to science and scientists has become increasingly common in literary fiction in the late twentieth and early twenty-first centuries. Powers is known for his many highly regarded novels in this vein—fiction not only about genetics and computer science but also about virtual reality, neurology, physics, and ecology. Powers is hardly alone, however, among novelists in taking a serious interest in the ideas, methods, and behavior of scientists. Even novels that satirize their scientist characters—such as Powers's later novel about genetics, *Generosity* (2009); Zadie Smith's *White Teeth* (2000); Ruth Ozeki's *All Over Creation* (2002); and Ian McEwan's *Solar* (2010)—still attend carefully to their scientists' ideas and ways of being in the world. It is this relatively new development in the literature of our time that this chapter surveys.[1]

The last three decades have seen a dramatic increase in realist fiction about science. Examples span a wide variety of disciplines—not only the three we concentrate on here (genetics, information technology, and ecology) but also physics, astronomy, pharmacology, neuroscience, robotics, nanotechnology, and other fields. Although one could point to a trickle of realist novels that addressed the social implications of science in the 1970s and 1980s—such as Thomas McMahon's *Principles of American Nuclear Chemistry* (1970), with its two generations of nuclear scientists, or Perri Klass's *Recombinations* (1985), with its story of a young female genetics researcher—by the 1990s the stream had become deep and steady, a forceful current that swept up readers, critics, and prizes alike in its flow. Indeed, many of these novels were shortlisted for or received the Man Booker Prize, National Book Award, Pulitzer Prize, James Tait Black Prize, or PEN/Faulkner Award. In the twenty-first century, the flood of titles—and prize nominations—has grown.[2] This development signals a social revaluing of the importance of science for society insofar as novels that win these prizes tend to thematize this relationship explicitly.

Novels about evolutionary science and genetics were among the earliest and most prominent in this vein, followed closely by novels about digital technology and artificial intelligence. In the last decade, climate fiction has become an important new subgenre of fiction about science. The advent of recombinant DNA and the first test-tube baby in the 1970s and the highly publicized cloning of Dolly the sheep in 1996 inspired writers to address urgent questions about the benefits and risks of pursuing research that could fundamentally alter life and to explore the historical origins of evolutionary science that made genetic engineering possible. The internet boom of the 1990s made breakthroughs in digital technology and AI compelling subjects of interest for a wider readership. Finally, the belated public recognition of climate change has prompted a surge of fiction focused on ecological disaster. Novelists were drawn to these topics as ways to fuse far-reaching ethical and social concerns with moving narratives about individual lives.

As we noted earlier, novelists have explored other fields too. There has been a steady pulse of physics novels, and nanotechnology and neuroscience also attract a fair amount of attention (Roxburgh, Kirchhofer, and Auguscik 2016; Freißmann 2011; Milburn 2008; and so on). Quantum physics has inspired impressive novels by Richard Powers, Rebecca Goldstein, and others. Regardless of the field, the goal of taking both the science and the fiction seriously has led to literary innovations in form, style, and perhaps most noticeably, character development. For much of the twentieth century, the construction of rich, compelling scientist characters—as opposed to more stereotypical representations of the mad scientist (Haynes 2017), the neutral authority figure, or the cold rationalist—had been the exception rather than the rule, not only in journalism, TV, film, and advertising but in much literary fiction as well. Now this situation has changed (Kirchhofer and Roxburgh 2016).

In what follows, we survey prominent examples of fiction that deal with genetics, information technology, and climate change. Other texts could have been chosen, but we have selected a few that we feel are illustrative of larger trends in the last three decades. While novels about climate change invite questions about a topic that has become politically contentious, revealing it to be clear, present, and socially salient, novels about genetic engineering tend to address risks associated with what it means to be human and to address the possible futures of society afforded by genetic engineering. Novels about information technology pose questions about the relationship of humans—or even of the concept of the "human"—to technology, especially insofar as technology has transformed communication, connection, and privacy.

Different types of science require different types of questions about the relationship between science and society. Like Michael Crichton's *Next* (2006) and Simon Mawer's *Mendel's Dwarf* (1999), two genetics novels we discuss in this chapter, many fictional works about genetic engineering feature the possibility of manipulating genes or cloning new humans. On one hand, social issues pertaining to genetic engineering have to do with questions of identity, the nature of the human, or the turn toward posthumanism. On the other hand, there is concern that those who can afford such technologies might come to have a godlike power. In some of these novels, such as Margaret Atwood's *MaddAddam* series (2003–13), David Mitchell's *Cloud Atlas* (2004), and Kazuo Ishiguro's *Never Let Me Go* (2005), cloning humans is a central aspect of the storyworld and plot. This aspect gives these novels more of a speculative feel because the storyworlds are not immediately recognizable as imitating the contemporary world even though there are many similarities. In other stories about genetics—such as Richard Powers's *The Gold Bug Variations* (1991) and *Generosity* (2009), Andrea Barrett's *Ship Fever* (1996), Michael Byers's *Long for This World* (2003), Jeffrey Eugenides's *Middlesex* (2003), and Ian McEwan's *Saturday* (2005)—the character of the scientist working in a contemporary research environment plays a more important role, allowing for reflection on the process of coming into knowledge.

Michael Crichton's *Next* (2006), called a "techno-thriller" by reviewers, features a storyworld much like our own, except that the progress of genetic engineering has continued to its next stages (hence the title). The novel features several plot threads based on the new possibilities afforded by unregulated market-driven technologies. Both the government and corporations spend large sums of money on genetics research, which has gotten out of control. One character, Frank Burnet, who has been treated for leukemia, finds out that his discarded cells have been used by a technology start-up called BioGen. In a development loosely based on the case of *Moore v. Regents of the University of California* (1990), the court rules through eminent domain law that he does not have the rights to his own cells, and he is later forced into hiding to prevent the forcible extraction of further tissue. In addition to this plot thread, the novel features transgenic characters, who are now under threat because of their distinctive characteristics: Dave, who is part chimpanzee and part human and whose existence is routinely threatened by his creators, and an African gray parrot called Gerard, who also has human genes and is able to converse with people. The wide variety of genetically modified life-forms and the lawsuits, violence, and criminal acts that take place within the novel reveal a society whose technologies have outpaced the ability of the law to keep up with them. An unintended consequence of genetic engineering, the novel suggests, is that new forms of life might emerge and require society to adapt its moral and ethical principles.

Next's multiple narrative threads, coupled with insights from diverse perspectives—including those of scientists, lawyers, and everyday citizens—reveal dangers that, if left unchecked, have the potential to create social, political, and legal chaos. The convenient way the various plots converge to reveal different aspects of the same problem gives the novel a somewhat didactic feel, one that is intensified by an afterword in which Crichton lists some of the nonfiction "conclusions" he arrived at after writing the novel, such as the need to "stop patenting genes" (2006, 529) (an activity the US Supreme Court did, in fact, put a stop to in 2013). A *New York Times* bestseller, the novel engages with the social aspects of genetic engineering by illuminating risks that could conceivably emerge from a legal system that looks very much like a present-day Western one. In Crichton's novel, and arguably in our world as well, legal institutions have not yet developed the capacity to handle the challenges posed by genetic engineering.

The scientist characters in *Next*, along with the portrayal of the practices of science, are rather flat, which tends to promote a simple and thus less realistic notion of what is at stake. Everett Hamner has suggested that this lack of depth in covering the practices of science promotes an idea of "genomic determinism," an age-old notion of predestination that too simply and even unscientifically associates particular genes with behaviors or attributes (2011, 415). In contrast to *Next*, other examples of what some have called "genomic fictions" feature more three-dimensional scientist characters and nuanced portrayals of science in order to represent genetics in a more realistic manner. These novels explore genetic engineering as a process of coming into knowledge about the fundamentals of life, human or otherwise. The implications of discoveries are covered in depth, often requiring narrative strategies that allow for a serious contemplation of the science from the perspective of knowledgeable characters. Examples include works such as *The Gold Bug Variations* and *Mendel's Dwarf*, both of which feature a two-generational plot structure that juxtaposes scientists in two different time frames (Clayton 2003a, 202).

Mendel's Dwarf is focalized through the character of Benedict Lambert, an achondroplastic dwarf and eminent geneticist who studies his own condition. Interspersed is an account of Gregor Mendel, focalized through an intradiegetic narrator who is also presumably Lambert. Flashing backward in time, the account of Mendel takes place in the period when he discovers some of the fundamental principles of genetic inheritance. Another instance of historical discourse in *Mendel's Dwarf* is a retelling of the unintended consequences of this discovery through the rise of eugenics that would ensue in the wake of Mendel's discoveries. In the present-day plot, the dramatic tension comes from Lambert's unscrupulous use of his scientific knowledge to exact personal revenge. At times, the narrator shifts into second-person voice (Mawer 1999, e.g., 133), conveying his area of expertise directly to the reader in an almost pedagogic manner. Lambert presents drawings, charts, and other visual references to provide the reader with a basic knowledge of genetics (e.g., 128, 193, 199, 219, 264). The deployment of different styles and narrative voices differs greatly from Crichton's novel in terms of narrative strategy.

Because Lambert is also afflicted with the syndrome he researches, the novel cannot avoid addressing the social consequences of the syndrome's possible eradication. His lover, Jean Piercy, aborts his baby because of the possibility that it will be a dwarf. Later, however, she asks him to be the donor for in vitro fertilization of her child and to choose a phenotypically "normal" embryo. The dramatic tension of the novel's conclusion revolves around whether he will choose the normal embryo or the one that would mean his child ends up like him. *Mendel's Dwarf*, by providing the historical perspective of Mendel and the contemporary perspective of Benedict Lambert, simultaneously examines the wonder of a particular scientific discovery (especially apparent when Lambert ruminates on the life of Mendel) and deals with the unintended consequences and potential applications of such a discovery. It asks what science can do to mitigate risks such as birth defects, but at the same time it presents the ethical issues that would result if the possibilities afforded by genetic engineering were to allow us to enforce our concepts of a "normal" human being. For this novel more than for *Next*, the construction of a compelling scientist character who understands not just the origins of genetic inheritance but also the nefarious, risk-producing uses to which this science has been put, is key.

Information technology and artificial intelligence research have been prominent in novels since the mid-1990s. Novels about AI often ask questions about the nature of the human, just as novels about genetic engineering do, but the questions are raised not as a result of biological interventions but as a result of the augmentation or replacement of human capacities by silicon chips (Clayton 2003b, 85–86). Other IT novels explore the impact of information technology on the social and cultural lives of humans. Powers's *Galatea 2.2* (1995), an early novel about AI, and *Plowing the Dark* (2001), about virtual reality, combine a virtuoso command of Western literary, artistic, and musical traditions with a thoroughgoing knowledge of digital technology; Neal Stephenson's *Cryptonomicon* (1999) establishes a genealogy for hacker culture by juxtaposing the exploits of codebreakers working with Alan Turing during World War II with present-day hackers setting up an IT firm in the Philippines; Kurt Anderson's *Turn of the Century* (2000) captures the frenzy of the dot-com years just before the bubble burst; Jeanette Winterson's *The PowerBook* (2000) flits through time and space, exploring virtual reality as a metaphor for the intangibility of love; Ellen Ullman's *The Bug* (2003) follows an obsessed computer programmer as he hunts for a bug in his code, entrancing his friend in the process with the mysteries of language—human and computer; Gary Shteyngart's *Super Sad True Love Story* (2010) constructs a social media society in which our mobile devices know everything about our health, finances, friendships, and sex lives; Scott Hutchins's *A Working Theory of Love* (2012) follows a technology start-up that is working on "affective computing," an AI that possesses feelings; Dave Eggers's *The Circle* (2013), set on the campus of a high-tech corporation, dramatizes the risk of losing all privacy to commercial data mining and corporate surveillance; and Ian McEwan's *Machines Like Me* (2019) imagines a mid-1980s England in which Alan Turing is still alive and robotics has advanced sufficiently to create an AI capable of love.

Powers's *Galatea 2.2*, published in 1995 before computers became common social tools, explores state-of-the-art research in artificial intelligence from the perspective of a novelist named Richard Powers, who loosely shares biographical details with the author. Using contemporary theory, such as machine functionalism, the novel stages the process of building an AI. The character Powers, who has just published his fourth novel, begins a research fellowship at the Center for the Study of Advanced Sciences, where he meets Phillip Lenz. Lenz is a cognitive neurologist who works on modeling the human brain through computer-based neural networking. The plot centers on teaching a machine to respond to literature in such a way that it can pass an MA exam in English literary history. Here the first-person narrator, along with the reader, learns about cognitive neuroscience from Lenz as he contributes to the project of building the machine, which is then gendered as female and called Helen, perhaps invoking Helen of Troy or one of the pioneering stories about robotics, Lester del Ray's "Helen O'Loy" (1938); one critic has even speculated that her name alludes to Helen Keller (Berger 2002).

Over the course of the novel, Powers and Lenz both develop an emotional attachment to Helen, who repeatedly asks Powers questions about the social and idiomatic contexts for the literature she is reading and who, late in the novel, turns to reading newspapers and magazines on her own. The novel's conclusion suggests that the hero's interactions with the AI turn out to have been the true subject of Lenz's experiment. Helen seems to pass the Turing test, but in the process of coming to understand the state of Western knowledge and her own condition—in which she possesses the wiring but not the evolutionary underpinnings of the human—she decides to turn herself off. The novel presents the problem of embodiment as a social-evolutionary one, which is perhaps what Lenz means when he says that "human knowledge is social" (Powers 1995, 148). *Galatea 2.2* thus examines the possibility of modeling human consciousness but also demonstrates a possible complication in doing so, namely, that collective thought might be required as we move forward in developing artificial intelligence since artificial humans do not share the biophysical evolutionary embodiment of natural ones.

Hutchins's *A Working Theory of Love* (2012) shares many plot similarities with *Galatea 2.2*. It is also written in first person and features a character, Neill Bassett, who is not a scientist but works with experts from a tech start-up in Silicon Valley in building an AI machine. Bassett has been chosen to work on this project because the materials used to design the machine's neural network include his father's journals. He assists cognitive scientist Henry Livorno, through whom he learns about the state of the art. Bassett comments, "When I first met my boss he told me that artificial intelligence sought to answer one question: what do you do in the face of uncertainty?" (18). Through asking the machine questions, Bassett comes to know his father in a very different way. The novel asks questions about the digitization of social experience and the way we come to know ourselves and our inherent uncertainties through interacting with computers. Further, lurking at the edges of the novel's main plot is the possibility that the work that Livorno and Bassett undertake will be used by companies who want to manufacture and market robotic sexual companions for humans, opening a Pandora's box of questions about the future of human connection. The practices of science are less prominent in this book than in *Galatea 2.2*, but the novel nonetheless presents science as a pertinent part of the social lives of humans.

Eggers's *The Circle*, in contrast to Powers's and Hutchins's novels, offers a different social assessment of IT. Written in third person, it is focalized by a young and talented female character, Mae Holland, who works for a Silicon Valley tech firm. State-of-the-art equipment is all-pervasive in the work complex known as The Circle, and at first Mae is enamored of the cutting-edge technology and sophisticated descriptions of how it works. After a while, however, Mae's experiences with these technologies—including SeeChange cameras that provide ubiquitous real-time video of private experiences and the advanced social networking platforms engineered by the mysterious IT tech, Kalden—take an ominous turn. Mae's private life is monitored and exposed, and her colleague, Mercer, is killed in a fruitless attempt to leave the totalitarian space of The Circle. Unlike the examples of Hutchins and Powers, *The Circle* makes an unsubtle link between IT and totalitarianism, showing the complex trade-offs between the benefits and risks of technology rather than portraying its ramifications ambivalently, as other novels have done.

Our final example, the genre of climate fiction, comes almost exclusively from the twenty-first century, although precursors such as J. G. Ballard's *The Drowned World* (1962) have been adduced. This group of works is the most explicit in dealing with a risk society and the reflexive modernization that it entails (see Beck, Giddens, and Lash 1994). It is here that the capacity of science to both produce and mitigate risk is most apparent. While science fiction writers such as J. G. Ballard, Ursula K. Le Guin, and Octavia Butler have been writing dystopian fiction about climate change since the 1960s and 1970s, the idea of climate change fiction as a category wasn't popularized until the twenty-first century. One of the striking features about some of the more recent works is that they are set in the world as we know it and employ more realist narrative strategies. Examples include Susan M. Gaines's *Carbon Dreams* (2001), Michael Crichton's *State of Fear* (2004), Kim Stanley Robinson's Science in the Capital trilogy (2004–7), Ian McEwan's *Solar* (2010), Jesmyn Ward's *Salvage the Bones* (2011), Barbara Kingsolver's *Flight Behavior* (2012), Nathaniel Rich's *Odds Against Tomorrow* (2013), and Richard Powers's *The Overstory* (2019). Some important works, including Jeanette Winterson's *The Stone Gods* (2007) and Paolo Bacigalupi's *The Windup Girl* (2009), are set in the near future (as of the time of publication), when global warming has already wrought environmental and social disaster. All these works share a concern with anthropogenic climate change and are informed by the science that provides evidence for it and proposes ways of dealing with it. Some, which we will discuss in more depth, explore the development of that science directly.

Whether climate change is an integral component of the plot or merely invoked in the storyworld, it looks very different in novels than it does in other discourses. As Adam Trexler writes, "Climate change does not come 'into' novels through special pleading on the part of the author. Instead, climate change spans an enormous, heterogeneous terrain that demands formal innovations of fiction. When climate change circulates through the novel, it is reshaped as a material, scientific, or cultural thing" (2015, 24). In other words, these novels show the multifaceted ways that climate change science is interwoven in society. Critics have especially noted how novels about climate change or anthropogenic global warming have focused on present-day issues in order to address the problem of societal risk. Sylvia Mayer calls such novels "risk narratives" (2014, 24). One strategy is to render the climate itself as a subject, as, for example, Dale Pendell does in *The Great Bay* (2010), which spans 160,000 years and details the impact of the rising seas on countries and continents around the world. Other examples are more character focused, and it is from the perspective of individuals that climate change science becomes pertinent.

Fiction about climate change often features realistically portrayed scientists whose voices contrast starkly with others in the novel—particularly those of the media. Gaines's *Carbon Dreams* (2001) employs a scientist as narrative focalizer, and the reader is exposed to scientific knowledge at the same time as the main character. Set in the early 1980s in California, the novel features an organic geochemist as the protagonist. Tina Arenas finds evidence for past global warming in the form of a high CO_2 concentration in the Cretaceous layer and explains what she finds out to her boyfriend, Chip. As she tells him what she—and by this point, the reader—has learned, it becomes apparent that there is a big gap between what she knows about climate change and what the media that Chip is exposed to have been reporting. The media, it turns out, have been guided by the research of an industrial scientist who has ties to an oil company and is offering assessments of the problem that are of questionable reliability: one needs the findings of basic science, not just a compromised version of industrial research, if one is to weigh all the evidence. *Carbon Dreams* illuminates a gap between what the public comes to believe about global warming and the process by which scientific knowledge is established. This gap is particularly significant in climate change discourse, for it has played a prominent role in thwarting political action that could minimize future risk.

In contrast to this early example, other works of climate fiction are less notable for their character constellations and place greater emphasis on their storyworlds. Kim Stanley Robinson's Science in the Capital trilogy, featuring the novels *Forty Signs of Rain* (2004), *Fifty Degrees Below* (2005), and *Sixty Days and Counting* (2007), engages with contemporary climate science and focuses on scientists from several different disciplines. Robert Markley has shown the way the trilogy takes science seriously in order to treat it as part of the solution to the environmental crisis (2012, 9), providing a "visionary reassessment of the assumptions and values that define contemporary science and politics" (8). This reassessment is not undertaken through one discourse alone but through many, including Buddhist beliefs, a rethinking of laissez-faire economic principles, and the public discourse of political actors grappling with imminent environmental disaster. Once again, we find science novels invoking multiple perspectives—through several scientist characters this time—in order to illustrate the role of science within a larger societal context.

Like Maggie Gee's *The Flood* (2004) and, at least metaphorically, Atwood's *The Year of the Flood* (2009), the Science in the Capital trilogy is about the coming of a great flood, which is anticipated by several scientists at the National Science Foundation (NSF) in Washington, DC. Because of the low-lying geographical location in DC where the trilogy is set, much of the city is destroyed after the flood, which takes place at the end of the first novel. The risk of increased flooding across low-lying coastal regions, which scientists call attention to in abstract terms at the beginning of the narrative, is transformed into a concrete reality, a plot feature that the trilogy shares with Rich's *Odds Against Tomorrow*. One of the trilogy's narrative focalizers, NSF scientist Frank Vanderwal, experiences the effects of the climate crisis firsthand. His ruminations on sociobiology, the difference between science and engineering, and economic factors that make taking action difficult are intertwined with a major crisis in his personal life—a crisis made immeasurably worse when he loses his home to the flood. The impacts of climate change thus become personal.

Vanderwal eventually moves to a tree house, where he not only befriends fellow homeless people who scavenge for food that has been discarded by corporations but also experiments with a paleo lifestyle. Through Vanderwal's dialogues with the Khembali (a group of refugee Buddhists) and with his associate, Charlie Quibler, multiple perspectives on the social impact of climate change are presented. Charlie is married to Vanderwal's superior, Anna Quibler, who leads the NSF's bioinformatics division and whose focalized perspective is also key. Charlie is a stay-at-home father who takes care of their toddler, Joe, and their older son, Nick, and, through phone and email, works as an environmental policy advisor to Senator Phil Chase. This connection becomes very important, as it is Charlie who prods Senator Chase into taking political action in the environmental arena.

Each section of Robinson's trilogy begins with an incipit written from an omniscient perspective that provides a discussion of a separate field of science—from mathematics to physics to climate science—and then critically assesses the type of knowledge and attempts to redirect it to function for the good of society. By the end of the second volume, scientists are at work on public engineering projects and are engaging with political parties involved in trying to implement their ideas. Throughout, the different perspectives exhibited by the characters' thoughts, blogs, and interviews convey the complexity of the relationship between climate change and society. More than other novels in our sample, which position science merely as an identifier of risk, the trilogy stages a scenario in which science can, with the right political coordination, also become a mitigator of climate-change-related risks. But, the trilogy suggests, long-term solutions require rethinking society's use of science and the way it is attached to capitalist imperatives. Such a reexamination calls forth critiques of conceptions of the Anthropocene that minimize the role that capitalism in particular—rather than humankind in general—has played in transforming the earth (Klein 2014).

A related example of what is sometimes called Anthropocene fiction is the novella by Vandana Singh, *Entanglement*, which was published in *Hieroglyph: Stories and Visions for a Better Future* (2014). The novella's title evokes its structure as well as its theme. It is about the way human beings are entangled with others: with nature, with animals, with technology, and with other humans. This perspective is perhaps best described as posthumanist; it is critical of the way science has sometimes understood the world as something to be mastered or controlled, as inherently separate from the human being. The narrative strategy is to show the way humans are interconnected not just with other humans but also with nonhumans and with the world around them.

The novella begins with a forty-something scientist, Irene Ariak, who is on an Arctic expedition to study climate change and to test devices she designed to ameliorate it. Like *Carbon Dreams* and the Science in the Capital trilogy, hard science is taken seriously, as a way of explaining and addressing climate change. In this case, the scientist character researches and experiments with methanotrophs, or unicellular organisms that metabolize methane. Indeed, the very organism Ariak researches has symbolic meaning for interpreting the novella: "Methanotrophs, like most living beings, didn't exist in isolation, but in consortia. The complex web of interdependencies determined behavior and chemistry" (Singh 2014, 356). Like these organisms, she finds that humans—and the human sciences—are also deeply interconnected, or entangled, with other agents. For this reason, the climate scientist cannot be a mere specialist: "The age of specialization is over," she ruminates (353). When she is saved from a near-fatal diving accident by a beluga whale, she finds herself remembering her childhood as an Inuit and reflects on the way Inuit philosophy considers the entanglement of humans and nature. Science teaches what indigenous people already know: that everything is connected (360). Like both *Carbon Dreams* and the Science in the Capital trilogy, *Entanglement* suggests that interdisciplinary work is necessary for collectively dealing with climate change. But *Entanglement* also emphasizes the necessity of understanding the interconnectedness of humans and other agents, a tenet of posthumanism, indigenous philosophy, and Buddhism (another angle it shares with Robinson's trilogy).

Entanglement reveals the effects of climate change through diverse personal experiences of those effects and through the way it connects science and technology to the stories of five very different characters with varying relationships. For example, Fernanda, another scientist who has been studying drought in the Amazon forests of South America, reflects on the way city life contributes to climate change as well as on the way climate change affects people differently according to class standing (Singh 2014, 364). One perspective her story opens up is the possibility of raising the awareness of ordinary people through art, which is achieved in the story via Fernanda's fascination with a graffiti artist as well as her saxophone performance at public events. This aspect of the novella renders it self-reflexive insofar as raising awareness through art is precisely what the narrative achieves through its five stories and narrative focalizers.

The novella starts and ends with a technological device in the form of an orange bracelet, whose significance is revealed in the last section when a young man named Yuan tells his story of having created these bracelets as a cure for emotional loneliness. He gives this account on a mountaintop to a man he believes to be a Buddhist monk. The experience of telling his story helps him to heal but also compels him to go back down the mountain and engage in the world, with all of its problems. Yuan's story of creating the bracelets challenges the reader to go back and reread to get a bigger picture of the characters' connections to one another through the device. Further, each section begins with a short reference to a previous section, interlinking the narratives in a way that parallels the work of the orange bracelet. The orange bracelet—a technological device—has transhumanist potential insofar as it offers a technological solution to the human problem of loneliness. But the novella also points to another solution by revealing human interconnectedness through art. It not only serves as a disaster story or cautionary tale but also does reparative work and offers hope. It attempts to spiritually remedy what it has diagnosed as a cause of the warming earth: a culture of destruction that takes the form of a sort of addiction. The personal solution to the political problem of climate change is to restore our knowledge of how we are already entangled with others: with other humans, with nature, and even with technology.

The examples we have selected for this chapter illustrate how recent novels take science seriously in a way they did not (or perhaps could not) for much of the twentieth century. The type of critical work found in recent fiction serves as evidence that the "two cultures" divide is no longer a fruitful means for understanding the relationship between the arts and the sciences. Novels are now representing scientific knowledge and issues with more detail and accuracy than ever before, presenting it next to—and in dialogue with—other types of knowledge.

This recent literary phenomenon is thus not what E. O. Wilson (1998) calls "consilience," in which the type of knowledge the humanities and arts produces becomes subsumed by (or incorporated within) the type of knowledge produced by the sciences. A key structural feature of the novels we have examined is that they retain multiple perspectives on science and society. These texts neither endorse a single truth nor simply promote better understandings of science. On the contrary, they insistently draw readers' attention to socioeconomic, educational, and cultural factors, demonstrating that science is only one important part of the equation. Interweaving science into objects of aesthetic enjoyment—making science personal and pleasurable—says much about science's changing place in Western culture as we move deeper into the twenty-first century.

Notes

1. Our goal here is to illuminate how realist fiction handles science as a topic. For a discussion of how science-in-society issues are being addressed in recent examples from the science fiction genre, which falls largely outside the purview of this survey, see chapter 8.

2. Examples include Margaret Atwood's *Oryx and Crake* (shortlisted for the Governor General's Award, Orange Prize, and

Booker Prize, 2003); Andrea Barrett's *Ship Fever* (National Book Award, 1996); William Boyd's *Brazzaville Beach* (James Tait Black Memorial Prize, 1990); Michael Byers, *Long for This World* (Friends of American Writers Literary Award, 2004); Karen Joy Fowler's *We Are All Completely Beside Ourselves* (PEN/Faulkner Award, shortlisted for Booker Prize and Nebula Award, 2013); Allegra Goodman's *Intuition* (shortlisted for Orange Award, 2006); Simon Mawer's *Mendel's Dwarf* (Los Angeles Times Book Prize, 1999); Ian McEwan's *Saturday* (James Tait Black Memorial Prize, shortlisted for Booker Prize, 2005); Ruth Ozeki's *All Over Creation* (American Book Award, 2003); Ann Patchett's *State of Wonder* (shortlisted for Wellcome Book Prize, Orange Prize, 2011); Richard Powers's *The Gold Bug Variations* (*Time Magazine* Book of the Year, National Book Critics Circle Award finalist, 1991), *In the Time of Our Singing* (Ambassador Book Award, shortlisted for National Book Critics Circle Award, 2002), *The Echo Maker* (National Book Award, 2006), *The Overstory* (Pulitzer Prize, 2018); and Weike Wang's *Chemistry* (National Book Foundation's 5 Under 35, 2017).

References

Beck, Ulrich, Anthony Giddens, and Scott Lash. 1994. *Reflexive Modernisierung: Eine Kontroverse*. Frankfurt am Main: Suhrkamp.

Berger, James. 2002. "Testing Literature: Helen Keller and Richard Powers' Implementation H[elen]." *Arizona Quarterly: A Journal of American Literature, Culture, and Theory* 58 (3): 109–37. https://doi.org/10.1353/arq.2002.0020.

Clayton, Jay. 2003a. *Charles Dickens in Cyberspace: The Afterlife of the Nineteenth Century in Postmodern Culture*. Oxford, UK: Oxford University Press.

———. 2003b. "Frankenstein's Futurity: Clones, Replicants, and Robots." In *The Cambridge Companion to Mary Shelley*, edited by Esther Schor, 84–99. Cambridge, UK: Cambridge University Press.

Cordle, Daniel. 1999. *Postmodern Postures: Literature, Science and the Two Cultures Debate*. Aldershot, UK: Ashgate.

Crichton, Michael. 2006. *Next*. New York: HarperCollins.

Eggers, Dave. 2013. *The Circle*. San Francisco: McSweeney's.

Freißmann, Stephan. 2011. *Fictions of Cognition: Representing (Un)Consciousness and Cognitive Science in Contemporary English and American Fiction*. Trier: Wissenschaftlicher Verlag Trier.

Gaines, Susan M. 2001. *Carbon Dreams*. Berkeley, CA: Creative Arts.

Hamner, Everett. 2011. "The Predisposed Agency of Genomic Fiction." *American Literature* 83 (2): 413–41.

Haynes, Roslynn D. 2017. *From Madman to Crime Fighter: The Scientist in Western Culture*. Baltimore: Johns Hopkins University Press.

Hutchins, Scott. 2012. *A Working Theory of Love*. New York: Penguin.

Kirchhofer, Anton, and Natalie Roxburgh. 2016. "The Scientist as 'Problematic Individual' in Contemporary Fiction." *Zeitschrift für Anglistik und Amerikanistik* 64 (2): 149–68.

Klein, Naomi. 2014. *This Changes Everything: Capitalism vs. the Climate*. Toronto: Alfred A. Knopf Canada.

Markley, Robert. 2012. "'How to Go Forward': Catastrophe and Comedy in Kim Stanley Robinson's Science in the Capital Trilogy." *Configurations* 20 (1–2): 7–27.

Mawer, Simon. 1999. *Mendel's Dwarf*. New York: Penguin.

Mayer, Sylvia. 2014. "Explorations of the Controversially Real: Risk, the Climate Change Novel, and the Narrative of Anticipation." In *The Anticipation of Catastrophe: Environmental Risk in North American Literature and Culture*, edited by Sylvia Mayer and Alexa Weik von Mossner, 21–37. Heidelberg, DE: Winter.

Milburn, Colin. 2008. *Nanovision: Engineering the Future*. Durham, NC: Duke University Press.

Powers, Richard. 1991. *The Gold Bug Variations*. New York: William Morrow.

———. 1995. *Galatea 2.2*. New York: Picador.

Robinson, Kim Stanley. 2004. *Forty Signs of Rain*. New York: Bantam Spectra.

Roxburgh, Natalie, Anton Kirchhofer, and Anna Auguscik. 2016. "Universal Narrativity and the Anxious Scientist of the Contemporary Neuronovel." *Mosaic: An Interdisciplinary Critical Journal* 49 (4): 71–87.

Singh, Vandana. 2014. *Entanglement*. In *Hieroglyph: Stories and Visions for a Better Future*, edited by Kathryn Kramer and Ed Finn, 352–97. New York: William Morrow.

Trexler, Adam. 2015. *Anthropocene Fictions: The Novel in a Time of Climate Change*. Charlottesville: University of Virginia Press.

Wilson, Edward O. 1998. *Consilience: The Unity of Knowledge*. New York: Vintage.

2.
From Individual to Collective Knowledge Production
A Brief Nonfiction History

Peter Weingart and
Luz María Hernández Nieto

The fictional images of science created by writers and the image of science prevalent in public discourse are shaped by contemporaneous as well as historical realities. Some of these historical realities—or the fictional depictions they inspired—have had a remarkable impact on the public imagination and have become entrenched as stereotypes. The images of scientists and scientific practice prominent in twentieth-century novels and movies were often based on stereotypes that reflected practices of medieval alchemists and early modern scientists, even when the stories drew on contemporary scientific knowledge and technology (Haynes 2017; Schummer 2006). From the perspective of institutional sociology, one of the most interesting developments observed in the recent fiction literature discussed in this volume is the way such literature reflects the contemporary social embeddedness and organization of science. In order to fully appreciate this development and how it has manifested in works of fiction, one should review key elements in the historic transformation of the organization of science—from an individual practice embedded in a socially stratified premodern society to a fully institutionalized collective practice within a functionally differentiated modern society. It's a transformation that began with prominent thinkers of the "scientific revolution" in the late sixteenth and early seventeenth centuries—Francis Bacon, Thomas Hobbes, Galileo Galilei, Johannes Kepler, René Descartes, and Robert Boyle, among others—and continued into the late nineteenth and early twentieth centuries.

From Lone Tinkerers to Sharing Knowledge:
The Royal Society and a Community of Gentlemen Scientists

The scientific revolution was as much epistemological as institutional. The transition from Aristotelian natural philosophy to the production of knowledge based on observation, experiment, and certification of empirical fact entailed interdependent epistemological and institutional change: the decline of scholasticism in institutions of higher learning, the split of natural philosophy and religion, and the evolution from alchemy to modern chemistry and pharmacology. The social roles and behavioral patterns congruent with premodern epistemology were those of the secretive alchemist, the lone experimenter and tinkerer known as a "virtuoso," but by the eighteenth century, these roles and patterns were giving way to modes of knowledge production based on interaction and open demonstration. Here, the connection between the objectivity of Baconian "facts" and observer impartiality was key: facts in themselves were not convincing but had to be verified by experiments that were witnessed and reported by impartial observers. But who could be trusted? During the seventeenth century, such trust was connected to social status and manners, generally reserved for the gentility and for familiar figures of authority (Daston 1994, 57; Shapin 1994, 60, 410). The new "experimental philosophy" relied on the king, nobles, and gentlemen—on people who were free to do as they wished and had sufficient financial means to invest in instruments and experiments (Shapin 1994, 44, 46). These were, in effect, amateurs who "turned to science, not as a means of livelihood, but as an object of devoted interest" (Merton [1938] 1970, 455).

It was these gentleman amateurs who founded the Royal Society in 1660, a year often designated as the beginning of modern science. The Royal Society operated under rules laid down by Robert Boyle: opinions must be separated from persons, and author must be separated from text. Truth would emerge from civil conversation and the building of consensus about what was to be accepted as "experimental fact" (Shapin and Schaffer 1985). The Royal Society became the model of cooperation among the amateur scientists, who met regularly to demonstrate their experiments and discuss which newly discovered phenomenon could be claimed as fact. In keeping with Bacon's *Novum Organon*, research progressed inductively from assembling particulars to asserting principles. The point was not whether the experiments were successful but that they were witnessed by all members in attendance and that detailed written reports were sent to absent members. In 1665, the society's first secretary, Henry Oldenburg, founded the first scientific journal, *Philosophical Transactions*, and established the basic principles of modern scientific publishing: the registration of submission dates, certification by peer review, and dissemination to interested parties. With this, the notion of the "scientific community" as an open, international communication network of scholars was born.

The Royal Society was not the only European effort to institutionalize and support the new natural philosophy: in Rome, a group of noblemen founded the Accademia dei Lincei in 1603, and in Florence, the Medici family founded the Accademia del Cimento in 1657. The French Académie des Sciences (1666) and the academies in Berlin (1700) and St. Petersburg (1725) were founded by the respective kings. It took some time to overcome conflicts about patents and priority of discovery, but the utopian model that Bacon had envisioned in his 1627 masterwork, *The New Atlantis*, ultimately prevailed, and collaboration within and between the academies became the basis for the eventual professionalization of scientific work. Whereas the Royal Society depended on a membership of gentlemen with independent financial means, the French king had allocated funds so that members of the Académie des Sciences, which also served as the patent office, received a regular income. The French academy thus served as a model for the professionalization of scientists as salaried employees of the state. The actual differentiation between amateur and professional members of the scientific community, however, would develop gradually (Bensaude-Vincent 2001, 102). Throughout the eighteenth century and into the nineteenth century, experiments continued to be performed not only in the academies but also in the salons of the aristocracy and at public gatherings and fairs. Aristocrats assembled "cabinets of curiosity," and members of the bourgeoisie—including physicians, pharmacists, and other members of the emerging scientific professions—also collected odd specimens of the natural world for study, classification, and demonstration.

The new experimental philosophy coexisted with the secret practice of alchemy for almost a century—both Robert Boyle and Isaac Newton practiced alchemy, even while developing the physical sciences (Principe 2000)—

but by the mid-eighteenth century, alchemy had been discredited and was popularly associated with charlatans claiming to create gold (Principe and Newman 2001, 386). The social organization of the new empirical scientific practice and its institutions was inextricably connected to the methods of knowledge production, and the kind of knowledge that counted was a result of the cooperative generation and open communication of research results rather than of the isolated, hidden experiments of the alchemists.[1]

Disciplines as a New Organizational Mode of Science

The organization of knowledge based on the accumulation and classification of objects and observations that characterized the late seventeenth century and the eighteenth century proved to be inherently limited. The development of Linnaeus's multivolume *Systema Naturae* illustrates the problem: the first edition was published in 1735 with 549 species, and the final edition, published from 1766 to 1768, listed 7,000. By the end of the eighteenth century, traditional methods of natural history based on the spatial ordering of knowledge were being replaced by new techniques of systematization based on sequential temporal developments (Lepenies 1976, 16, 18). The problems of overload and integration of experiential data increased the pressure to treat data selectively according to increasingly specific scientific criteria. This set the stage for specialization and the disciplinary differentiation of knowledge production and organization (Stichweh 1984, 42).

Slowly, the differentiation into disciplines began to transform both the internal operations and the social organization of science. Increasingly, knowledge was categorized and recorded according to the emerging disciplinary divisions, but it took some time for this to affect the structure of universities (14–15). Eighteenth-century textbooks typically contained as much knowledge as their authors could master, and a student moved upward through a hierarchy from philosophy to medicine and then to law and theology. Universities had been structured into faculties based on this hierarchy since the Middle Ages, but by the beginning of the nineteenth century, such structures, and the classification of knowledge that had informed them, were obsolete.

The emergence of disciplines had several implications. Disciplines were organized into communities of scholars who communicated with one another and generated research questions from such interactions rather than from contributions from the "external" society. Within these closed circles of communication, specialized languages and modes of social organization developed. The mere accumulation of observations and artifacts gave way to research that was aimed at discerning and understanding patterns or effects and at discovering the laws of nature. The scientist's goal was to be original and discover something *new*, and a seemingly endless universe of research questions presented itself. As the philologist August Boeckh observed in the mid-nineteenth century, "No problem was too small not to be worthy of a serious scientific analysis" (quoted in Daston 1999, 74). The differentiation into disciplines also produced an increasingly fine-grained division of labor among scientists. Observing this process in 1882, Emil du Bois-Reymond commented that "a thousand busy workers, renouncing high fame, are daily bringing in a thousand details, unconcerned about inner and outer completeness" (1882, 21).

By the end of the eighteenth century, it had become clear that the academies were organizationally incapable of dealing with the many disciplinary cultures and heterogeneous forms of doing research. Although they retained their function as places for the collection and recording of knowledge, they ultimately lost their authority as the primary purveyors of scientific knowledge, and the universities replaced them as organizations for research and the dissemination of information (Stichweh 1984, 73; Weingart 2010).[2] In 1809, the University of Berlin was founded as a model for the new research-oriented university, based on Wilhelm von Humboldt's concept that teaching and research should be integrated, with students and professors learning and doing research together. It was still structured around the traditional faculties—theology, law, philosophy, and medicine—but the natural sciences, which were part of the philosophy faculty, had room to develop into multiple self-contained disciplines.

The development of the modern research and teaching laboratory accompanied the transition from eighteenth- to nineteenth-century science and its institutionalization in the university. At the end of the eighteenth century, private research and teaching facilities—set up in the homes of enterprising university teachers—were widespread. As experiments and scientific instruments became more complex and sensitive, these laboratories were professionalized and integrated into the universities. One of the first prototypes for the modern teaching laboratory, for example, was organized by the chemist Justus Liebig, who started out with a private laboratory in Giessen but by 1852 had taken a university position in Munich that came complete with a new laboratory building and attached home (Schmidgen 2011).

Gradually, the formal university structure was reorganized into faculties or departments with their own teaching curricula and degrees. These degrees then connected research and study to the labor market. The faculties were based on the newly defined disciplines, and as these became more and more specialized and developed their own technical languages, communication across disciplinary boundaries became difficult. Reporting of new discoveries and theoretical advances had already shifted from the academies to general scientific associations—the German Association of Naturalists and Physicians (Gesellschaft deutscher Naturforscher und Ärzte) was founded in 1822, the British Association for the Advancement of Science in 1831, and the American Association for the Advancement of Science in 1848. Discipline-specific associations were quick to follow. These were professional membership organizations in the modern sense rather than general scholarly honorary societies like the academies. The Chemical Society of London was first, in 1841, followed by the German Physical Society (Deutsche physikalische Gesellschaft) in 1845, the German Chemical Society (Deutsche chemische Gesellschaft zu Berlin) in 1867, and the Physical Society of London in 1874. They provided forums for discussion of new findings, set professional standards, made recommendations on teaching curricula, represented the discipline in political contexts, and, above all, published discipline-specific journals.

The emergence of disciplines and their ongoing differentiation also indicated a new place for science in society. Scientific research and university teaching became respected, paid, institutionalized professions.[3] At the same time, the idea that scientific discoveries and their benefits should be made widely accessible led to new cultural formats: the first world's fairs showed off the achievements of science and technology, and popularizing articles and books were published in great numbers. In fact, popularization became a profession in its own right and generated a new genre of literature. Journals such as *Scientific American*, founded in 1845, and *Nature*, in 1869, attempted to bridge the gap between specialized science and the general public that had developed along with the progressing specialization of science. Science also became a topic of coverage in the general news and entertainment media. Practical new technologies and applied sciences such as agriculture and medicine were of particular interest, but by the turn of the century, the focus was on astronomy and geology as well as on electricity (Bensaude-Vincent 2001, 104). Thus, although the popularization movement itself reflected a growing distance between the lay public and professional scientists—with their increasingly specialized languages and complex practices—the public remained remarkably engaged with science throughout the nineteenth century.

The Emergence of Science Policy

Until the early twentieth century, the concept of science policy per se was nonexistent, and state support for science was tantamount to its support for higher education. In Europe the universities were founded, financed, and governed by the state, which dictated departmental structure and hired the professors. But as scientific knowledge became increasingly relevant for existing arenas of state regulation, such as public health and infrastructure, industrialization and modernization generated new regulatory needs (Lundgreen et al. 1986, 17). From the 1870s onward, governments in most of the industrializing countries established research entities. To cite just a few examples, in Germany, the National Materials Testing Office was founded in 1871;[4] in the United States, the Hygienic Laboratory, which later became the National Institutes of Health, was established in 1887; and in the United Kingdom, the National Physical Laboratory was established in 1900. These were followed by more institutes dedicated to meteorology, public health, agriculture, food technology, forestry, and so forth. In contrast to the academic research system, in which researchers are free to determine their topics and focus on basic science, these government institutions have focused mandates and predefined research goals.

Science in Government, Industry, and the Military

By the early twentieth century, scientific research had become a major force in the industrialization of the economy, and the practice of science itself had become industrialized—that is, it had turned into a collective enterprise with a marked division of labor. Although scientists such as du Bois-Reymond had worried that "the stream of knowledge is continually dividing itself into more numerous and smaller rills, and there is danger of its getting lost in the sands and marshes" (1882, 21), those rills and trickles added up to a torrent of discovery. Advances in physics and chemistry such as the discovery of electromagnetism, the design of a synthesis for potassium nitrate (used in gunpowder and fertilizer), and the invention of chemical dyes had led to the development of new industries. Large chemical and electrical engineering companies emerged around this time; examples include BASF, Hoechst, Siemens, and AEG in Germany, and Dow Chemical and Edison General Electric in the United States.

The modern entanglement of scientific knowledge production with its uses and consequences—both benevolent and destructive—became apparent during the two world wars. The chemical process used to synthesize ammonia fertilizer and save people from starvation (the Haber Process) was also used in producing the nitrates for explosives during World War I, and the man who won the Nobel Prize for inventing it, Fritz Haber, also became known for pioneering the use of chlorine gas and phosgene as weapons. If World War I had demonstrated the utility of science—notably chemistry—for warfare, World War II proved to be the physicists' war (Kevles 1987, 302–23). The basis for this was the discovery of nuclear fission by Otto Hahn and Fritz Strassmann in 1938, although unlike Haber neither of them was complicit in the wartime uses of their discoveries. Leo Szilard, a Jewish European physicist who had escaped to the United States, realized the destructive potential of the discovery and, worried the Nazis would harness it, joined forces with Albert Einstein and other immigrant physicists to convince President Roosevelt to support a massive research effort to develop an atomic bomb. The result was the Manhattan Project, which, led by the physicist Robert Oppenheimer, successfully designed the bombs that were dropped on Hiroshima and Nagasaki in 1945. Physicists were also involved in the military development of radar systems, jet-powered aircraft, and rockets, which later laid the groundwork for the postwar space programs in the United States and Soviet Union. Other scientific disciplines were mobilized for the war effort as well, and the social sciences and psychology were used to determine the best methods of training soldiers, boosting their morale, and improving the effectiveness of propaganda (Geuter 1984; Stouffer 1949). This signaled the fact that science had generally proven to be instrumental for the military, albeit not equally across all fields.

The development of weapons of mass destruction irreversibly entangled scientists in political and ethical issues. In the United States, they were deeply involved in and affected by the Cold War and the McCarthy-era persecution of communists and political critics. Oppenheimer and his fellow Manhattan Project scientists, along with many other influential scientists around the world, spoke out against further nuclear arms testing and the international nuclear arms race. When the Atomic Energy Commission revoked Oppenheimer's security clearance in 1954, he became a symbol of the government repression of scientists in politically sensitive positions (Polenberg 2002). Another early member of the Manhattan Project, Edward Teller—considered the father of the H-bomb—was ostracized by the scientific community and became known as the "real Dr. Strangelove" when he implicated Oppenheimer in security hearings and spoke out for nuclear armament and a tough stance against the Soviet Union (Goodchild 2004). The atomic bomb is just one of many examples of the ethical and political dilemmas that scientists face when their knowledge proves to be instrumental for political or military purposes.

World War II and its aftermath provoked changes in the ways scientific research was funded and organized that reflected the emergence of systemic science policies in Europe and North America. These changes were particularly apparent in the governmental institutions that were established specifically to provide funding for basic research and allow the scientific community to set its own research agendas and conduct its own quality assessments. In the United States, expenditures for military research had increased fiftyfold by the end of World War II, and the first political objective after the war was to demobilize research that had been deployed for the war effort. Vannevar Bush, head of the Office of Scientific Research and Development, which had overseen the Manhattan Project, argued in his postwar report to President Truman that basic research was an important source of technological innovation; he recommended significant government support for university-based research and a new federal agency to administer it (Bush 1945).

After years of debate, the US Congress established the National Science Foundation (NSF) with the mandate to support basic research, adding to the diverse US research funding system in which numerous agencies and departments exercise jurisdiction over parts of the federal science budget, and political oversight is provided by an array of committees in both houses of Congress. In this arrangement, basic research is mostly funded in the form of individual projects, the relevance and quality of which are determined by the respective disciplinary communities. But political priorities have also manifested themselves in the form of overarching funding programs for specific topics. In the 1970s, for example, the threat of economic competition from new Japanese products led to support for technology-focused, university-industry partnerships, whereas from the 1980s onward, "mission-oriented basic research" gained priority. In the late 1990s, medical research and the life sciences assumed supremacy, and between 1998 and 2003, the National Institutes of Health budget doubled (Smith 1990; Stokes 1997).

In Europe, as in the United States, science emerged as a new policy arena in the postwar years, and many countries established national ministries in addition to research-funding councils.[5] The perception that science policy and economic policy went hand in hand—that scientific research was essential to technological innovation and economic growth—was international. Although economic theory did not yet support this assumption, the international Organisation for Economic Co-Operation and Development (OECD) assembled the leading industrial countries in the West under a science policy agenda that was, in fact, based on it.

The Manhattan Project as Model for the Industrial Organization of "Big Science"

The Manhattan Project introduced the new concept of research as a large-scale industrial-style organization in which there is substantial division of labor, intense time pressure, and a culture of secrecy even within the organization. Some one hundred thousand people worked on the project, with more than two thousand physicists in Los Alamos alone (Kevles 1987, 329; Rhodes 1986). In the postwar period, most industrialized countries began to adopt this type of large-scale research organization, setting up state-funded research installations devoted to the design and construction of nuclear reactors. Because of their size—both in terms of instrumentation and the personnel and funds required—such efforts were dubbed "big science" (Weinberg 1967).

Science policy-makers around the world followed the model of nuclear energy facilities, particularly in fields in which state-of-the-art scientific instruments outgrew the capacities of even the largest universities or in which exceptionally large numbers of researchers and extended periods of time were needed to produce results. Examples include the various particle accelerators used in high-energy physics, the huge telescopes used in optical and radio astronomy, the International Space Station, the fusion reactor, and the 1000 Genomes Project—all of which are, of necessity, financed by international consortia of research organizations. The creation and management of such facilities produce intricate, highly complex organizations, both in their internal workings and their engagement with local, national, and international politics. Their existence depends on the support of local communities that have their own traditions and economic interests, on convincing national governments that the large investments will pay off in terms of economic development, and on the creation of international consortia that can be sustained over extended periods of time.

Although not characteristic of science as a whole, big science has become the organizational model for certain fields of scientific research, effectively transforming their social structures. For example, the professional standing of scientists depends on peer recognition of their achievements, which, of course, requires that achievements can be linked to individual scientists. In the case of industrialized big science, however, experiments and observations can involve hundreds or even thousands of researchers, all of whom may share coauthorship of a journal article (Birnholtz 2008).[6] In such projects, attribution can be assigned only to an institution or research group, not to an individual—a development with far-reaching and still unclear implications for science.

The political and social conditions of science have been affected not only by big science per se but also by the overall growth of science systems.[7] In the OECD countries, there are currently 7.7 scientists on average per 1,000 full-time employed individuals, and national expenditures range from 2.07 percent of GDP (in China) to 2.90 percent (in Finland) (World Bank 2017). Expenditures for science require political legitimation, policies, and regulation and, with no guarantees that basic research will have useful economic or beneficial societal outcomes, a considerable measure of trust on the part of politicians and taxpayers; legitimation, policy, regulation, and trust are thus all elements of what has been called a "social contract for science" (Guston and Keniston 1994).

The Changing Relationship Between Science and the Public

Since the 1970s, the "social contract" established in the postwar years has changed in a number of respects. One change involves the closer coupling of science to the economy, or the "economization" of science. Although the promise of the practical utility of science goes back to the beginnings of modern science, the actual translation of research into economically profitable applications had mostly been limited to fields such as chemistry and solid-state physics. As the size of the sums involved made public funds for research more and more politically sensitive, science policy began to emphasize the direct transfer of a wider spectrum of fundamental research from universities to industrial applications and marketable products, with biotechnology being the paradigmatic example. Inspired by the example of a few highly successful cases, universities in the United States and Europe established "technology transfer centers" to promote such activities and earn revenues from patents, licenses, and intellectual property rights. The logic of private research, with its competitive drive for profit and its culture of secrecy, thus began to invade the universities (Slaughter and Rhoades 2009).[8]

National science policies have also responded to a perceived erosion of public trust in the innate worth and utility of basic research by introducing fine-tuned funding schemes, evaluation methods, and performance measures designed to focus academic research on politically and economically justifiable applications—namely, technological innovation and health. This further subjects universities and research laboratories to a market logic that encourages competition—both among academic institutions and among individual scientists—and is likely to have even stronger long-term impacts on the academic culture of collaboration, transparency, and publicly oriented research than technology transfer has had (Geuna and Nesta 2006).

By the 1970s, public awareness of the risks associated with apparently beneficial scientific discoveries and applications such as pesticides and, in particular, nuclear energy had also begun to undermine the uncritical confidence in scientific experts that prevailed during the first half of the twentieth century. The nuclear reactor accident at Three Mile Island in 1979 showed how misleading statistical projections of accident probability could be. A critical news media exposed the internal debates between scientists and demonstrated to the general public that the experts were uncertain about some of the issues and appeared at times to be partisan or politically motivated in their pronouncements. This destroyed the myth of science having exact answers to all questions, and the distrust that erupted paved the way for the green political parties that began to emerge around the world (Agar 2008). Public awareness of the risks inherent in new discoveries and technological developments—and the role of science in detecting and mitigating those risks—has grown steadily over the last half century. Issues such as nuclear waste storage, the safety of genetically modified corn, climate change, and, more recently, the dangers of fracking have ignited citizens movements that are attentive to and often critical of scientific developments and new technologies, forcing scientific communities, corporations, and politicians to enter into a dialogue with the public.

Another change in the social contract with science concerns the ways that science and the public interact. As early as the late 1950s, science associations, policy organizations, and government ministries were running campaigns designed to gain public support for science expenditures and legitimacy for scientific institutions and knowledge. Under the banner of "public understanding of science," such campaigns reflected a paternalistic teacher-student relationship between science and the public. In recent years, however, they have taken a more democratic approach—now under the banner of "public engagement with science and technology" or "dialogue with the public"—that recognizes the role of public opinion in determining policy and takes the public's engagement with scientific knowledge seriously. This changing relationship also reflects a dramatic change in the demographics of education since the 1970s, with an increasing proportion of the population obtaining secondary (i.e., high school) and tertiary (i.e., college) education that involves at least rudimentary contact with scientific knowledge and practices. Clearly this means that ever-larger numbers of citizens are likely to be interested in science and capable of forming critical opinions about scientific issues.

Science and the Media

The pressure to validate scientific research to the public and the market-style competition resulting from the introduction of "new public management" have also changed the relationship between science and the media, with scientific institutions as well as individual scientists seeking out and attempting to manage media attention. Universities now have dedicated media relations offices that not only produce press releases about new discoveries but also generate sophisticated PR materials aimed at raising their profiles and promoting their institutional images (Kohring et al. 2013). Scientists communicate freely with the media and, in adapting to the media's "news values," may end up compromising the standards of science (Rödder, Franzen, and Weingart 2012). With the advent of social media, the quest for popular attention and acclaim has expanded to blogs, Twitter, and Facebook, which generally lack any system of quality control but do allow for rapid and direct two-way communication. The public can now keep close watch over developments in science—citizens can comment on the ethical, political, and social implications of discoveries; criticize and scandalize scientific misconduct; and even occasionally contribute to research efforts. Clearly, social media has given the public a new role and presence in the realm of scientific research.

Conclusion

Over the past two hundred years, the number of people involved in science has grown exponentially: 80–90 percent of all scientists who have ever lived are alive now, making science a very present phenomenon (Price 1971; Weingart 2003, 186). During this time, science has evolved from an individual practice to a global professional network of millions of individuals and thousands of institutions—all governed by remarkably similar norms and standards that transcend vast cultural differences and language barriers. The scientist's role has changed from that of the individual genius tinkering in an attic to that of a nameless researcher in an army of researchers, performing experiments with instruments that, in some cases, cost billions of dollars and require thousands of technicians to build and operate. The lone explorer working, as Alexander von Humboldt proclaimed, in "solitude and freedom" (*Einsamkeit und Freiheit*)[9] is a figure of the distant past. As science has developed into a central institution of modern society, it has both shaped and been shaped by economics, politics, and social innovation—to such an extent that sociologists have started referring to contemporary society as the knowledge society. Scientific developments and their consequences are now debated in wide-reaching and sophisticated public discourses that engage scientists, politicians, and the general public across all forms of media. It should come as no surprise that this public engagement is also apparent in the nuanced explorations of science and its complex social interactions—with politics, news media, the economy, the military, and the general public—that have been appearing in mainstream fiction media. More surprising and, as we discuss in the next chapter, more interesting are the ways that ancient stereotypes of scientists have withstood the tides of time and appear within and alongside these multifaceted contemporary stories about science.

Notes

1. Our focus here is on institutional transformations as they affected the embeddedness of early modern European science systems. For nuanced discussions of Bacon's model, see, for example, Keller 2018 and Manzo 2006. For detailed accounts of epistemological issues during this period, see, for example, Jacob and Stewart 2004 and Cohen 1981.

2. Science systems differed internationally, as did the exact fate of the academies. In Europe, there was a revival of science academies in the early 2000s, and national governments have given them new advisory functions (Lentsch and Weingart 2011).

3. In 1833, William Whewell coined the term "scientist" to replace "natural philosopher," but it didn't come into widespread use in the United States and Great Britain until the end of that century.

4. Staatliches Materialprüfungsamt, which later became the Bundesanstalt für Materialforschung und -prüfung.

5. In Germany, the precursor to today's Deutsche Forschungsgemeinschaft (the German Research Foundation) was actually established much earlier, in 1920, as the Notgemeinschaft der deutschen Wissenschaft (Emergency Association of German Science).

6. A 2008 article describing the Large Hadron Collider, the twenty-seven-mile-long particle accelerator on the French-Swiss border, boasted 2,926 authors from 169 research institutions (The ATLAS Collaboration 2008). Some papers have so many authors that they cannot be listed at all.

7. Science has grown exponentially since the eighteenth century and, contrary to predictions, is still growing: between 1980 and 2012, for example, global scientific publications increased at a rate of approximately 3 percent annually (Bornmann and Mutz 2015).

8. See chapter 7 for a detailed discussion of portrayals of economization in contemporary science novels.

9. See Wilhelm von Humboldt's famous "Denkschrift über die äußere und innere Organisation der höheren wissenschaftlichen Anstalten in Berlin" of 1809–10.

References

Agar, Jon. 2008. "What Happened in the Sixties?" *British Society for the History of Science* 41 (4): 567–600. https://doi.org/10.1017/S0007087408001179.

The ATLAS Collaboration. 2008. "The ATLAS Experiment at the CERN Large Hadron Collider." *Journal of Instrumentation* 3 (8). https://doi.org/10.1088/1748-0221/3/08/S08003.

Bensaude-Vincent, Bernadette. 2001. "A Genealogy of the Increasing Gap Between Science and the Public." *Public Understanding of Science* 10 (1): 99–113. https://doi.org/10.1088/0963-6625/10/1/307.

Birnholtz, Jeremy. 2008. "When Authorship Isn't Enough: Lessons from CERN on the Implications of Formal and Informal Credit Attribution Mechanisms in Collaborative Research." *Journal of Electronic Publishing* 11 (1). https://doi.org/10.3998/3336451.0011.105.

Bornmann, Lutz, and Rüdiger Mutz. 2015."Growth Rates of Modern Science: A Bibliometric Analysis Based on the Number of Publications and Cited References." *Journal of the Association for Information Science and Technology* 66 (11): 2215–22.

Bush, Vannevar. 1945. *Science, the Endless Frontier.* Washington, DC: US Government Printing Office.

Cohen, I. Bernard. 1981 *The Newtonian Revolution.* Cambridge, UK: Cambridge University Press.

Daston, Lorraine. 1994. "Baconian Facts, Academic Civility, and the Prehistory of Objectivity." In *Rethinking Objectivity,* edited by Allan Megill, 37–63. Durham, NC: Duke University Press.

———. 1999. "Die Akademien und die Einheit der Wissenschaften: Die Disziplinierung der Disziplinen." In *Die Königlich Preußische Akademie der Wissenschaften zu Berlin im Kaiserreich,* edited by Jürgen Kocka, Rainer Hohlfeld, and P. T. Walther, 61–84. Berlin: Akademie Verlag.

Du Bois-Reymond, Emil. 1882. "The Science of the Present Period." Address delivered at the Academy of Sciences, Berlin, March 23, 1882. Translation in *Popular Science Monthly* 22 (November 1882). Originally published as *Über die wissenschaftlichen Zustände der Gegenwart: Festrede gehalten in der Sitzung der Akademie der Wissenschaften zur Geburtstagsfeier seiner Majestät des Kaisers und Königs am 23. März 1882.* Berlin: Ferd. Dümmlers Verlagsbuchhandlung, 1882. https://en.wikisource.org/wiki/Popular_Science_Monthly/Volume_22/November_1882/The_Science_of_the_Present_Period#cite_note-1.

Geuna, Aldo, and Lionel J. J. Nesta. 2006. "University Patenting and Its Effects on Academic Research: The Emerging European Evidence." In "Property and the Pursuit of Knowledge: IPR Issues Affecting Scientific Research," edited by P. A. David and B. H. Hall. Special issue, *Research Policy* 35 (6): 790–807. https://doi.org/10.1016/j.respol.2006.04.005.

Geuter, Ulfried. 1984. *Die Professionalisierung der deutschen Psychologie im Nationalsozialismus.* Frankfurt am Main: Suhrkamp.

Goodchild, Peter. 2004. *Edward Teller: The Real Dr. Strangelove.* Cambridge, MA: Harvard University Press.

Guston, David H., and Kenneth Keniston, eds. 1994. *The Fragile Contract: University Science and the Federal Government.* Cambridge, MA: MIT Press.

Haynes, Roslynn D. 2017. *From Madman to Crime Fighter: The Scientist in Western Culture.* Baltimore: Johns Hopkins University Press.

Jacob, Margaret C., and Larry Stewart. 2004. *Practical Matter: Newton's Science in the Service of Industry and Empire, 1687–1851.* Cambridge, MA: Harvard University Press.

Keller, Vera. 2018. *Knowledge in the Public Interest.* New York: Cambridge University Press.

Kevles, Daniel J. 1987. *The Physicists: The History of a Scientific Community in Modern America.* New York: Knopf.

Kohring, Matthias, Frank Marcinkowski, Christian Lindner, and Sarah Karis. 2013. "Media Orientation of German University Decision Makers and the Executive Influence of Public Relations." *Public Relations Review* 39 (3): 171–77. https://doi.org/10.1016/j.pubrev.2013.01.002.

Lentsch, Justus, and Peter Weingart, eds. 2011. *The Politics of Scientific Advice: Institutional Design for Quality Assurance.* Cambridge, UK: Cambridge University Press.

Lepenies, Wolf. 1976. *Das Ende der Naturgeschichte.* Munich: Hanser.

Lundgreen, Peter, Bernd Horn, Wolfgang Krohn, Günter Küppers, and Rainer Paslak. 1986. *Staatliche Forschung in*

Deutschland 1870–1980. Frankfurt am Main: Campus Verlag.

Manzo, Silvia. 2006. "Francis Bacon: Freedom, Authority and Science." *British Journal for the History of Philosophy* 14 (2): 245–73.

Merton, Robert K. (1938) 1970. *Science, Technology and Society in Seventeenth-Century England*. New York: Harper Torchbooks.

Polenberg, Richard, ed. 2002. *In the Matter of J. Robert Oppenheimer: The Security Clearance Hearing*. Ithaca, NY: Cornell University Press.

Price, Derek J. de Solla. 1971. *Little Science, Big Science*. New York: Columbia University Press.

Principe, Lawrence M. 2000. "The Alchemies of Robert Boyle and Isaac Newton: Alternate Approaches and Divergent Deployments." In *Rethinking the Scientific Revolution*, edited by Margaret J. Osler, 201–20. Cambridge, UK: Cambridge University Press. https://doi.org/10.1017/CBO9780511529276.011.

Principe, Lawrence M., and William R. Newman. 2001. "Some Problems with the Historiography of Alchemy." In *Secrets of Nature: Astrology and Alchemy in Early Modern Europe*, edited by Anthony Grafton and William R. Newman, 385–431. Cambridge, MA: MIT Press.

Rhodes, Richard. 1986. *The Making of the Atomic Bomb*. New York: Simon and Schuster.

Rödder, Simone, Martina Franzen, and Peter Weingart, eds. 2012. *The Sciences' Media Connection: Public Communication and Its Repercussions*. Sociology of the Sciences Yearbook 28. Dordrecht, NL: Springer.

Schmidgen, Henning. 2011. "The Laboratory." European History Online (EGO). Institute of European History (IEG), August 8, 2011. http://www.ieg-ego.eu/schmidgenh-2011-en.

Schummer, Joachim. 2006. "Historical Roots of the 'Mad Scientist': Chemists in Nineteenth-Century Literature." *Ambix* 53 (2): 99–127.

Shapin, Steven. 1994. *A Social History of Truth: Civility and Science in Seventeenth-Century England*. Science and Its Conceptual Foundations. Chicago: University of Chicago Press.

Shapin, Steven, and Simon Schaffer. 1985. *Leviathan and the Air-Pump*. Princeton, NJ: Princeton University Press.

Slaughter, Sheila, and Gary Rhoades. 2009. *Academic Capitalism and the New Economy*. Baltimore: Johns Hopkins University Press.

Smith, Bruce L. R. 1990. *American Science Policy Since World War II*. Washington, DC: Brookings Institution Press.

Sprat, Thomas. 1959. *History of the Royal Society*. St. Louis: Washington University Press. Facsimile edition of the 1667 publication, London: Routledge and Kegan Paul.

Stichweh, Rudolf. 1984. *Zur Entstehung des modernen Systems wissenschaftlicher Disziplinen: Physik in Deutschland 1740–1890*. Frankfurt am Main: Suhrkamp.

Stokes, Donald E. 1997. *Pasteur's Quadrant: Basic Science and Technological Innovation*. Washington, DC: Brookings Institution Press.

Stouffer, Samuel A. 1949. *The American Soldier*. Princeton, NJ: Princeton University Press.

Weinberg, Alvin Martin. 1967. *Reflections on Big Science*. Cambridge, MA: MIT Press.

Weingart, Peter. 2003. *Wissenschaftssoziologie*. Bielefeld, DE: Transcript-Verlag.

———. 2010. "A Short History of Knowledge Formations." In *The Oxford Handbook of Interdisciplinarity*, edited by R. Frodemann, J. Thomson Klein, and C. Mitcham, 3–14. Oxford, UK: Oxford University Press.

World Bank Development Indicators. 2017. "Research and Development Expenditure (% of GDP)." United Nations Educational, Scientific, and Cultural Organization (UNESCO) Institute for Statistics. https://data.worldbank.org/indicator/GB.XPD.RSDV.GD.ZS.

3.

Between Mad and Mundane
Mixed Stereotypical and Realistic Portrayals of Science in Contemporary Fiction Media

Luz María Hernández Nieto
and Peter Weingart

The representations of science in the mainstream and literary science novels that have been amassing over the past few decades (see chapter 1) appear to depart from earlier cultural representations in at least two interrelated ways. First, they represent science in its social, political, and economic contexts, drawing a seemingly more realistic picture than we saw in novels and films during most of the twentieth century. Second, they seem to have replaced prototypes of isolated, obsessed, generally dangerous, and sometimes foolish, mad, power-hungry, or downright evil male scientists with protagonists who more closely resemble the diverse assortment of down-to-earth individuals one might find in any university or research lab in the United States or Europe—people with ordinary hopes, anxieties, passions, and chores rather than grandiose ambitions to rule the world or take revenge by destroying humankind. Haynes has noted that the "entrenched stereotype of the mad, bad scientist has been progressively eroded" over the past couple of decades (2014, 5). Roxburgh and Clayton hold that "the last three decades have seen a dramatic increase in realist fiction about science" (chapter 1, 22). Kirby observes that "contemporary portrayals have become more complex and far less negative than previous stereotypes. Even the most recognizable stereotype of the 'mad scientist' has evolved and no longer resembles the maniacal, evil, obsessed one of decades past" (2017, 292). While maintaining that the "mad scientist is the most enduring scientist stereotype and the one that has had the greatest impact on popular perceptions of scientists," Kirby also points out that "portrayals of mad scientists in contemporary entertainment media are most often associated with emerging, complex, and unregulated areas of science" (293). All these authors seem to agree that depictions of scientists (and science) have changed in the sense that they have become "more realistic," that old stereotypes have "evolved" or been "eroded."

Other studies indicate that stereotypical representations still dominate in some media (see, for example, Haynes 2003; Hernández Nieto 2016; Pansegrau 2009; Flicker 2003; Van Gorp, Rommes, and Emons 2013).[1] But few if any of these studies define or discuss the concept of *stereotype* that underlies their assessments. There is also an implicit assumption that stereotypes and complex, realistic portrayals of science are mutually exclusive. Indeed, such an assumption is pervasive among scholars, scientists, and government entities concerned about public perceptions of science. Also pervasive is the idea that people who come into contact with scientists or "realistic" fictional representations through communications media understand what scientists really do and therefore have a more positive view of science. The relationship between media exposure to science and interest in or knowledge about science is, however, complex,[2] and various studies show that familiarity with science may lead to a critical stance on particular issues (see, for example, Allum et al. 2008; Evans and Durant 1995).[3] A "realistic" portrayal of scientists is not necessarily a "positive" one. In *Solar*, Michael Beard is represented realistically, but the overall portrayal of him as a researcher is negative. Likewise, positive portrayals of scientists can also be stereotypical, and portrayals of the "heroic scientist" (Pansegrau 2009) or "noble scientist" (Haynes 2003) are common in fiction. Indiana Jones and Sam Becket from the TV series *Quantum Leap* are perhaps two well-known examples of fictional benevolent scientists who use their knowledge and expertise for the benefit of society.

Both the appearance and persistence of stereotypes, which vary in form and complexity, are related to the material medium, conventions, and audience of a particular media and genre. Novels, for example, tend to portray more fully developed, complex characters and contextual scenarios than do animated cartoons. Similarly, market-oriented commercial novels and cartoons may be more prone to the use of stereotypical characters than is literary fiction. Stereotypical features may be used to facilitate the audience's quick identification of a character as a scientist (Kirby 2017), or they may simply make the characterization process easier for authors, screenwriters, or character designers. In serial media and comedy genres in particular, stereotypes contribute to creating and breaking the audience's expectations, providing viewers with both constancy and variation through the episodes.

A sociological account of stereotypical representations of science, however, requires not only a description of the recurrent features of scientist characters but also a reconstruction of the underlying social critique that stereotypes articulate and convey. In their different variations, stereotypes and their respective recurrent narratives offer views about the role of science in society and reveal controversial aspects of, or risks associated with, scientific developments. For instance, the mad scientist stereotype, which has its roots in the literary representations of alchemists (Schummer 2007; Haynes 2007) and has been notably stable across media, genres, and time, has embodied a number of societal concerns (see Frayling 2006; Hernández Nieto 2016; Haynes 2007; Pansegrau 2009; Skal 1998; Tudor 1989; Van Gorp, Rommes, and Emons 2013). The most common are perhaps related to the emergence of new knowledge or technology, but the internal organization of science has also been the object of literary observation and critique. The mad scientist stereotype of nineteenth-century literature, for example, expressed concerns about the emergence of modern science. More specifically, it reflected preoccupations with the emergence of chemistry as a separate discipline and the fragmentation of scientific knowledge that accompanied the differentiation of science into disciplines (Schummer 2007). Stereotypes such as the "eccentric" professor (Pansegrau 2009) or the "foolish scientist" (Haynes 2003), while benevolent and sympathetic, have been used to criticize the distance between science and society created by the specialization of scientific knowledge and language.

In this chapter, we examine how stereotypes—some old and some new—*coexist* with relatively complex representations of science in recent fiction directed at various audiences. The prevalence and persistence of many of the old stereotypes of science and scientists has been explained by the separation between the scientific sphere and the rest of society as well as by the public's deep-seated ambivalence toward science and the production of new knowledge. What, then, explains the shift in representations that we now observe? Is the shift toward realism in the representation of science limited to the new science novels, or can it also be observed in recent films, TV series, or popular literature? To what extent have the old cultural stereotypes of scientists persisted, been replaced by new ones, or become more sophisticated in appearance? In order to address these questions, we must first discuss the nature and sociological functions of stereotypes as they pertain to perceptions and representations of science.

Stereotypes as Schemata

The term *stereotype* comes from social psychology, where it is used to denote the reduction of the conception of a group to a limited, relatively stable, and persistent set of properties. These conceptions derive from a process of abstraction and categorization in which certain features are differentiated and selected from among the many apparent in the individual members of a group and other features are excluded. Stereotypes thus serve to reduce complexity when evaluating and interacting with different groups of individuals (Scheufele 2013). As Walter Lippmann writes, "They are an ordered, more or less consistent picture of the world, to which our habits, our tastes, our capacities, our comforts and our hopes have adjusted themselves. They may not be a complete picture of the world, but they are a picture of a possible world to which we are adapted. In that world people and things have their well-known places, and do certain expected things" (1922, 95).

When thinking about stereotypes, two different but interrelated issues arise. The first pertains to the conditions of human cognition, because stereotypes are inherent to thinking; the second concerns the role of media—as the basis of communication in society—in producing and circulating stereotypes. Luhmann employs the term *schema* interchangeably with other terms such as *stereotype, cognitive map*, or *prototype*. According to him, observing the world necessarily means distinguishing and selecting what to emphasize and what to omit from a thing or a person observed in our reality (2000, 108). Schemata are then recurrent forms of making those distinctions and selections. The schema of the mad scientist constitutes a fixed form of observing and communicating about scientists that emphasizes and makes salient certain characteristics, such as lunacy, megalomania, or arrogance, and suppresses others. This particular schema is also linked to a particular script—to what Luhmann would call a schematization of events across time (109)—in which the "mad scientist" is likely to misuse science to take over the world and wreak havoc on society.

The formation of schemata is the memory's way of coping while perceiving the world—of processing the flood of impressions and of regulating what is to be acknowledged and remembered versus what is to be ignored and forgotten (108). Schemata facilitate perception and communication by allowing us to filter information about an individual or a character in a story and develop expectations about his or her behavior or motivations. Luhmann maintains that the autopoietic nature of human cognition and the "unobservability of the world and the non-transparency of individuals to themselves and to others" make the formation of schemata unavoidable (114). Lippmann (1922) likewise argues that we cannot observe every single event taking place in the world, and even if we could, it would be impossible to give an exact account of any of them because each observation would always involve a certain degree of selectivity specific to the observer. If schemata are inherent to perception and communication, it follows that *stereotype*, even if occasionally used as a pejorative term, is actually neutral.

Human perception of the world is in large part mediated. "The subtlest and most pervasive of all influences," Lippmann writes, "are those which create and maintain the repertory of stereotypes. We are told about the world before we see it. We imagine most things before we experience them. And those preconceptions, unless education has made us acutely aware, govern deeply the whole process of perception" (1922, 89–90). Both the volume and the types of media available to tell us about the world have increased steadily since antiquity: from the itinerant storyteller to the first printed Bible and on to newspapers and mass media, photographs and movies, and finally, the internet and social media—all carry representations of the world that influence our perception of it. As Luhmann says, "All we know about the world we know through the mass media" (2000, 1).

With the evolution of media—its sheer growth and differentiation—the role of stereotypes in reducing complexity has become even more important. The differentiation of media goes along with a differentiation of publics and thus also with a differentiation of stereotypes. Movies, for example, are directed to different publics more than are novels and comics. Although stereotypes are relatively stable simplifications, specific details of a given stereotype may vary or change over time. Stereotypes may be reinforced by self-observation within the mass media (i.e., communication about media by the media)—for example, when a character in a movie or novel refers explicitly to Frankenstein or mentions an established stereotype such as the mad scientist.

Thus, by asking whether the depiction of scientists and of science has become more realistic and less stereotypical, one is actually invoking a misplaced dichotomy. Schematic descriptions of science and scientists can be present in complex representations, and elements from different schemata can coexist. Furthermore, the use of the phrase *stereotypical character* as a synonym for a flat or oversimplified character is often derogatory. This implies a judgment of the quality of the depiction, but one cannot evaluate the quality of a depiction without taking into account the conventions and audience of a specific medium or genre. Rather than judging the quality of a character depiction, it is more fruitful to compare stereotypes used in different media or different time periods.[4] As Luhmann notes, there is no reason why we cannot ask "about the social conditions of the plausibility of such schemata" (2000, 114). Stereotypes may also differ in their level of abstraction, which may serve different functions in a narrative. Central to our research is the question of what different stereotypical depictions of scientists and science tell us about the ways the media portray the place of science in society. For example, if scientists are now depicted in their institutional contexts, with all of their links to politics, the economy, and the media, then their central place in contemporary society may be more closely reflected than was the case when they were represented as individuals working outside a scientific community or organization.[5]

The concept of stereotypes allows us to observe what aspects of the scientific realm are omitted or picked up by fictional narratives across time and media, providing insight into the ways the media observe science and its function and place in society. In the following, we examine the content of selected examples in which stereotypical characters coexist with complex representations of science, including a small cross section of genres and media directed at different audiences—literary fiction, commercial novels, and TV programs—and we discuss how such fiction represents the place of science in contemporary society.[6]

New Depictions of Science and the Persistence of Stereotypes in Novels

As we see in other chapters of this volume, two of the most notable characteristics of recent novels about science are the diversity of science-related topics and the detailed views of the internal world of science. Novels such as *Intuition* (Goodman [2006] 2010), *Brazzaville Beach* (Boyd 2009), *Cantor's Dilemma* (Djerassi 1991), and *The Honest Look* (Rohn 2010) describe the everyday life of researchers in different disciplines, giving detailed accounts of the pressures they are subjected to, from individual financial problems and worries about their careers to collective concerns such as securing funding for research and the survival of research institutions. Through the portrayal of internal crises—in these particular cases the suspicion of data manipulation or fraud—they make visible the reward system and control mechanisms of science. Through the diverse perspectives of their scientist characters and narrators, these novels portray the political, economic, and media influences in the production of knowledge and technology and describe the social fabric of the research community. They carefully explore different aspects of the internal organization of the domain of science as well as its relationship with the world around it.

In science novels such as these, it appears that science has indeed left the isolation of the home laboratory and become embedded in contemporary society. In this sense, these novels reflect the institutional development of science from an individual practice to a collectively organized one that has taken place over the last century and a half (see chapter 2). Yet some of the entrenched stereotypes are still used to portray scientists in popular fiction media, and elements of these stereotypes may also be incorporated into more complex depictions. How do the modern versions of the "heroic," "mad," "adventurous," or "evil" scientist differ from earlier versions? Which characteristics remain and which have disappeared? And what do these stereotypes express about contemporary fears and hopes regarding science?

Michael Crichton's commercial thriller *State of Fear* (2009) puts its emphasis on plot and action and portrays most of its characters in two dimensions. Thus, a stereotypically "heroic" (Pansegrau 2009) and "adventurous" (Haynes 2003; Van Gorp, Rommes, and Emons 2013) scientist character named Richard John Kenner is described in *State of Fear* as a "fit-looking man with prematurely gray hair and heavy horn-rim glasses" who is young, highly intelligent, physically attractive, athletic, and intrepid:

> Doctorate in civil engineering from Caltech at age twenty. Did his thesis on soil erosion in Nepal. Barely missed qualifying for the Olympic ski team. A JD from Harvard Law School. Spent the next four years in government. Department of the Interior, Office of Policy Analysis. Scientific advisor to the Intergovernmental Negotiating

Committee. Hobby is mountain climbing; he was reported dead on Naya Khanga peak in Nepal, but he wasn't. Tried to climb K2, driven back by weather. . . . Anyway, he then went to MIT, where I'd say his rise has been spectacular. (Crichton 2009, 71, 72)

Kenner, who is also an undercover law enforcement agent, has had a successful and reputable professional career inside and outside the scientific community. The novel's detailed account of his work as a researcher and governmental advisor emphasizes the relationship between political, economic, and science systems. He is portrayed as a figure of authority and as an objective and credible voice in the discussion of climate change and the politicization of science that are at the heart of the story. Kenner is skeptical about climate change and travels around the globe trying to uncover and stop the plot of an ecoterrorist organization that seeks to re-create natural disasters and then attribute their existence and impact to climate change. Kenner is not alone in his quest, and—like many heroic characters—he is accompanied and supported by his sidekick, a graduate student named Sanjong Thapa.

In addition to these two heroic characters, the novel portrays a social scientist who fits the stereotype of the eccentric professor. Professor Norman Hoffman is described as "an elderly man in a tweed coat and tie" who is "messily shaven, unkempt, his hair wild" (560–61). The "notorious" sociologist is "extremely critical of environmental beliefs. A bit of a mad dog" (560). Hoffman seems chaotic and unfocused: "He talks a mile a minute and goes off on tangents—in every direction." Nicholas Drake, who is the president of an environmental organization and who also turns out to be behind the ecoterrorist group, refers to him as "crazy," a "nut," and a "cuckoo" (564).

The story is simple and, in many aspects, does not seem essentially different from other thrillers involving heroic scientists. The overall depiction of science is more complex than it at first seems, however. The heroic characters villainize the terrorists and hold them responsible for several attacks, but they also blame the institutional conditions that affect science—namely, political influences on the production, interpretation, and dissemination of scientific knowledge. In the novel, these influences are part of a broader dynamic that is set in motion by the politico-legal-media complex, which aims to instigate fear in citizens in order to control their behavior (571). It is actually the sociologist Hoffman who openly denounces the emergence of a "state of fear," but because he is portrayed as an eccentric professor,[7] his thesis is not at first taken seriously.

In *State of Fear* the dependence of research on external funding is portrayed as a significant vulnerability of the science system, since it threatens objective, independent scientific inquiry. This is exemplified when a researcher is pressured by the president of the NGO funding his research to interpret data in a manner that complies with the organization's objectives and political line (Crichton 2009, 56). The issue is emphasized again at the end of the novel when George Morton, a philanthropist who had previously funded scientific projects through research organizations, concludes that "scientists are in exactly the same position as Renaissance painters, commissioned to make the portrait the patron wants done. And if they are smart, they'll make sure their work subtly flatters the patron. Not overtly. Subtly. This is not a good system for research into those areas of science that affect policy. Even worse, the system works against problem solving. Because if you solve a problem, your funding ends" (712). Morton goes on to describe how science should be independent and autonomous and what must be changed in order to improve the internal control mechanisms of science and to prevent political criteria from interfering: "Make scientists blind to their funding. Make assessment of research blind. We can have major policy-oriented research carried out by multiple teams doing the same work. Why not, if it's really important? We'll push to change how journals report research. Publish the article and the peer reviews in the same issue. That'll clean up everybody's act real fast. Get the journals out of politics. Their editors openly take sides on certain issues. Bad dogs" (712).

It could be argued that one-dimensional, and in this case also stereotypical, characters are typical of commercial novels, even if they deal in more detail with science or incorporate current scientific debates. But stereotypical depictions of science are still present in more complex novels and characters. Margaret Atwood's *Oryx and Crake* portrays a strongly mediatized and economized society ([2003] 2004). The logic of commercialized science is extrapolated to its extreme in a society in which almost every aspect of social life is regulated by the logic of the market. Profit-making has become the sole engine of society and the goal of scientific practice, regardless of its potential or manifest negative effects on society.[8] It is in this context that Crake—a brilliant but obscure scientist who works for a company with limitless resources—secretly develops a virus that will annihilate the world population and, at the same time, creates a new species of transgenic humans to repopulate the planet. Like a "mad scientist" (Pansegrau 2009; Haynes 2003; Van Gorp, Rommes, and Emons 2013) or an "evil" alchemist (Haynes 2003), he conducts ethically questionable experiments, engages in criminal activities, and eventually dies while achieving his goal. Crake's actions are not attributed to madness or an inherently evil self. Rather, the novel meticulously describes the childhood events and societal context that produced Crake, who has rationally and analytically observed a world in which humans appear to have, among other things, an intrinsically conflictive and destructive nature. In keeping with his own nature, he has taken it to its logical conclusion: Crake is "intellectually honorable" and "doesn't lie to himself" (Atwood 2004, 79), and the reader understands that he came to the logical conclusion that humans should be eradicated and replaced by an improved—peaceful and innocent—species. Crake's friend, who is known as Snowman and appears to be the last human left on Earth, draws an explicit analogy between Crake and Victor Frankenstein as well as between himself and Frankenstein's monster. "Crake!" he whimpers. "Why am I on this earth? How come I'm alone? Where's my Bride of Frankenstein?" (199).

Like stereotypical scientists of the past, Crake works in secret on an ambitious project, but in *Oryx and Crake* this secrecy is standard practice in private companies, which go to great extremes to protect their trade secrets. OrganInc Farms, for example, keeps its transgenic "pigoons" in "heavily secured" special buildings because "the kidnapping of a pigoon and its finely honed genetic material by a rival outfit would have been a disaster" (29; see also 60). Such secrecy also makes it easier to develop illegal products, as Snowman learns when Crake takes him into his confidence:

> "But don't they keep discovering new diseases?" [Snowman asks.]
> "Not discovering," said Crake. "They're creating them."
> "Who is?" said Jimmy. Saboteurs, terrorists, is that what Crake meant? . . .
> "HelthWyzer," said Crake. "They've been doing it for years. There's a whole secret unit working on nothing else. . . . Naturally they develop the antidotes at the same time as they're customizing the bugs, but they hold those in reserve, they practise the economics of scarcity, so they're guaranteed high profits." (247)

In this novel the dangers and risks associated with science stem primarily from the economization of science and the institutional conditions created by the dominance of economic logic over scientific logic, wherein scientific innovation is driven only by its commercialization potential and the projected profitability of its products. The pressure to make new and lucrative products results in unethical or even illegal scientific practices. Crake explains that subjects for clinical trials are drawn "from the poorer countries. Pay them a few dollars, they don't even know what they're taking. Sex clinics, of course—they're happy to help. Whorehouses. Prisons. And from the ranks of the desperate, as usual" (349). Crake understands this logic and easily circumvents the company's almost nonexistent regulations and internal control mechanisms. In this sense, the acts of scientific hubris that characterize the evil and mad scientist stereotypes transcend the individual level and become systemic, and researchers take part in such acts, whether reluctantly or enthusiastically: "There'd been a lot of fooling around in those days: create-an-animal was so much fun, said the guys doing it; it made you feel like God" (57).

The tension between the agency of an individual scientist and the institutional and social dynamics is illustrated in a discussion between Jimmy's parents, both professional researchers:

> "Don't you remember the way we used to talk, everything we wanted to do?" [said Jimmy's mother]. "Making life better for people—not just people with money. You used to be so . . . you had ideals, then."
>
> "Sure," said Jimmy's father in a tired voice. "I've still got them. I just can't afford them." . . .
>
> "Be that as it may, there's research and there's research. What you are doing—this pig brain thing. You're interfering with the building blocks of life. It's immoral. It's . . . sacrilegious." (64)

The religious language in these two quotes evokes another of the established schemata for portraying science in fiction (the first makes direct reference to Frankenstein's pronouncement in James Whale's film: "In the name of God, now I know what it feels like to be God!" [1931]). Indeed, *Oryx and Crake* explores the moral and ethical dimensions surrounding scientific practice and the application of scientific and technological products in an economized society. It goes beyond depicting the catastrophic effects that one scientist's invention has on the population and describes in detail the impacts of scientific developments on the science system and the organization of society in general. The novel portrays, for instance, a commercialized science that reinforces prevailing social inequality structures and favors the emergence of a new form of eugenics: Ramona "was doing her 'research' because of course they wanted the best for their money. Terrific, thought Jimmy. They'd have a few trial runs, and if the kids from those didn't measure up they'd recycle them for the parts, until at last they got something that fit all their specs—perfect in every way, not only a math whiz but beautiful as the dawn" (Atwood 2004, 293).

As in *Oryx and Crake*, the concern surrounding eugenics in *Mendel's Dwarf* shifts from the political to the commercial and from "top-down" to "bottom-up" in the novel's portrayal of late twentieth-century practices (Mawer 1999). The narrator, Benedict Lambert, is a geneticist who himself suffers from achondroplasia (dwarfism) and is well aware of the ethical issues raised by new scientific knowledge. At the end of the novel, as he recounts a speech he gave to his colleagues at the Masaryk University of Brno, he refers to the ethical dimensions and social consequences of developing and applying tests to detect genetic diseases as well as procedures to select embryos according to genetic characteristics: "'Are we really such intellectual dwarfs'—ah, they shiver at that one—'as to imagine that the laws of supply and demand can be elevated to the level of a philosophy? Because that is what we have done. We have within our grasp the future of mankind, and as things are going the future will be chosen according to the same criteria as people now choose silicone breast implants and liposuction and hair transplants. It will be eugenics by consumer choice, the eugenics of the marketplace. All masquerading as freedom'" (286).

Mendel's Dwarf also portrays the negative side of a too-close interrelation between science and political power.[9] The novel refers to several historical events to illustrate the disastrous consequences of involving political ideology in the production of scientific knowledge (e.g., 191, 245, 246, 282), among them the ban in the USSR on Mendelian genetics and the persecution of its supporters (248) and the instrumental use of genetics for political purposes by the Nazi regime (245).

Like many scientists in fiction, Benedict Lambert is confronted with ethical dilemmas and the temptation to abuse scientific knowledge for a personal motive. When his ex-lover Jean asks him to conceive a child for her through artificial insemination—without her husband's knowledge—Lambert suddenly finds himself in a position of power: should he use his expertise to gain revenge? Regardless of his decision, Lambert's consent to Jean's proposal entails ethically questionable actions and scientific misconduct.

Like an "accidental mad" scientist (Pansegrau 2009) and a "helpless" scientist (Haynes 2003), Lambert's personal moral transgressions and a final fit of arrogance have tragic consequences for him, for Jean, and for their baby.

The work-obsessed, even maniacal, researchers characteristic of the deeply rooted "inhuman" (Haynes 2003) or "mad" scientist stereotypes (Haynes 2003; Pansegrau 2009; Van Gorp, Rommes, and Emons 2013; Hernández Nieto 2016) are still apparent in novels depicting scientists who develop a mental illness in connection with their work. In *Brazzaville Beach*, the young, ambitious, brilliant mathematician John Clearwater develops a pathological obsession with his research. In spite of working at a university, surrounded by colleagues and friends, John gradually isolates himself and begins to behave erratically, picking up new research topics every couple of weeks and developing all kinds of peculiar habits. His failure to produce long-term innovative results ends his dream of making history in mathematics and drives him into depression and eventually suicide.

In *Properties of Light*, the physicist Samuel Mallach breaks away from his research institute because his revolutionary scientific propositions are being openly ignored by fellow physicists (Goldstein 2001). Although employed by a university, the disillusioned and resentful Mallach continues his theoretical work in a cluttered office at home, breaking off every social contact with other members of the physics department: "Mallach's hatred was as intense as anything else he had ever thought or felt. He hated those who had frozen him out, who had closed ranks around their chosen dogmas and frozen him and his hidden variables out" (68–69). This is, of course, the archetypical pattern of the Frankensteinian narrative: the scientist who withdraws from his community and the world altogether to pursue his research in isolation. Mallach becomes consumed by jealousy when he learns that his greatest enemy has won the Nobel Prize, and he believes that Justin, the young colleague who is his only supporter and friend, has betrayed him. Like Clearwater, Mallach loses his mind and commits suicide. In comparison with classical mad scientists, Mallach and Clearwater appear to have modest ambitions. Certainly they don't seek to take over the world, but they have a profound desire for scientific acknowledgment: "How much Mallach must have wanted the world's love, with how much terrible passion, to have answered the world's indifference with such a shape of bitterness as this. He must have loved the world quite madly, madly. All along he must have loved, always desperately longing for the world to love him back" (205). Similarly, Clearwater "longed for his name to merit a separate entry in dictionaries of mathematics. 'John Clearwater, English mathematician, inventor of the Clearwater Set'" (Boyd 2009, 253). Unlike mad scientists in films or cartoons, who often reveal their plans and motives in dramatic monologues, Clearwater is cautious when allowing himself to express his ambitions out loud:

> "I think I'm close, this time. There's something taking shape. A new set."
>
> A set? Hope thought. What was a set? But she humored him. With her spread fingers she framed an invisible title, a plaque in the air. "The Clearwater Set," she proclaimed. She saw she had said exactly the right thing.
>
> He smiled, momentarily exhilarated, then lowered his gaze, immediately modest. "If only," he said quietly. "My God, if only." When he looked up, she saw the ache of his ambition in his eyes for a second or two. (248)

While Clearwater's psychological instability becomes evident only gradually, Samuel Mallach's characterization as a "loon" and a "lunatic" is explicit and recurrent throughout the novel (Goldstein 2001, 267, 346). He is a man with "the odor of the old insanity still wafting faintly about him. Each madness has an odor of its own, and most of them are nasty" (19–20).

The "madness" of Clearwater and Mallach is attributed not only to individual features (e.g., a megalomaniac or paranoid personality) but also to structural conditions in the world of science. In the case of Clearwater, these are publication and time pressures in a competitive field. For Mallach, it is the exclusion from scientific discourse that marks the beginning of his psychological deterioration. Their ambitions and high expectations in combination with their failed academic careers turn out to be more dangerous for the scientists themselves than for society: "Samuel Mallach was a great physicist, but with a wound to the soul that proved eventually fatal. His death, the second one, the one more final, was not, in the end, my [Justin's] fault" (16).

As we have seen, the presence of stereotypical features in scientist characters does not necessarily imply a simplistic representation of science or of scientists. The heroic scientists in *State of Fear* defend not only the world against ecoterrorists but also the autonomy of science against its politicization.[10] *Oryx and Crake* portrays the risks posed by an individual scientist "going rogue" but also those posed by the commercialization of science and the conditions that enable it. In *Mendel's Dwarf*, we observe the scientific misconduct of an individual researcher but also take a close look at the relationship of science with other societal spheres and at the emergence of new technologies. The "mad" researchers portrayed in *Properties of Light* and *Brazzaville Beach* go beyond the traditional depictions of this kind and offer an inside view of the world of science, its social organization, and its reward mechanisms. They differ markedly from the alchemist-inspired mad scientists typical of older works, who were generally isolated scientists working alone in secret laboratories.

Science and Scientists on TV

New depictions of science can also be found in TV series, some of them in unexpected genres such as sitcoms and cartoons for children. In *Marsupilami*, a cartoon series for children, the botanist Diane Forster is a stereotypical noble scientist who bravely protects the jungle against the invasive activities of a private company. The goal of her research is to produce knowledge about an endangered plant. Unlike the scientists typically portrayed in cartoons, who produce a new invention in each episode, Forster works on one long-term project over the course of two seasons of the series. Although she works in a remote location, her scientific community becomes visible when she attends a congress of women in science to present her research. The series is atypical of its media genre in that it deals with complex science and society issues. The treatment is simple and geared for children, but the episodes often touch on the ethical and moral dimensions of scientific research, especially in relation to the influences of market logic on scientific work and society. In one episode, Forster concludes that "science without a conscience is nothing more than life without a soul" (Allix and Enard 2011). The antagonism between Diane Forster and Felizia Absahn—an ambitious and unscrupulous businesswoman—is employed to explore the social responsibility of scientists and to criticize the exploitation of science for the acquisition of wealth or ownership of nature (Hernández Nieto 2016).

The animated series *Kim Possible* (Schooley and McCorkie 2002), which is geared to a preteen audience, contrasts Dr. Drakken, a stereotypical "mad scientist," with Dr. Tim Possible, an intelligent though slightly geeky rocket scientist who is represented as a normal guy doing a regular job. Dr. Drakken is an amateur scientist who dropped out of college and works secretly in remote or inaccessible places, whereas Dr. Possible is a professional scientist doing his work openly at a research institution with many other researchers. Through Dr. Possible, science is depicted within society, and this integration is indicated, among other things, by his efforts to communicate science to the public, particularly children. The series also touches briefly, if superficially, on several issues related to the internal organization of science, including the specialization of scientific knowledge into disciplines, the publication system, gender discrimination in the scientific community, and scientific misconduct. Here the presence of a stereotypical character such as Dr. Drakken has an important function, as it helps viewers to distinguish between the story's fictional science and the realistic science embodied by Dr. Possible (Hernández Nieto 2016).

One last example is the sitcom *The Big Bang Theory* (Lorre and Prady 2007), which is geared to a general adult audience. Four of the five main characters (eventually they become seven) are portrayed as nerdy or geeky scientists from different disciplines in the physical sciences: Sheldon (a theoretical physicist), Leonard (an experimental physicist), Rajesh (an astrophysicist), and Howard (an aerospace engineer) are all intelligent but socially inept and childlike young professionals.[11] They love their console games, superhero comics, and Star Wars memorabilia as much as they love science and technology; they have equal admiration for Stephen Hawking and Leonard Nimoy. In spite of this, these four young researchers are different from the stereotypical nerds and geeks we are used to seeing in fiction. As the episodes progress, the characters change and gain complexity through the inclusion of biographical information and detailed descriptions of their professional desires, worries, and dilemmas. Science and technology play an important role in their lives and in the series as a whole. As in many science novels, scientific knowledge is portrayed and incorporated into the plot in various ways. Physical theories and models are represented visually through equations on whiteboards at Sheldon and Leonard's apartment, and the characters often discuss mathematical or physical problems, theories, models, and experiments, such as the famous thought experiment known as Schrödinger's cat. The series makes numerous references to contemporary science, with cameo appearances by real scientists (e.g., Stephen Hawking and George Smoot), and the episodes deal with current theories and debates in physics and other disciplines. Through the characters of Sheldon and his mother, the series confronts religious beliefs with scientific knowledge, joking, for example, about creationism and the theory of evolution (Lorre and Prady 2009a).

Perhaps the most significant aspect of the representation of science in *The Big Bang Theory* is the diverse view that it offers of the world of academic science. The series considers a wide variety of topics, such as scientists' contributions to society throughout history, the establishment of a scientific career, the acquisition and loss of a scientific reputation, the politics of research institutions, the difficulties of interdisciplinary collaboration, the importance of project funding and grants, the difficulties faced by international researchers, the scientific publication system and internal communication of scientific results, and the popularization of science, among others. The comic situations surrounding science depart from traditional depictions. The series leaves behind slapstick jokes involving explosive and colorful substances in a research lab. Instead, humorous situations are created from the everyday conditions of contemporary scientific work. *The Big Bang Theory* often takes a stab at the hierarchies of scientific work, as, for example, when Sheldon mocks Howard for studying engineering and not having a doctorate (as in Lorre and Prady 2008a, 2008b, and 2009b). The negative aspects of contemporary scientific work, such as failing to obtain innovative results or reaching a dead end in a line of research, are also a constant source of comic material (e.g., Lorre and Prady 2009c).

Conclusion

Luhmann's notion of schemata has allowed us to identify various ways in which realistic and stereotypical representations of science coexist in contemporary fiction as well as to deduce the ideas about science that these representations convey. The characteristic features of stereotypical researchers have not disappeared entirely, but scientist characters have generally gained complexity, and the persistent stereotypes do not form an obstacle to conveying new, more diverse and differentiated images of science. We have found indicators of these new descriptions of science in popular media genres such as cartoons and commercial thrillers, which typically employ two-dimensional—and in many cases stereotypical—characters, as well as in mainstream and literary fiction. These new representations focus not only on scientists but also on the institutional and societal contexts of science. It is precisely in this last aspect that they have changed significantly and may both reflect the practice of science and contribute to demystifying it.

These changes in the way science is represented do not necessarily translate into more "positive" images of science. Rather, as fiction media explore the conditions under which contemporary scientific work takes place, scientists are losing their attributed divine or magical as well as diabolical auras. In looking so closely at the world of science, these literary and entertainment products make visible its internal organization, emphasizing both positive and negative attributes—including the bureaucratic and tedious aspects of research, the difficulties of establishing a career in science, the underside of research financing, and, not least, scientific misconduct. The mad, noble, heroic, and nerdy scientists in these contemporary depictions must deal with much more than their own motivations, obsessions, and peculiarities: we now see work-obsessed researchers forced to take vacation days, evil scientists who are actually fulfilling their job mandates to develop profitable research products for companies, mad scientists succumbing to publication pressures and the weight of their own professional expectations, and heroic scientists fighting against the media, economic, and political influences over science and society. These fictional scientists have finally moved from the isolated laboratory of the fifteenth-century alchemists—which dominated literature well into the twentieth century—to the contemporary research center, where they are now busy writing grant proposals or managing financial resources. They have replaced their quests to rule or destroy the world with more mundane goals, such as a patent, a Nobel Prize, the quest for recognition from their peers, or a tenured position at a university.

Even in these more realistic contexts, the persistence of stereotypes of mad, obsessed, evil, or amoral scientists alongside stereotypes of heroic or noble scientists suggests that the ambivalence toward science and its products is still deeply rooted in our society. This ambivalence, however, is no longer always linked to the use and abuse of knowledge or technology by an individual scientist, and new technologies do not necessarily threaten an innocent and vulnerable society. The examples discussed here indicate a departure from the traditional narratives of separation between science and society that were embodied by classic stereotypical characters. In these examples, science is shown in constant interaction with other societal institutions—an indicator that public discourse has finally recognized that science is an integral part of society rather than the prerogative and product of isolated geniuses and madmen.

Notes

1. For studies on children's and adolescents' perceptions of science, see Chambers 1983; Sala de Gómezgil 1975; Manzoli et al. 2006; and Mead and Métraux 1957.

2. Research on the topic gives mixed results: according to Takahashi and Edson, "Interest in science is negatively related to using television as source for science information" (2015, 685), whereas Brossard found that use of online sources and TV reduces the gap between groups with different levels of education, which is the most important demographic predictor of both TV use and interest in science (2013, 14099).

3. There are also substantial differences in perceptions of and knowledge about science in different countries and among different demographic groups. These are captured by polls and segmentation analyses. For three examples among the vast literature, see Besley 2013; Schäfer et al. 2018; and Guenther, Weingart, and Meyer 2018.

4. The literature review done by Kirby constitutes an effort in this direction (2017).

5. The history of science, and to an extent the philosophy of science, also focused on scientists as individuals (the genius, discoverer, heroic figure, etc.) until well into the 1970s. When Thomas Kuhn first introduced the "disciplinary matrix" as the duality of the cognitive and social structures of science, he met with harsh resistance from his community (see Kuhn 1962; compare Lakatos and Musgrave 1970).

6. This discussion draws from the results of qualitative content analyses of some two dozen contemporary novels about science and from a reconsideration of past studies of TV series portrayals.

7. See, for example, Pansegrau, for a description of the eccentric professor stereotype (2009). A similar stereotype is the foolish scientist (Haynes 2003). Colloquially, this stereotype is known as the absent-minded professor.

8. For example, the development and commercialization of the Happicuppa coffee bean leads to a war (Atwood 2004, 210). See chapter 7 for an account of how the novel dramatically extrapolates and highlights the economization of science, and see chapter 5 for a discussion of reader and media reactions to the science in the novel.

9. The novel also represents an ambivalent relationship between science and the media. In *Mendel's Dwarf*, Benedict Lambert's boss considers the relationship to the media innocuous for scientific practice: "A bit of publicity never does anyone any harm" (Mawer 1999, 74). For Benedict, however, the contact with the media is personally embarrassing, and he is willing to "play the circus clown" only if his boss supports his research project (74).

10. In Appendix I of the novel, Crichton explicitly warns the reader about the dangers of the politicization of science and the use of scientific knowledge for political purposes (2009, 723–31).

11. Two other characters, Leslie Winkle and Dr. Amy Farrah Fowler, resemble the stereotypical depictions of women scientists found by Flicker (2003).

References

Allix, Claude, and Moran Caouissin Enard, dir. 2011. *Marsupilami houba houba hop!* "Da ist was faul" [Something fishy]. Aired October 2 on ARD/ZFD.

Allum, Nick, Patrick Sturgis, Dimitra Tabourazi, and Ian Brunton-Smith. 2008. "Science Knowledge and Attitudes Across Cultures: A Meta-Analysis." *Public Understanding of Science* 17 (1): 35–54.

Atwood, Margaret. (2003) 2004. *Oryx and Crake*. New York: Anchor.

Besley, John C. 2013. "The State of Public Opinion Research on Attitudes and Understanding of Science and Technology." *Bulletin of Science, Technology, and Society* 33 (1–2): 12–20. https://doi.org/10.1177/0270467613496723.

Boyd, William. 2009. *Brazzaville Beach*. London: Penguin.

Brossard, Dominique. 2013. "New Media Landscapes and the Science Information Consumer." *PNAS* 110, suppl. 3: 14096–101.

Chambers, David Wade. 1983. "Stereotypic Images of the Scientist: The Draw-a-Scientist Test." *Science Education* 67 (2): 255–65. https://doi.org/10.1002/sce.3730670213.

Crichton, Michael. 2009. *State of Fear*. Reprint ed. New York: Harper.

Djerassi, Carl. 1991. *Cantor's Dilemma*. New York: Penguin.

Eggers, Dave. 2013. *The Circle*. New York: Alfred A. Knopf.

Evans, Geoffrey, and John Durant. 1995. "The Relationship Between Knowledge and Attitudes in the Public Understanding of Science in Britain." *Public Understanding of Science* 4 (1): 57–74. https://doi.org/10.1088/0963-6625/4/1/004.

Flicker, Eva. 2003. "Between Brains and Breasts—Women Scientists in Fiction Film: On the Marginalization and Sexualization of Scientific Competence." *Public Understanding of Science* 12 (3): 307–18. https://doi.org/10.1177/0963662503123009.

Frayling, Christopher. 2006. *Mad, Bad, and Dangerous: The Scientist and Cinema*. London: Reaktion Books.

Goldstein, Rebecca. 2001. *Properties of Light*. New York: Mariner Books.

Goodman, Allegra. (2006) 2010. *Intuition*. London: Atlantic Books.

Guenther, Lars, Peter Weingart, and Corlia Meyer. 2018. "'Science Is Everywhere, but No One Knows It': Assessing the Cultural Distance to Science of Rural South African Publics." *Environmental Communication* 12 (8): 1046–61. https://doi.org/10.1080/17524032.2018.1455724.

Haynes, Roslynn. 2003. "From Alchemy to Artificial Intelligence: Stereotypes of the Scientist in Western Literature." *Public Understanding of Science* 12 (3): 243–53. https://doi.org/10.1177/0963662503123003.

———. 2007. "The Alchemist in Fiction: The Master Narrative." In *The Public Image of Chemistry*, edited by Joachim Schummer, Bernadette Bensaude-Vincent, and Brigitte van Tiggelen, 7–36. Singapore: World Scientific.

———. 2014. "Whatever Happened to the 'Mad, Bad' Scientist? Overturning the Stereotype." *Public Understanding of Science* 25 (1): 31–44.

Hernández Nieto, Luz María. 2016. "What Do Cartoons Tell Children About Science? A Qualitative Study of the Representation of Science and Scientists in Animated Television Series." PhD diss., Universität Bielefeld. https://pub.uni-bielefeld.de/publication/2904323.

Kirby, David A. 2017. "The Changing Popular Images of Science." In *The Oxford Handbook of the Science of Science Communication*, edited by Kathleen Hall Jamieson, Dan M. Kahan, and Dietmar A. Scheufele, 291–300. Oxford, UK: Oxford University Press. https://doi.org/10.1093/oxfordhb/9780190497620.013.32.

Kuhn, Thomas S. 1962. *The Structure of Scientific Revolutions*. International Encyclopedia of Unified Science, vol. 2, no. 2. Chicago: University of Chicago Press.

Lakatos, Imre, and Alan Musgrave, eds. 1970. *Criticism and the Growth of Knowledge*. Proceedings of the International Colloquium in the Philosophy of Science 4. Cambridge, UK: Cambridge University Press.

Lippmann, Walter. 1922. *Public Opinion*. New York: Harcourt Brace. http://archive.org/details/publicopinion00lippgoog.

Lorre, Chuck, and Bill Prady. 2007. *The Big Bang Theory*. CBS.

———. 2008a. "The Jerusalem Duality." *The Big Bang Theory*. Aired April 14, on CBS.

———. 2008b. "The Bat Jar Conjecture." *The Big Bang Theory*. Aired April 21, on CBS.

———. 2009a. "The Electric Can Opener Fluctuation." *The Big Bang Theory*. CBS. Aired September 21, on CBS.

———. 2009b. "The Vengeance Formulation." *The Big Bang Theory*. Aired November 23, on CBS.

———. 2009c. "The Pirate Solution." *The Big Bang Theory*. Aired October 12, on CBS.

Luhmann, Niklas. 2000. *The Reality of the Mass Media*. Oxford, UK: Blackwell.

Manzoli, Federica, Yurij Castelfranchi, Daniele Gouthier, and Irene Cannata. 2006. "Children's Perceptions of Science and Scientists: A Case Study Based on Drawings and Story-Telling." Paper presented at the 9th International Conference on Public Communication of Science and Technology, Seoul, Korea, May 2006. https://pcst.co/archive/pdf/Manzoli_et_al_PCST2006.pdf.

Mawer, Simon. 1999. *Mendel's Dwarf*. New York: Penguin.

Mead, Margaret, and Rhoda Métraux. 1957. "Image of the Scientist Among High-School Students: A Pilot Study." *Science* 126 (3270): 384–90. https://doi.org/10.1126/science.126.3270.384.

Pansegrau, Petra. 2009. "Zwischen Fakt und Fiktion—Stereotypen von Wissenschaftlern in Spielfilmen." In *Frosch und Frankenstein: Bilder als Medium der Popularisierung von Wissenschaft*, edited by Peter Weingart and Bernd Huppauf, 373–86. Bielefeld, DE: Transcript.

Rohn, Jennifer L. 2010. *The Honest Look*. Cold Spring Harbor, NY: Cold Spring Harbor Laboratory Press.

Sala de Gómezgil, Maria Luisa Rodriguez. 1975. "Mexican Adolescents' Image of the Scientist." *Social Studies of Science* 5 (3): 355–61. https://doi.org/10.1177/030631277500500306.

Schäfer, Mike, Tobias Füchslin, Julia Metag, Silje Kristiansen, and Adrian Rauchfleisch. 2018. "The Different Audiences of Science Communication: A Segmentation Analysis of the Swiss Population's Perceptions of Science and Their Information and Media Use Patterns." *Public Understanding of Science* 27 (7): 836–56. https://doi.org/10.1177/0963662517752886.

Scheufele, Bertram. 2013. "Stereotyp." In *Lexikon Kommunikations- und Medienwissenschaft*, edited by Günter Bentele and Hans-Bernd Brosius, 327. Wiesbaden, DE: Springer Verlag.

Schooley, Bob, and Mark McCorkie. 2002. *Kim Possible*. Disney Channel.

Schummer, Joachim. 2007. "Historical Roots of the 'Mad Scientist': Chemists in Nineteenth-Century Literature." In *The Public Image of Chemistry*, edited by Joachim Schummer, Bernadette Bensaude-Vincent, and Brigitte van Tiggelen, 37–80. Singapore: World Scientific.

Skal, David J. 1998. *Screams of Reason: Mad Science in Modern Culture*. New York: Norton.

Takahashi, Bruno, and Tandoc C. Edson Jr. 2015. "Media Sources, Credibility, and Perceptions of Science: Learning About How People Learn About Science." *Public Understanding of Science* 25 (6): 674–90.

Tudor, Andrew. 1989. *Monsters and Mad Scientists*. Oxford, UK: Blackwell.

Van Gorp, Baldwin, Els Rommes, and Pascale Emons. 2013. "From the Wizard to the Doubter: Prototypes of Scientists and Engineers in Fiction and Non-Fiction Media Aimed at Dutch Children and Teenagers." *Public Understanding of Science* 23 (6): 646–59. https://doi.org/10.1177/0963662512468566.

Whale, James, dir. 1931. *Frankenstein*. Los Angeles: Universal Pictures.

Part 2
Embedded Science
Societal Impacts on Scientific Work and Knowledge

4.
Scientists at Risk

Roslynn D. Haynes
and Raymond Haynes

As outlined in chapter 2, the development of science over the last five centuries has involved a radical change in the position and role of the professional scientist. The lone alchemist—autonomous, secretive, and possessed of a knowledge to which no one else was privy (Haynes 2006, 5–29; Haynes 2017, 14–18)—was superseded by the member of a large team, working on classified research funded either by governments or by corporations. Although modern scientists, like their predecessors the alchemists, still dealt in knowledge that was unavailable to nonscientists and were therefore perceived to wield an unchallengeable degree of power, they were themselves increasingly subject to a hegemonic system based on principles of economization rather than the dictates of pure research.[1] In the current phase of postmodernity, scientific knowledge is paradoxically both prized for its economic and political value and contested in the sociopolitical arena, in which diverse power blocks continually attempt to enlist, exploit, or denigrate science for their own agendas. While this has been most apparent in relation to the antismoking and the climate change lobbies and their opponents, these are not the only arenas of disputation.

In this context, scientists are no longer, as characterized by previous generations of writers and filmmakers, mainly perpetrators of risk to humanity as a result of their chemical, physical, or biological research. Although such stereotypical figures are still found sporadically in novels[2] and, more frequently, in films, their prevalence in fiction has diminished considerably in the last two decades. In the science novels under consideration here, they are outweighed by more complex depictions of scientists as themselves being subject to a unique set of career-specific risks and dangers, largely undocumented and unrecognized by the wider society. In these novels, the vulnerability of the scientist characters is a recurrent theme and an integral part of both plot and characterization. The adverse forces confronting the individual scientist may be overt and external (physical dangers contingent on fieldwork, threats from militant demonstrators, demands imposed by team leaders or funding agencies, or pressure to publish results prematurely) or internal (conflicts between organizational processes and the individual researcher's moral values and ideals or mental depression resulting from failure to produce new research results or to receive peer recognition).

We have chosen to consider three kinds of risk to scientists as depicted in the selected novels. First are the physical dangers, rare in science carried out in an institution but not unusual in fieldwork situations in which nature becomes a significant threat, as in *Wegener's Jigsaw* (2003), *The Hungry Tide* (2005), and *Measuring the World* (2005), or in which the isolation of the location permits threatening behavior on the part of some team members toward others (*Brazzaville Beach* [2009]). Second are challenges to the integrity of the researcher arising from pressure from peers or superiors within the discipline to engage in practices that run counter to her or his ethical values. And third are risks to intellectual identity and mental health resulting from pressure, whether imposed or self-generated, to perform at an ever-higher standard. We argue that these scenarios function as more than merely plot material. By exposing the complex web of socioeconomic, political, and psychological factors within which contemporary science and scientists are embedded in the "world risk society" (Beck 1999), they engender reader empathy for the scientist protagonists and present a new image of the scientist as a potentially well-intentioned, albeit often disempowered, fellow human being who is sympathetic to the reader rather than yet another example of the obsessed, power-hungry scientist stereotype.[3]

Physical Risks

Physical risks may arise from dangerous fieldwork, from the products of the science itself, or because possession of politically powerful or commercially profitable intellectual property renders the scientist a target for kidnapping, intimidation, or exploitation. Although portrayal of such risk was not unknown in earlier novels (Jules Verne's scientist-adventurers encountered successive dangers in their quest for knowledge, and Frankenstein is the prototype of numerous fictional scientists menaced by their own creations),[4] the focus in the past was rarely on the scientist as victim and more often on the sequence of disasters initiated by his hubris and obsession.

With increased awareness of environmental issues, contemporary novelists have turned their attention to scientists engaged in fieldwork that proves dangerous or even life-threatening, exploring what motivates them to take such risks. In these cases, nature is associated with unpredictable dangers and inherent violence, far from the regimen of "safe" science conducted within the walls of an institution. The dangers encountered may be intrinsic to the research location and even well recognized as such but still willingly accepted by the scientists as the necessary price of knowledge.

In his historical novel *Measuring the World* (2005), Daniel Kehlmann depicts the adventurer, naturalist, explorer, and geographer Alexander von Humboldt (1769–1859) as determined to experience the extreme conditions of the Andes by climbing Mount Cimborazo, then thought to be the highest peak in South America, and lowering himself into volcanoes. Arguing that "the man who deliberately undergoes pain nevertheless learns things" (Kehlmann 2005, 25), he experiments on his own body, measuring the effects of curare, the paralyzing plant poison used by the indigenous South Americans, and electric shocks from eels. Kehlmann's Humboldt is supremely confident and careless of risk, driven by a passion to discover the unity of nature by establishing interconnections between science and the natural world, and between physical and biological systems, as epitomized in his all-encompassing five-volume work *Cosmos* ([1845–62] 1864).

Similarly, in *Wegener's Jigsaw* (2003), Clare Dudman portrays the geophysicist and meteorologist Alfred Wegener, who first proposed the theory of continental drift, as being a risk taker from childhood on because of his innate curiosity about the world. When he has just learned to walk, he eludes the grasp of his siblings and, rushing forward to catch a bright patch of light on the water, falls into the cold, dark water of the canal. From hot air ballooning for meteorological studies to his three grueling expeditions to Greenland, the last of which would kill him, exploration for the cause of science was the high point of his life. His compulsion to return to the Arctic was fueled by its potential to provide new data for his theory of glaciation via ice-core drilling and the measurement of polar air circulation; by the company of others similarly driven to sacrifice comfort, and possibly their lives, for knowledge; and not least by the exhilaration of the journey and the sheer beauty of the frozen world. He notes the different colors of the ice: "Sometimes it's not even blue, but yellow or maybe orange. That's when the sun is setting. . . . Often it is so low that all the light is scattered, and for a small while, just a few seconds, it is so beautiful you could forget to breathe" (1). During his final journey in Greenland, Wegener feels reinvigorated and as youthful as he was at twenty-six. "And now a strange thing happens: I become young. . . . Along with the overwhelming feelings of accomplishment and satisfaction, there was something else: an unexpected sense of rejuvenation" (339–40).

Kehlmann's Humboldt and Dudman's Wegener are physically strong and fully aware of, even elated by, the dangers to be confronted; accompanied by support teams, they survive the rigors of their respective research journeys over many years. Other novelists, however, have chosen to examine the vulnerable situation of young twentieth-century women scientists in dangerous and isolated situations that they did not knowingly choose. Although many of these female protagonists triumph over adversity, it may be indicative of residual gender stereotyping that such women are more frequently portrayed as being, at least initially, victims who rely on a male figure for support.

In William Boyd's *Brazzaville Beach* (2009), the recently widowed Hope Clearwater appears to have no instinctual forewarning of the dangers involved when, on the suggestion of her former supervisor, she applies to study chimpanzees at an African research station, Grosso Arvore, directed by Eugene Mallabar. Although a novice in primate studies, she finds that her observations of the violent relations between the chimpanzees, including infanticide, cannibalism, and gratuitous torture, run counter to the image of benign primate behavior on which Mallabar has built his international reputation. When informed of her findings, Mallabar systematically sets out to destroy her field notes and her researcher status and then orchestrates an attempt on her life. Finally, forced to observe the primates willfully killing each other, Mallabar furiously attacks Hope's person in actions that resemble those of the chimps. Fleeing from Grosso Arvore, Hope is caught up in a civil war in the Congo and held prisoner by UNAMO dissidents. In the real world, these situations are rare but do happen. Remote field stations can be dangerous places, as evidenced in the experiences of Jane Goodall observing chimpanzees in Tanzania, and of Dian Fossey, murdered in her Rwandan camp while studying mountain gorillas.

Piyali Roy, the young marine biologist of Amitav Ghosh's *The Hungry Tide* (2005), chooses, out of necessity, a research location that is beset by dangers of both natural and human origin. Her object of study is the rare and endangered Irrawaddy river dolphin *Orcaella brevirostris*, found only in the Bay of Bengal in the tidal river channels between the Sundarbans. Attacks by tigers and crocodiles, unpredictable tidal floods, and political turmoil among the inhabitants make life here precarious for people and for the dolphins. From the outset, Piyali is menaced by the guard assigned to her, and she is pushed into crocodile-infested water. Later, while she is reaching over the side of the boat to measure the water depth, a crocodile almost removes her hand. "Suddenly the water boiled over and a pair of huge jaws came shooting out of the river, breaking the surface exactly where Piya's wrist had been a moment before. . . . A second later the boat shook under the impact of a massive underwater blow" (174). Piyali has framed a conjecture, however, that the Sundarbans dolphins have found a novel means of adapting to their tidal environment, performing twice a day the migration that other river dolphins undertake only annually, and this "hypothesis of stunning elegance and economy—a thing of beauty" (124) impels her to continue her research, whatever the risks. "It would be as fine a piece of descriptive science as any. It would be enough; as an alibi for a life, it would do" (127).

A more unusual scientist role and the danger it involves are explored by Michael Ondaatje in *Anil's Ghost* (2011). Anil Tissera is a Sri Lankan forensic pathologist who has been educated in Britain and the United States. As part of a United Nations human rights investigation, Anil returns to Sri Lanka in the 1980s to identify the victims of the carnage sweeping the country as the result of a civil war that involves the government and two different ethnic groups. Anil and her colleague Sarath, a local archaeologist, become determined to reveal the identity of one representative skeleton that was found in an ancient burial site but that they believe is the remains of a victim of recent violence. Their investigation is fraught with political danger, as the nature and number of the murdered are being suppressed, but Anil pursues the inquiry using every means, forensic and artistic, at her disposal. Called on to make a report to the government about her work, she launches into an accusation, saying, "I think you murdered hundreds of us" (269), thereby publicly identifying herself with the victims. This puts her life at stake when she delivers her report to the government and refuses to retract her accusations. "The skeleton I had was evidence of a certain kind of crime. That is what is important here. 'One village can speak for many villages. One victim can speak for many victims'" (272). Anil is driven to engage in this dangerous dialogue, fully aware of the risk she runs, partly because of her professional integrity but mainly because of her determination to seek justice and recognition for the victims of the massacre. Ultimately, however, she is powerless without Sarath's assistance and his complicity in engineering her escape at the cost of his own life.

Of these fictional characters, Humboldt and Wegener clearly foresaw and even courted danger but counted it as nothing compared with the delight of scientific discovery. The female scientists Hope Clearwater, Piyali Roy, and Anil Tissera, though initially less aware of the risks entailed in their research, were nevertheless determined to pursue it in spite of the dangers and are shown as growing in confidence and determination as a result.

Such physical dangers are to be expected in remote field stations, but some science novels also depict urban laboratory scientists threatened by human antagonists. In Jennifer Rohn's *Experimental Heart* (2009), the biotechnology company Geniaxis, where mice are used in experiments, is blockaded by animal rights demonstrators, and Gina Kraymer, a biochemist working there, is threatened by the protesters and later attacked at her home. A bottle of blood is thrown over her by an animal liberationist, who also delivers a death threat: "This is the last time we'll ask nicely, Dr. Kraymer! . . . If you keep experimenting on animals, you're *dead*!" (182). Gina is also in danger from her senior colleague Richard Rouyle, who, when she tries to prevent premature escalation of their research to clinical trials, physically overpowers her and then sedates and kidnaps her. Although Gina is introduced as a confident and outstanding researcher, she is unable to survive in the menacing, profit-driven world of commercialized biotechnology and intellectual property theft without the protection of a supportive male scientist.

In these novels exposure to physical risk is used not only to create suspense but also to gauge the degree of dedication of the scientist characters to the integrity of their findings and to trace their development from insecurity to confidence. The writers also contest the view that science is a sheltered profession, protected by the power of the institution in which it is carried out. As we shall see, the institutional hierarchy engenders many of the more insidious dangers confronting individual scientists.

Ethical Risks

Less overt but no less pervasive is the danger to scientists of having their moral integrity and ethical values compromised. Individual scientists may feel pressured to resort to some form of scientific misconduct in order to achieve job security or fame; they may be trapped in immoral ventures devised by employers with an undisclosed political, financial, or ideological agenda; or they may experience a combination of these factors. In the first case, a desire for fame or fortune may appear to be the fundamental cause of professional corruption, but on closer examination, that apparent motive may prove to be the consequence of other factors—personal, social, or economic (see chapter 7).

Dr. Benedict (Ben) Lambert, protagonist of Simon Mawer's *Mendel's Dwarf* (1999), is a world authority on Mendelian genetics and himself a bearer of the gene for achondroplasia (dwarfism). Believing that fate has dealt him a mean hand, Ben has no compunction in agreeing to the request of the woman he loves to substitute his own sperm for that of her husband during an in vitro fertilization process, but he intervenes far beyond this. Without the knowledge of the medical or scientific fraternity, he illegally tests the resulting embryos for the achondroplasia gene. Ironically, by choosing whether to select for or against an achondroplastic offspring, he participates in the same market-driven genetic selection he had publicly condemned as the new socially acceptable eugenics when announcing, "At least the old eugenics was governed by some kind of theory, however dreadful it may have been. The new eugenics, *our* eugenics, is governed only by the laws of the marketplace. You get what you can pay for" (273). In Ben's case, the currency of the marketplace is his knowledge of genetics, but the outcome is the same. He secretly manipulates results to achieve his own purposes—not professional advancement, because he already has that, but the acquisition of power over those who implicitly despise or pity him.

A more widely known form of scientific misconduct involves instances of negligence, in which scientists themselves have been deceived by preliminary results into making claims for desired outcomes that later proved false;[5] have failed to check results, a scenario explored in depth by C. P. Snow in *The Search* ([1934] 1979); or have failed, professedly by accident, to acknowledge another researcher's results, a condition known as "citation amnesia" (Robinson and Goodman 2011). Ethically more serious is scientific fraud, involving deliberate fabrication or falsification of research results, selection of data to support the author's thesis, suppression of results that are contrary to the interests of the author or his or her sponsors, or intentional plagiarism. There have been numerous real-life examples of such bogus research claims in relation to cancer research and cloned human stem cells (Pincock 2006; Wade and Sang-hun 2006). Significantly, the research areas of such fraud align not only with funding opportunities but also with the potential cures that the public *wishes* to believe in, about which the gatekeepers (referees and the media) are correspondingly less rigorous. Ellen Schrecker notes that "in almost every instance, the unethical behavior within academe reflects off-campus pressure" (2002, 2). David Goodstein supports this: "Among the incidents of scientific fraud . . . three motives, or risk factors, have been present. In all cases the perpetrators (1) were under career pressure, (2) knew, or thought they knew, what the result would be if they went to the trouble of doing the work properly, and (3) were in a field in which individual experiments are not expected to be precisely reproducible. This tempts the researcher to dispense with experimental rigor and assume the desired results" (2002, 29).

The form of scientific misconduct most frequently explored in science novels arises from the pressure that research institutes place on early-career scientists to gain funding or to publish prematurely in prestigious journals, especially if the results apparently promise breakthroughs in high-profile areas of the discipline. The resulting false or unsubstantiated claims rebound upon the individual scientists as well as the laboratory. Yet although the scientific edifice pays lip service to disinterested rigor, whistle-blowers of alleged scientific misconduct are rarely rewarded and may themselves be professionally penalized and rejected by other research institute directors who doubt their team loyalty.

Allegra Goodman explores just such a scenario in *Intuition* ([2006] 2010).[6] Cliff Bannaker, a young postdoc who has spent years trying unsuccessfully to find a cure for breast cancer tumors in mice using a genetically modified strain of virus, faces losing his research position, which would end his scientific career. Suddenly and inexplicably, one strain of the virus appears to have cured three mice. This is considered sufficient reason to continue the project. Amid general jubilation in the laboratory, Cliff allows himself to be drawn into premature publication of his work by one of the institute directors, whose influence secures advance publication in *Nature* and a popular article in *People* under the sensationalist headline, "Will This Man Cure Cancer?" As a result, the institute receives large-scale government funding, even before there has been any attempt to reproduce the results. Subsequently, doubt is cast on the validity of Cliff's observations by a fellow postdoc, leading to a humiliating retraction of the *Nature* paper. Goodman does not present a clear-cut case of scientific fraud, however. Cliff consistently denies having falsified or manipulated his results, and Goodman focalizes Cliff's thoughts, indicating that he genuinely believed his results: "Perhaps his work with R-7 had been more about ideas than concrete fact; perhaps findings had been intuitive rather than entirely empirical. . . . Still aspects of his data were so compelling that in his mind they outweighed everything else. He had sifted out what was significant, and the rest had floated off like chaff" (321–22). Cliff's rationalization fits closely with the controversial picture that Latour and Woolgar ([1979] 1986) advanced for the socially constructed procedures of scientific culture, wherein inconclusive results are passed through the researcher's subjective filter to determine which data to keep and which to reject on the basis of what supports the desired outcome.

In *Intuition* an appeal panel eventually dismisses the charge of fraud, calling for reform of ethics oversight: "Poor record-keeping does not necessarily indicate a desire to mislead. . . . Faulty, or even false conclusions do not necessarily connote fraudulent claims" (Goodman 2010, 328). Because Goodman provides the perspectives of all parties—directors, postdoc, and whistle-blower—we understand how each operates, as not just a scientist but also a flawed human being, subject to the pressures and temptations of issues unrelated to the actual science. Goodman's scenario mirrors closely the real-life Baltimore case of 1986, in which a postdoc queried the published results of a senior immunologist in her laboratory and was dismissed (Charles 1991).

Other ethical risks arise from pressure to sidestep the agreed protocols and procedures of science, especially those involving human subjects. The requirement for animal trials preceding clinical trials is mandatory, although pharmaceutical companies would like to dispense with this lengthy and expensive procedure before releasing a lucrative product on the market. In some cases, third-world subjects, unaware of their rights, are used for the clinical trials. This situation is also a major focus of Rohn's *Experimental Heart*. Here, Richard Rouyle, senior scientist with the struggling start-up Geniaxis, hears of Gina Kraymer's use of a strain of herpes virus as a vector to carry a gene for combating Vera Fever infection in African villages and sees an opportunity to secretly substitute a behavioral modulator and test it by delivering it into the nervous system of the Africans. Uwe Schimank has argued that "the more a researcher understands himself as doing basic research, the more he suppresses reflections about the technological applications of the knowledge he produces and the potential societal risks involved" (1992, 328). Significantly, Rouyle "loathes applied research . . . [and] thought it right to use volunteers and prisoners for fundamental research" (Rohn 2009, 328). He pressures the company to proceed immediately to clinical trials, dispensing with in vitro tests and animal trials. Desperate to recoup its finances by gaining credibility in the gene transfer field, the company agrees, and Gina, torn between her knowledge that this is ethically wrong and a desire to avoid waiting years for tissue culture and animal trials, tacitly agrees. In order to save Gina, to whom he is attracted, Andy O'Hara, a scientist in a neighboring laboratory, persuades his colleagues to engage in secret and unauthorized research to publicly denounce Rouyle. Thus, the novel shows how an ethical breach is rarely an isolated affair; it draws in other unsuspecting scientists, usually juniors, who have little alternative but to acquiesce in what their superiors request.

Rohn explores a different aspect of scientific misconduct—suppression of unfavorable results—in *The Honest Look* (2010). Claire Cyrus, a new recruit at the biotechnology company Neurosys, observes an accidental but crucial sampling of proteins sourced from outside the cell rather than from the interior as intended. The result from this wild-card sample clearly indicates that the company's hoped-for cure for Alzheimer's, the "zapper," is ineffective, thereby throwing the whole project into doubt. Yet Claire delays reporting her observation until it becomes an issue of misconduct and prejudices the company's already advanced plan to proceed to clinical trials. Like Andy O'Hara in *Experimental Heart*, another scientist, Joshua, becomes involved in her deceit, endangering his position in the company. Claire's secrecy arises partly from her insecurity as a new postdoc promoted above her experience and resented by most of her colleagues and partly because of her romantic liaison with one of the senior scientists, whom she does not want to disappoint. But the depiction of Claire as the timid, vulnerable heroine leads to too-easy forgiveness by the company director and other senior colleagues and to her voluntary departure from science to write poetry. As in *Experimental Heart*, the ethical issue of scientific misconduct, although raised so pertinently, is dissipated in the romantic elements of the novel, leading to a simplistic conclusion that absolves the female scientist and perpetuating the well-worn stereotype of the helpless female in need of a male champion to save her from the consequences of her own failings and even, in Claire's case, to offer her an easy release from a demanding career in science.

A more sinister instance of suppressed observations occurs in William Boyd's *Brazzaville Beach*, when a powerful research director attempts to coerce a junior scientist to deny or conceal results that conflict with the director's own theories and research credibility. As we have noted, Hope Clearwater is pressured to discount or reinterpret her observations of ferocious, cannibalistic behavior by the chimpanzees at Grosso Arvore in order to support the theory of the benign, peaceful primate on which the director, Eugene Mallabar, has built his reputation. At first, he offers only a veiled threat, but Hope knows that "to go further would have been the end of my career" (2009, 235).

Direct plagiarism of results is rare in science, although a less overt form of this underlies the tacitly accepted practice by some senior researchers of placing their name on publications as first author, even if the majority of the work was carried out by junior colleagues—the so-called Matthew effect, whereby more fame accrues to the already famous (Merton 1968). Although this is often justified as facilitating publication, it effectively precludes junior researchers from becoming known. The accrediting of the work of female postdocs to their male colleagues, which carries the additional complication of gender discrimination, has been called the Matilda effect (Rossiter 1993).

A deliberate and blatant instance of such plagiarism occurs in *Brazzaville Beach*, when Mallabar and his colleagues, finally convinced of the validity of Hope's observations, revise his magnum opus as *Primate: The Society of the Great Ape*, incorporating her observations as his own and merely acknowledging in a footnote "the invaluable work of Dr. Hope Clearwater." In Ian McEwan's *Solar* (2010), Michael Beard, after the accidental death of a junior colleague, quickly takes steps to appropriate the colleague's research on a solar cell that would perform artificial photosynthesis. Passing it off as his own idea, Beard lodges an application for patents and gains sufficient funding to perfect the design and finance its mass production in a solar power plant in New Mexico. When subsequently hailed as an environmental savior, Beard shows no remorse or embarrassment for exploiting this stolen research.

Even when a patent lawyer discovers the plagiarism, Beard's business partner abandons him to multimillion-dollar debts, and a vandal (whose life Beard ruined) destroys the demonstration solar panels, he fails to accept responsibility and is merely bewildered by the turn of events against him.

Medical science involves a particular ethical risk to researchers in the treatment of human subjects. In *The Echo Maker* (2006), Richard Powers explores one aspect of this through the character of cognitive neuroscientist Gerald Weber, for whom Powers's acknowledged model was the neurologist Oliver Sacks. Throughout his long career, Weber has opposed the "medical model," which reduces psychology to a mechanistic understanding of the brain, believing instead that "consciousness works by telling a story" (234) and that encouraging his clients to construct their personal narrative is a therapeutic practice. He has also achieved a level of public acclaim by transferring his cases into popular books for general readers, the fictional counterpart of Sacks's best-selling *The Man Who Mistook His Wife for a Hat* (1985). More recent trends in psychotherapy have veered sharply toward clinical procedures, however, and Weber's methods are now regarded as unscientific. More seriously, he is accused in the media of using his patients' stories without permission. A reviewer of his latest book claims that "his stories border on privacy violations and sideshow exploitation. . . . Seeing such a respected figure capitalize on unacknowledged research and unfelt suffering borders on the embarrassing" (Powers 2006, 221). Weber finds himself assailed by the combined power of the profession and the press with accusations of ethical malpractice. Powers here points to the ephemeral nature of ethical norms within a profession, such that a researcher who conforms to one mode of research can be condemned not only as outdated but also as unethical when the accepted parameters suddenly change. Such paradigm shifts can be triggered by a change in "fashion" initiated by a popular figure in the discipline or by a desire to denigrate and exclude those not versed in the latest techniques, as is the case with Weber.

More problematic is the situation in Michael Byers's *Long for This World* ([2003] 2004). Henry Moss, a medical geneticist, researches possible treatments for the genetically transmitted Hickman Syndrome (a fictional version of progeria, which causes children to age prematurely and die before they are twenty). Moss coincidentally discovers, in an unaffected but genetically liable sibling of a Hickman patient, an enzyme that apparently overrides the Hickman effect. Moss takes regular blood samples from this boy and synthesizes the enzyme; then, without waiting for preclinical trials, which would take years, he injects it into his favorite patient, William, who is close to death. In thus violating ethical procedures Moss knowingly risks his whole career. William experiences a temporary reprieve of his symptoms but subsequently dies. Although compassion for William is his overriding motivation, Moss is not unaware of the lucrative market potential of an antiaging factor in a public eager for a youth drug. He reflects: "Who would suspect Henry himself of so entirely disregarding the tenets of his profession? Who could see into his heart and see the greed, the disregard, all of it stained with such a fearful love?" (217). Moss quickly takes steps to patent and on-sell the enzyme to a pharmaceutical firm with resources to conduct the appropriate trials and thus avoids discovery of misconduct. Nevertheless, he experiences "a strange, slightly dirty, uncomfortable feeling, as though he were negotiating to sell a memory, or a limb" (378).

Although known instances of scientists violating ethical norms are relatively rare, novelists have focused on such incidents partly to engender plot interest and the suspense of potential discovery but also to explore for readers the personal and sociological complexities involved in cases of ethical misconduct as well as the pressures and seductions inherent in a contemporary science that is dependent on funding for its existence. Consequently, these writers hope to evoke empathy for scientists who are caught in such ethical dilemmas.

Risks to Intellectual Identity and Mental Health

In previous centuries, the single most recurrent stereotype of the scientist, and of his conceptual ancestor, the alchemist, was a deranged and usually evil researcher who isolated himself from the rest of humanity (Haynes 2017). No explanations were offered for the madness of this character; he (and it was always *he*) was simply presented as such, with the implicit understanding that his obsession with his research goal was mentally unhealthy. He was almost invariably a figure of condemnation (although occasionally one of satire), who received his due punishment in the end. The best-known examples of such characters are, of course, Dr. Faustus, Victor Frankenstein, and

Doctor Moreau, but in much of twentieth-century literature and especially film, this stereotype was, as Peter Weingart and his colleagues have shown, practically the norm (Weingart, Muhl, and Pansegrau 2003).

In recent literature, however, the scientist afflicted with intellectual insecurity, anxiety, or, in extreme cases, madness is rarely condemned or satirized. Obsession is rebadged and respected as devotion to a higher cause, even though that cause may be opaque to most others. Even "madness" may be treated as an inescapable consequence of the science that is pursued with such dedication, aligning the scientist with the divine frenzy of the classical and Romantic poets.[7] In such fiction we are invited into the mental states of these characters to experience empathy and understanding rather than judgment.

The character's mental distress may arise from factors not initially related to the discipline—for example, heredity or a contracted illness—but may be exacerbated by an obsessive focus on research. This was possibly the case with the behavioral abnormalities and auditory hallucinations exhibited by the brilliant mathematician John Forbes Nash, subject of Sylvia Nasar's biography *A Beautiful Mind* (1998).[8] But more frequently novelists focus on an exploration of the mental states arising from the scientist's obsession with research. Often this obsession is associated with desire for recognition by peers and with extreme frustration and disappointment when such recognition is withheld or awarded to others. It may also arise when the scientist's results run counter to the prevailing paradigm and are ignored or viciously attacked (as in Rebecca Goldstein's *Properties of Light*, 2001); when experiments, theories, or proofs fail to produce an acceptable result; or when the scientist experiences a loss of certainty about the validity of his research, his intellectual powers (as in Rebecca Goldstein's *The Mind-Body Problem* [1983], Apostolos Doxiadis's *Uncle Petros and Goldbach's Conjecture* [1992], and Pippa Goldschmidt's *The Falling Sky* [2013]), or his own mental state (as in David Auburn's *Proof* [2000],[9] Tom Petsinis's *The French Mathematician* [1998], and William Boyd's *Brazzaville Beach* [2009]). Whatever the cause, the scientist character's mental distress is portrayed as an occupational hazard deserving our pity rather than our condemnation or ridicule.

In the novels we focus on here, the authors have used different methods to explore these issues phenomenologically, that is, by asking what this experience is like or by allowing the reader imaginative access to the scientist's mental state. Tom Petsinis's historical novel *The French Mathematician*

(1998) traces in detail the life of the nineteenth-century mathematics prodigy Évariste Galois, who died at age twenty as the result of a duel he initiated, and offers a rationale for this illogical behavior and extreme mental state. Galois was certainly a mathematical genius: while still at school he determined the conditions for solving a polynomial equation by radicals, a problem unsolved for 350 years, and his work became the foundation for Galois Theory and group theory, both fundamental principles of abstract algebra.

His easy mastery of algebra and geometry led Galois to despise all other subjects as well as his teachers and fellow students, and this arrogance prevented him from passing the entrance exam for the École Polytechnique, since he could not be bothered to give the reasons for his answers and insulted the examiner. But still obsessed with the purity of abstract math (a concept that is also explored in Max Frisch's play *Don Juan, or The Love of Geometry* [(1953) 1969]), Galois wrote, "There are times when 'I *am* mathematics—emotions, memories, self-awareness all vanish'" (Petsinis 1998, 101). Like Nash, he was devastated to find that someone else, in his case the Norwegian Niels Abel, had preempted (albeit by a different method) his work on quintic equations in the previous year; later, a paper he submitted to the French Academy was ignored and subsequently lost. In Galois's conspiracy-ridden mind, this was a deliberate act on the part of inferior mathematicians to deny him recognition. Thus, even a scientist who professes to despise the establishment, caring for nothing but the purity of the math, suffers intense depression when acknowledgment and honors are withheld. To his contemporaries, this appears to be at the very least intermittent madness.

In his last hours, Galois frenetically records all his mathematical ideas in mystical language: "In an idea lasting no more than a fraction of a second I have apprehended the full beauty and significance of elliptical integrals" (416). His heart is "now susceptible only to imaginary numbers. It can grasp the meaning of the square root of negative one, feel the presence of the elusive *i*. By tonight it will renounce these for the transcendental, the mysterious π. And by tomorrow it will renounce even these for the holy zero" (420).

Is Galois mad? Or is his obsession a necessary prerequisite for the expression of his genius? Impatient with his arrogance, his rejection of humanity, and his seemingly self-induced failures, we are nevertheless intrigued by the purity of his dedication to an abstract ideal and persuaded to feel compassion for this visionary struggling against the sociopolitical forces of the time. Petsinis's Galois is far from being the stereotypical mad scientist.

Rebecca Goldstein's *Properties of Light* (2001) presents three pure mathematicians, each arguably mad. Justin Childs, a brilliant young mathematician and one of the narrators, is clearly anxious about his own mental state since he repeatedly tries to justify his sanity and rationalize his actions. "My hatred is my cause. . . . Would an obsessive person even pose the possibility of his own delusion?" (2). Since childhood, he has focused on "constructing truth tables" (5) and compulsively decoded the signs around him. Confronted by the prevailing paradigms in physics, which had "abandon[ed] reality to stuff more spectral than material" (16) and used "difficulties in the fundamental theory of matter as a license to malign the objectivity of matter" (33), he discovers an alternative view in a paper by the little-known physicist Samuel Mallach, proposing "hidden variables" that purport to "save the phenomena" by reconciling quantum mechanics with relativity theory. Goldstein's acknowledged model for Mallach was the theoretical physicist David Bohm, who, like Mallach, published a paper on a "hidden variables" formulation of quantum mechanics.

When Justin finally meets Mallach, the latter appears to conform in many ways to the traditional stereotype of the mad scientist: he is isolated, embittered, and noncommunicative with anyone except his mathematically gifted daughter Dana. And yet he is also, paradoxically, attracted to the rarified world of the Romantic poets. Justin soon concludes that Mallach is, indeed, mad: "Having lost his physics, together with his senses, to the devastations of vast sorrow, he was desperately seeking it in poetry" (21). But he nevertheless determines to exploit Mallach's mind for his own purposes, to "get the glorious physics out from him" (22). Thus, in the triad of Mallach, Justin, and Dana, each intends to exploit one or both of the others, but in so doing they have all, through their intellectual intensity, placed themselves in a situation of mental risk that ultimately destroys them.

Like Bohm, Mallach has been mentally and emotionally devastated by the disregard of his seminal publication. Justin concludes, "What had driven him so near the edge of madness (and was he not still mad?) but the enmassed indifference of his peers?" (52). This resonates with what Bohm wrote in a personal letter: "I seem to have only one strong emotion left, and that is hatred for the forces that have destroyed so many human beings, including myself."[10] His ignominy is exacerbated by the disdain projected by the head of school, Dietrich Spencer, who has demoted him to teaching the department's most unpopular course, Physics for Poets. But through this course, Mallach enters further into a world of nonreality, since the Romantic poets valued the imagination and access to supernatural states through dreams, trance, and madness more highly than they valued the material world. Eventually he kills himself, believing that Justin, too, has betrayed him. Paradoxically, Mallach, Justin, and Dana are all trying, by fundamentally irrational means, to rationally establish (through mathematics, the ultimate logical tool) that the material world is real and predictable, as opposed to the nebulous quantum model of chance and uncertainty. Mallach speaks of "scientists of ecstasy" (164) and claims that Einstein told him he "felt equations in his muscles, in sensations that lay deeper than reason" (102). Dana also "feels" truth in this way (103), and both believe in dancing their way to truth. Interestingly, Nash also declared that he arrived intuitively at a proof before he could provide the steps of the process (Goodstein 1998).

Eventually even Justin, the rationalist, comes to believe that "there is some way of seeing we have not yet seen, a seeing still unsighted in the long corridors of links, and without it even the deepest most powerful mathematics gropes blind" (Goldstein 2001, 146). Yet, ironically, all three characters believe they need mathematics to secure their Romantic vision. Thus, Goldstein uses the trope of madness to focus on the tension between reason on one hand and inspiration or ecstasy on the other. By confining the reader within the mental anguish of these characters, entangled within the ambiguity of quantum mechanics and the uncertainty principle yet passionately desiring certainty, she re-creates for us the intellectual problem that all three are obsessively and incestuously focused on resolving, evoking our understanding and empathy rather than our judgment.

Achieving mathematical insights through nonrational means has allegedly been the experience of a significant number of mathematicians. Werner Heisenberg acknowledged the help of Indian poet and mystic Rabindranath Tagore in formulating quantum theory,[11] and the Indian mathematician Srinivasa Ramanujan, a devout Brahmin, claimed to receive visions of scrolls containing complex equations from the Hindu goddess Maha'lakshmi of Namakkal (Kanigel 1991).[12] Ramanujan himself could provide no formal evidence for the visions, believing that "an equation has no meaning for me unless it represents a thought of God" (Ranganathan 1967, 8). It seems noteworthy that for mathematicians immersed in Eastern philosophy or religion, this visionary basis for arriving at mathematical truths, far from producing mental anguish or a threat to personal identity, was taken as a confirmation of certainty.

This importing of intuition into the highly logical, axiom-based procedures of mathematics has intrigued a number of novelists and playwrights and issued in a range of novels, plays, and films: David Leavitt's novel *The Indian Clerk* (2007), Jagat Narain Kapur's play *Ramanujan's Miracles: A Drama to Demystify Mathematics* (1997), Ira Hauptman's play *Partition* (2000), David Freeman's drama *A First Class Man* (2007), Simon McBurney's play *A Disappearing Number* (2008), and two films based on Ramanujan's life, *Ramanujan* (2014) and *The Man Who Knew Infinity* (2015).

In *Brazzaville Beach*, mathematician John Clearwater is attempting to find patterns in turbulence that might illuminate other disorderly systems in the universe. Presumably influenced by contemporary interest in chaos theory as proposed by Edward Lorenz in 1961 and revived by Benoit Mandelbrot in 1982, he is planning to "write the book of the unruly world we live in" (Boyd 2009, 62) by focusing on Divergent Syndromes, the erratic behavior avoided by most mathematicians, who are seeking an orderly, explanatory system. During a holiday he has a flash of insight into an equation while burying the rubbish and, confusing precedent for cause, tries to retrieve his inspiration by digging more and more holes. His wife, Hope, is shocked by this irrational behavior: "The thought came to her, unbidden, unwelcome, that perhaps her husband was going insane" (112). She realized that "eccentricities were becoming problems and that quirks of behavior were developing into warning signs" (162). John suffers a mental breakdown and depression and undergoes electric shock therapy, but eventually he drowns himself, a victim of madness produced by a passionate desire to be a great mathematician despite his lack of genius and to coerce the complexity of nature into a model of order.

In terms of mental health, mathematical genius Noam Himmel in Goldstein's *The Mind-Body Problem* (1983) bears some resemblance to John Clearwater, although, unlike the latter, he has received worldwide acclaim for his early work. Nevertheless, like most mathematicians in fiction and film, he does not readily relate to people and does not understand or "read" human behavior: "I discovered early that I liked ideas much better than people" (28–29). The more he becomes encased in a mental bubble of math, the less he can, or even wishes to, converse with others who are less informed, until his social skills degenerate. This is equally true of Galois, Mallach, Clearwater, and, as we shall see, of Milo Andret. Himmel's approach to mathematics, like that of Galois, Ramanujan, Fermat, and many others, is intuitive rather than rational. He claims that he has known mathematical proofs before he saw why they were valid and that he is merely remembering them. "I wish I were able to describe the beauty and excitement when it's working, when I'm seeing it. . . . I suppose any creative act makes one feel powerful, but in math the power seems absolute. . . . It's truth" (91, 93). But as his wife, Renee, observes, "There's a certain degree of danger involved in the life of the pure mathematician, in his intimacy with the inhumanly perfect and the consequent liberation from mortal concerns. Insanity is an occupational hazard, a sacrifice the mathematician risks in his solipsistic splendor" (202). Because math is his whole world, Himmel, like Clearwater, is devastated to find he has lost his mathematical powers and, with them, his identity, which has been partly foisted on him and partly self-generated: "All I have ever been to anyone, including you, including myself, for that matter, had been defined by my mathematical gifts. It was all anyone asked of me. It was my justification" (262).

Ethan Canin's novel *A Doubter's Almanac* (2016) traces three generations of gifted mathematicians—at least one of whom frequently appears mad—and concludes that in males, being a genius, at least in the field of math, leads to mental instability and degenerative behavior. Milo Andret has a natural facility for recognizing spatial relationships in both the real world (even as a child he could find his way home through the woods from a great distance) and in pure math. Throughout a lonely childhood on a farm in the 1950s, raised by disaffected parents, he takes little account of his gift. But on proceeding to UC Berkeley he falls prey to the multiple risks arising from his mathematical talent. As a young assistant professor, he proves the famously difficult Malosz Conjecture (fictional), a long-unsolved theorem in the field of topology. For this he receives the Fields medal, the mathematics equivalent of a Nobel Prize, and is appointed as distinguished professor at Princeton. Mathematical ability is widely believed to deteriorate rapidly after the age of thirty, however, and Andret is pressured by his head of school to embark on a new challenge, preferably greater than the Malosz, as he may have only five to ten years to do great work.

After briefly considering the famous Goldbach Conjecture, he starts work on the Abendroth Conjecture (also fictional), and like the other mathematicians considered here, he believes in alternatives to rationalism: "Though it was considered part of algebraic topology, Andret had a feeling that its solution—if it was going to be solved at all—would not come through equation but through the ability to visualize strange and unearthly shapes. At this he was quite adept" (Canin 2016, 95). His confidence is shattered, however, when the proof is discovered by a fourteen-year-old schoolboy with access to a home computer—a tool that Andret had despised as irrelevant to math. His genius, inherited by his son Hans, becomes a curse (298–99), made worse by his appalling arrogance, his contempt for social civilities, and his sexual exploitation of women, on whom he is obsessively dependent. Hans lists his father's characteristics as being "his logical brilliance, his highly purified arrogance, his Olympian drinking, his caustic derision, his near autistic introversion, and his world-class self-involvement" (210). Most of these traits can be observed to a lesser degree in the other fictional mathematicians discussed here. Milo lapses into decline and despair when it is shown that even his acclaimed proof of the Milosz Conjecture was, after all, flawed. He isolates himself in a cabin in the woods (a return to childhood), pretending to work on the Abendroth but passing his days in an alcoholic stupor. His violent and erratic behavior toward his wife and children signals his declining mental state, which is confirmed by his son's psychologist, who says, "Genius is a degenerative psychosis . . . belonging to the group of moral insanity. . . . Fewer dopamine receptors, or something like that. Psychosis and inventiveness seem to run along a kind of continuum" (424). Through the three generations of the Andret family, Canin explores the relative importance of genetic and environmental inheritance and the role of women in the life of a mathematical genius. The female mathematicians in the family, Milo's daughter, Paulette, and Hans's daughter, Emmy, both possibly more brilliant than their brothers, seem not to be afflicted with the "curse," suggesting that the arrogance and mental extremes exhibited by the males of the family may result from hormonal interaction with "dopamine receptors, or something like that." In effect, the Andret family history counterpoints genius with curse, ambition with arrogance, obsession with destructiveness, and the highest intelligence with infantile dependence.

Although the majority of fictional scientists suffering from mental anguish are mathematicians, they are not the only ones. Neuroscientists are also depicted as victims of anxiety, self-doubt, and a sense of meaninglessness. We have seen in the previous section the mental devastation experienced by psychologist Gerald Weber when he is suddenly pilloried by his colleagues and the media and reviled by a formerly admiring public. In their study of the anxious neuroscientist in contemporary fiction, Roxburgh, Kirchhofer, and Auguscik (2016) conclude that "Weber's case studies emphasize the humanity that manifests itself in the disorders from which patients suffer" (79). After a series of humiliations at a conference, during TV interviews, and in reviews of his latest book, Weber reflects that "he had humiliated himself abroad. Back home, hundreds of subjects awaited him, real people he'd used as mere thought experiments. Every one of them throbbed in him and could not be cut out. The world had no place left, real or imagined, where he might put down" (Powers 2006, 260).

Conclusion

Unlike earlier fiction in which scientist characters were viewed through the observations of others, the science novels discussed in this chapter invite readers to enter the minds of contemporary scientists and reach a degree of empathic understanding of their inner lives. Novelist Barbara Kingsolver, whose *Flight Behavior* is discussed in chapter 10, asserts that "all fiction has the power to create empathy for the theoretical stranger. It has the power to bring the reader inside the mind of another person. Only fiction can do that. Journalism can't do that. Journalism describes from the outside. Photography describes from the outside, but in fiction, really, you put down your life. You enter the mind of another person" (Walsh 2012). Cognitive psychologist Steven Pinker argues that the "*philosophes* of the Enlightenment extolled the way novels engaged a reader's identification with and sympathetic concern for others" and that "whether or not novels in general . . . were the critical genre in expanding empathy, the explosion of reading may have contributed to the Humanitarian Revolution in getting people into the habit of straying from their parochial vantage points. And it may have contributed in a second way: by creating a hothouse for new ideas about moral values and the social order" (2011, 177).

By focusing on the physical, ethical, and mental risks that assail their scientist characters and on the courageous efforts of those characters to meet such challenges, the novelists considered here fulfill a similar function in creating the "deep intersubjectivity" that Rita Felski (2008) claims as one of the three achievements of literature. They indicate the degree to which scientists, far from being powerfully autonomous and able to pursue the research of their choice, are enmeshed in complex political, social, and economic interactions and restraints that may, and increasingly do, determine the research projects they can undertake. The prevailing culture of science, which legitimizes an institutional hierarchy as rigid as that of a business corporation, creates another contingent set of limitations, often gender based, which may either encourage or condemn the early-career scientist. In addition to these external career risks, many scientists suffer internal self-judgment regarding their professional abilities and individual mental state. Although most of the protagonists of the novels discussed here survive the external risks, few are able to overcome the self-doubt and devastating sense of failure they experience. This may prove a critical factor in producing in readers an empathic understanding of scientists, domesticating and normalizing emerging scientific concepts and promoting dialogue about controversial ethical issues.

Notes

1. For a detailed discussion of the economization of science, see chapter 7.
2. For example, the brilliant geneticist Crake in Margaret Atwood's *Oryx and Crake* ([2003] 2004), the scientists of Michael Crichton's *Jurassic Park* (1990) and *Prey* ([2002] 2008), and the scientists of Greg Bear's *Darwin's Radio* (1999). See also the discussion in chapter 3.
3. There are, of course, also ill-intentioned scientists in modern fiction— for example, Eugene Mallabar in William Boyd's *Brazzaville Beach* (2009), Richard Rouyle in Jennifer Rohn's *Experimental Heart* (2009), and Michael Beard in Ian McEwan's *Solar* (2010), but they are increasingly rare.
4. Other examples from among many are found in Ambrose Bierce's story "Moxon's Master" (1899), Robert Louis Stevenson's *Dr Jekyll and Mr Hyde* (1886), H. G. Wells's *The Island of Dr Moreau* (1896), and Karel Čapek's *R.U.R.* (1921).
5. The best-known case was the cold-fusion report in 1989 by Pons and Fleischmann (see Close 1991).
6. See also Schimank, chapter 7.
7. In *Ion* (1987), Plato identified poetic inspiration as arising from divine frenzy, insisting that it preceded consciousness. When uttering his rhapsodic words, the poet was believed to be divinely possessed.
8. Nash's behavioral abnormalities are well documented, and the earlier label of schizophrenia is now disputed (see, for example, Shorter 2015).
9. For a detailed analysis of these issues in *Proof*, see Henke, Schaffeld, and Voigt 2017.
10. Quoted in Peat 1996.
11. Quoted by Fritjof Capra, interviewed by Renee Weber in Wilber (1982).
12. Kanigel 1991.

References

Auburn, David. 2000. *Proof: A Play*. London: Faber and Faber.

Beck, Ulrich. 1999. *World Risk Society*. Cambridge, UK: Polity Press.

Boyd, William. 2009. *Brazzaville Beach*. London: Penguin.

Brown, Matthew, dir. 2015. *The Man Who Knew Infinity*. New York: Pressman Film.

Byers, Michael. (2003) 2004. *Long for This World*. New York: Houghton Mifflin.

Canin, Ethan. 2016. *A Doubter's Almanac*. London: Bloomsbury.

Čapek, Karel. (1921) 1923. *R.U.R.* Translated by Paul Selver. Garden City, NY: Doubleday, Page.

Charles, D. 1991. "Last Act of American Science 'Soap Opera.'" *New Scientist* 129 (March 30): 8.

Close, F. 1991. *Too Hot to Handle*. Princeton, NJ: Princeton University Press.

Doxiadis, Apostolos. 1992. *Uncle Petros and Goldbach's Conjecture*. New York: Bloomsbury.

Dudman, Clare. 2003. *Wegener's Jigsaw*. London: Sceptre Books.

Felski, Rita. 2008. *Uses of Literature*. Oxford, UK: Blackwell.

Ghosh, Amitav. 2005. *The Hungry Tide*. London: HarperCollins.

Goldschmidt, Pippa. 2013. *The Falling Sky*. Edinburgh: Freight Books.

Goldstein, Rebecca. 1983. *The Mind-Body Problem*. London: Penguin.

———. 2001. *Properties of Light*. Boston: Houghton Mifflin.

Goodman, Allegra. (2006) 2010. *Intuition*. London: Atlantic Books.

Goodstein, David. 1998. "Mathematics to Madness, and Back." *New York Times*, June 11, 1998.

———. 2002. "Scientific Misconduct." *Academe* 88 (1): 29–32.

Hauptman, Ira. 2000. *Partition*. New York: Playscripts.

Haynes, Roslynn. 2006. "The Alchemist in Fiction: The Master Narrative." *HYLE: International Journal for Philosophy of Chemistry* 12 (1): 5–29.

———. 2017. *From Madman to Crime Fighter: The Scientist in Western Culture*. Baltimore: Johns Hopkins University Press.

Henke, Jennifer, Norbert Schaffeld, and Kati Voigt. 2017. "Mathematicians, Mysteries and Mental Illness: The Stage-to-Screen Adaptation of *Proof*." *Adaptation* 10 (3): 322–37. https://doi.org/10.1093/adaptation/apx017.

Humboldt, Alexander von. (1845–62) 1864. *Cosmos: A Sketch of a Physical Description of the Universe*. Vol. 1, translated by E. C. Otte. London: Henry G. Bohn. https://archive.org/details/cosmoso1humbgoog.

Kanigel, Robert. 1991. *The Man Who Knew Infinity: A Life of the Genius Ramanujan*. New York: Charles Scribner's Sons.

Kehlmann, Daniel. 2005. *Measuring the World*. New York: Pantheon.

Kingsolver, Barbara. 2012. *Flight Behavior*. New York: HarperCollins.

Latour, Bruno, and Steve Woolgar. (1979) 1986. *Laboratory Life: The Construction of Scientific Facts*. Princeton, NJ: Princeton University Press.

Mawer, Simon. 1999. *Mendel's Dwarf*. New York: Penguin.

McEwan, Ian. 2010. *Solar*. New York: Random House.

Merton, Robert K. 1968. "The Matthew Effect in Science." *Science* 159 (3810): 56–63.

Nasar, Sylvia. 1998. *A Beautiful Mind*. New York: Simon and Schuster.

Ondaatje, Michael. 2011. *Anil's Ghost*. London: Vintage Books.

Peat, F. David. 1996. *Infinite Potential: The Life and Times of David Bohm*. Reading, MA: Helix Books.

Petsinis, Tom. 1998. *The French Mathematician*. New York: Walker.

Pincock, Stephen. 2006. "*Lancet* Study Faked." *Scientist*, January 16, 2006. http://www.the-scientist.com/?articles.view/articleNo/23607/title/Lancet-study-faked.

Pinker, Steven. 2011. *The Better Angels of Our Nature: The Decline of Violence in History and Its Causes*. New York: Farrar, Straus and Giroux.

Plato. 1987. *Ion*. Edited and translated by T. J. Saunders. London: Penguin.

Powers, Richard. 2006. *The Echo Maker*. London: Vintage.

Rajasekaran, Gnana, dir. 2014. *Ramanujan*. Chennai, IN: Camphor Cinema.

Ranganathan, Shiyali Ramamrita. 1967. *Ramanujan, the Man and the Mathematician*. Delhi: Gyan.

Robinson, Karen A., and Steven N. Goodman. 2011. "A Systematic Examination of the Citation of Prior Research in Reports of Randomized, Controlled Trials." *Annals of Internal Medicine* 154 (1): 50.

Rohn, Jennifer. 2009. *Experimental Heart*. Cold Spring Harbor, NY: Cold Spring Harbor Laboratory Press.

———. 2010. *The Honest Look*. Cold Spring Harbor, NY: Cold Spring Harbor Laboratory Press.

Rossiter, Margaret E. W. 1993. "The Matthew/Matilda Effect in Science." *Social Studies of Science* 23 (2): 325–41.

Roxburgh, Natalie, Anton Kirchhofer, and Anna Auguscik. 2016. "Universal Narrativity and the Anxious Scientist of the Contemporary Neuronovel." *Mosaic: An Interdisciplinary Critical Journal* 49 (4): 71–87.

Schimank, Uwe. 1992. "Science as a Social Risk Producer." In *The Culture and Power of Knowledge: Inquiries into Contemporary Societies*, edited by Nico Stehr and Richard V. Ericson, 215–33. Berlin: Walter de Gruyter.

Schrecker, Ellen. 2002. "What's Right?" *Academe* 88 (1): 2.

Shorter, Edward. 2015. "A Beautiful Mind: What Did John Nash Really Have?" *Psychology Today*, May 27, 2015. https://www.psychologytoday.com/blog/how-everyone-became-depressed/201505/beautiful-mind-what-did-john-nash-really-have.

Snow, C. P. [1934] 1979. *The Search*. Harmondsworth, UK: Penguin.

Wade, Nicholas, and Chloe Sang-hun. 2006. "Researcher Faked Evidence of Human Cloning, Koreans Report." *New York Times*, January 10, 2006. http://www.nytimes.com/2006/01/10/science/10clone.html.

Walsh, Bryan. 2012. "Barbara Kingsolver on *Flight Behavior* and Why Climate Change Is Part of Her Story." *Time*, November 8, 2012. http://entertainment.time.com/2012/11/08/barbara-kingsolver-on-flight-behavior-climate-change-and-the-end-of-doubt/#comments.

Weingart, Peter, Claudia Muhl, and Petra Pansegrau. 2003. "Of Power Maniacs and Unethical Geniuses: Science and Scientists in Fiction Film." *Public Understanding of Science* 12 (3): 279–87.

Wilber, Ken, ed. 1982. *The Holographic Paradigm and Other Paradoxes: Exploring the Leading Edge of Science*. Boulder, CO: Shambhala/Random House.

5.
Speculative Fiction and the Significance of Plausibility
Dystopian Science in the Critical Response to Margaret Atwood's *Oryx and Crake*

Anna Auguscik,
Sina Farzin,
Emanuel Herold,
and Anton Kirchhofer

Published in 2003, Margaret Atwood's *Oryx and Crake* has become one of the most widely discussed science novels of the new century. It is set partly in a dystopian near-future world and partly in a postapocalyptic future world. In the near-future world, contemporary trends toward the privatization and profit orientation of scientific work and toward the neoliberal subjection of all areas of society to economic imperatives have become dominant, and all forces counter to these trends have become completely marginalized and delegitimized. In the postapocalyptic world, the few human survivors live alongside the Crakers, a genetically modified, posthuman race.

Although Atwood herself has discussed conceptions of utopia and dystopia in various contexts, her own preferred genre term for *Oryx and Crake* has been, emphatically and insistently, "speculative fiction."[1] Her definition at the time of publication[2] emphasized how the negative features of the near-future world need to be conceived as plausible consequences of conditions and developments in contemporary society. It is this *criterion of plausibility* that Atwood defines as the cardinal distinction between speculative fiction (which must be plausible in this way) and science fiction (which is not required to be).

Ever since it was published, *Oryx and Crake* has been discussed in general and literary review media, in science magazines and academic journals, and more recently in online and social media, with regular participation by the author. Our contribution will explore the dynamics of this discussion. What aspects of the novel are addressed in these diverse forms of reception? Do they differ according to the various media contexts? Specifically, we examine the extent to and manner in which the *science-related* aspects of the novel are addressed—the representation of scientists, their institutions and laboratory practices, and the depiction of the material products of science and of the social, cultural, and economic contexts that shape all of these. *Oryx and Crake* was the first novel in the MaddAddam trilogy, and while the later publication of the second and third novels—*The Year of the Flood* (Atwood 2009b) and *MaddAddam* (Atwood 2013a)—has modified readings of the entire MaddAddam world, we are interested here in the representation and discussion of laboratory science against the background of genre debate and will therefore focus on *Oryx and Crake*.[3]

Our findings suggest that in many cases, reception is focused almost exclusively on those elements of the novel concerned with technological innovations. To substantiate this general observation, we will start with a brief recapitulation of the thematic and narrative entanglement of science and society in the novel and follow that with an outline of Atwood's conception of speculative fiction in the context of her participation in critical debates about her fiction. A general analysis of the novel's reception in various media contexts will form the backdrop to an analysis of the discussions of one specific biotechnological innovation presented in the novel, the artificial meat product ChickieNobs. Our conclusion will revert to the question of the potential contributions of narrative fiction to ongoing debates about science and society.

Reading *Oryx and Crake* as a Vision of Dystopian Science

Snowman, formerly known as Jimmy, is a lonely survivor of a pandemic that appears to have completely wiped out human life on Earth. Struggling to eke out his existence in loose contact with a group of genetically modified post-humans, he recalls the world in which he grew up and revisits the facts that led to its collapse. This preapocalyptic society is represented as being split into two separate spheres. One sphere consists of gated communities, the so-called compounds, owned and run by private biotechnological corporations who dominate society. These are research centers that provide a high standard of living for their resident employees. They are policed by a privately owned paramilitary security force (CorpSeCorps) and shuttered off from their surrounding areas—the "pleeblands," where the disenfranchised and underprivileged consumer population work and live. The pleeblands comprise the second sphere, and they provide a vast additional market for financially lucrative applications of biotechnological research, ranging from plastic surgery and cosmetics to medications and organ transplants, all developed by the scientists employed in the compounds.

The all-encompassing commercialization of genetic and biotechnological research has produced a corresponding split in the education system. Whereas the sciences, which develop profitable commodities, are privileged and generously funded, societal interest in the humanities and in literary or artistic pursuits is limited to their potential usefulness in advertising and marketing. The relative educational careers of Jimmy, a "word person," and Crake, his hyperintelligent scientist friend, reflect this split.

The families of both men have been partly destroyed by the moral corruption of society: Jimmy's mother disappeared under mysterious circumstances and seems to have been executed for taking part in environmentalist protests against corporate interests; Crake's father "commits suicide" before he can turn whistle-blower and expose the destructive effects of a popular health product. Jimmy's response has been to escape into sex and alcohol. Crake, however, uses his scientific expertise to beat the system with its own means, initiating a pandemic that destroys humans and leaving Jimmy with the role of guide to the new genetically modified type of human that Crake has designed (with great ingenuity but mixed success) to populate the earth in peace and harmony.

Through a range of signals the novel invites us to read this society as a not-so-distant possible future version of our own. To establish this, we will pick out three indications. First, the protagonist's parents are described as having grown up in a society that contemporary readers would recognize as their own: "Everyone's parents moaned on about stuff like that. *Remember when you could drive anywhere? Remember when everyone lived in the pleeblands? Remember when you could fly anywhere in the world, without fear? Remember hamburger chains, always real beef . . . ? Remember when voting mattered? . . . it was all so great once. Boohoo"* (Atwood 2003, 72). Second, the privatization of public concerns such as education and research is well known in today's social sciences, as is the economization[4] of all areas of human existence. Third, the novel contains scientific developments that may sound futuristic but that have already been or are close to being implemented (for example, luminescent rabbits, spider-goats, and genetically engineered lab meat, which we will discuss later).

The dystopian science in the novel is depicted as a symptom rather than as the cause of the emergence of a dystopian society. The fact that science can be exploited in such a way is the result of a *social* failure. It would be an understatement to say that science in the novel is driven by marketability or profitability: in Atwood's scenario the boundaries between science and the economy have practically collapsed. The commercialization of scientific research is so sweeping that other external factors, such as political or legal regulation, have been eliminated. Dystopian science in *Oryx and Crake* is the product of a dystopian society that was made possible by a sociostructural failure resulting from socioeconomic tendencies already visible in the current phenomenon of economization. When we talk about dystopian science, social as well as technological aspects of scientific practice are implied. Intertwining social and technological conditions of science in this way, however, is not merely a contingent feature of the novel. It is core to Atwood's understanding of speculative fiction.

Atwood's Notions and Strategies Regarding Speculative Fiction

Atwood's discussion of her work as *speculative fiction* predates *Oryx and Crake*, and the term has a history that goes back much further. First recorded in 1889 in *Lippincott's Monthly Magazine*, it was propagated by author Robert A. Heinlein in 1947 ([1947] 1965) and has been used by literary scholars since the 1950s. Its relation to other genre labels such as science fiction, utopian, and dystopian has been a matter of discussion ever since. Atwood's ideas about speculative fiction update this older discourse. As we shall see, her understanding of the term has evolved over time, not least as a response to the effect that her strong initial positioning had on genre debates about science fiction. While academic criticism has generally adopted *speculative fiction* as an umbrella term (see, for example, Booker 2013), the distinction between the various genre terms and the individual positioning is strong in public media and in statements by contemporary writers themselves. Atwood's controversial conception of speculative fiction is far narrower than the widespread use in academic criticism, and it shifts the focus of the genre debate within and about science fiction from an emphasis on the distinctions between science fiction and fantasy toward the relations between science fiction and literary fiction. Her positioning on the "literary" side of science fiction has touched on questions of high versus popular culture, but other writers have joined and expanded the subsequent debate. China Miéville, as leader of "radical SF's invasion of the mainstream" (D. G. Walter 2011), argues for an erosion of strict subgenre boundaries between estranging forms of fiction such as fantastic, science fiction, and utopian writing (Miéville 2009, 244). Similarly controversial positions were articulated around the same time by Kim Stanley Robinson, who speaks of science fiction as "the realism of our time" (Flood 2009), and by Ursula K. Le Guin in relation to Jeanette Winterson, whom she sees as "trying to keep her credits as a 'literary' writer even as she openly commits genre" in her novel *The Stone Gods* (Le Guin 2007).

Atwood first defined the concept in the wake of the reception of *The Handmaid's Tale* (1985). She points out that, in contrast to narratives involving time travel, Martians, or unknown galaxies, "in *The Handmaid's Tale*, nothing happens that the human race has not already done at some time in the past, or that it is not doing now, perhaps in other countries, or for which it has not yet developed the technology" (Atwood 2005b, 92). Atwood thus claims plausibility for her extrapolations, which are historically informed and comprise social as well as technological developments. In statements linked to the publication of *Oryx and Crake*, she insists that the novel "is speculative fiction, believe me" (Gussow 2003).[5] By assigning the novel to a literary tradition that is associated with works such as George Orwell's *1984*, among others, Atwood reinforces any reception of the novel that sees it as a critique of the economization of science.[6] What she is offering in this way is an interpretive framing, what we may call a "hermeneutic orientation": she outlines a certain conceptual frame for an ideal reception of her novel.

As the discussion progresses, however, Atwood herself tends to undermine this initial framing of the novel in several ways. The literary references she invokes appear to change over time and to move toward a greater stress on technology rather than on societal frameworks: "For me, 'speculative fiction' means plots that descend from Jules Verne's books about submarines and balloon travel and such—things that really could happen but hadn't just completely happened when the authors wrote the books" (2011a, 6). In her interviews, she shifts the focus increasingly toward the plausibility of her technological speculation (see Case and McDonald 2003; Kellogg 2009; Hoby 2013; Doherty 2013). Moreover, Atwood's own comments frequently shy away from spelling out a social critique. Remarkably, comments on the specific social and economic contexts of scientific practice are more prominent in the questions of the interviewers than in Atwood's own statements. In response to such questions, Atwood only occasionally addresses problems relating to the *social* context in which science operates, as is evident, for example, in this comment: "When pressed for present-day concerns in science ethics that prompted her book, Atwood says she feels particularly strongly about the loss of independence of scientists, citing the suppression of negative data by corporate sponsors" (Louët 2005).[7] Instead, she invokes very general notions on the relation between science and the nature of human *morality*: "Science is a tool, like a hammer. You can use it for good or ill, to build a house or to murder your neighbor. . . . It's not science you have to look at but the human beings that use it" (Akbar 2009; see also Hoby 2013).

Thus, in the decade following the publication of *Oryx and Crake*, a complex picture emerged from the evolving genre debates around science fiction, literary fiction, and speculative fiction and the reception of what we call dystopian science. Since the early 2000s, there has been a lively debate involving numerous contemporary novelists about the changing relationship between science fiction and literary fiction. The position for which all participants appear to compete, regardless of the genre terms and definitions they may champion, is that of *writing fiction that has a claim to relevance as social critique*. This is true whether they promote a certain reading of speculative fiction (Atwood), claim that science fiction has always had this function (Le Guin), or maintain that science fiction has only recently acquired this function (Robinson). If we look at Atwood's evolving positions in this debate, we can highlight three striking observations: (1) she is particularly emphatic and insistent on her definition of speculative fiction in the years immediately following the publication of *Oryx and Crake*; (2) she is considerably less dogmatic in the debates after 2009;[8] and (3) paradoxically, she consistently eschews taking any position of concrete social critique that would validate social critique as a genre feature (of literary fiction or speculative fiction) rather than as a direct authorial social intervention. Like Atwood's shift from focusing on societal plausibility to focusing on technological plausibility, this position appears to run counter to her emphatic claims for speculative fiction. We can construe these somewhat contradictory findings in two ways: They might be seen as undermining her texts' impact by effectively reducing their social critique to a genre feature rather than embracing their potential to engender societal debate. Or, on a more positive note, we might read them as Atwood's way of assigning responsibility for the critique of specific sociotechnological developments portrayed in her texts to readers and commentators rather than allowing the public to portray the author herself as an activist.

We now turn to an analysis of the novel's reception in different media contexts in order to see how reviewers, interviewers, and readers deal with the relation between technological and social plausibility. The question, to us, is less whether the reception generally follows Atwood's hermeneutic orientation than whether similar tensions occur in the discussion of the social and technological aspects of *Oryx and Crake* and to what extent such tensions can be attributed to the specific conditions of the respective media.

Dystopian Science in the Reception of *Oryx and Crake*

We can generally distinguish two phases of reception. During the first phase, lasting from 2003 to 2009, *Oryx and Crake* received sustained attention in academic criticism, in general and literary reviews, and (less frequently) in science journals. The second phase, starting in 2009 with the publication of the second installment of the trilogy and the beginning of Atwood's online media presence, still shows a sustained relevance of *Oryx and Crake* in connection with Atwood's new publications (*The Year of the Flood* [2009b]; *In Other Worlds* [2011a]; *MaddAddam* [2013a]). In the earlier phase, the interest in the novel's critical perspective on contemporary society and contemporary science is remarkably strong both in general and literary reviews and in science journals. When the second volume of the trilogy appears, however, this aspect receives considerably less attention, while the novel's relation to continuing biotechnological developments remains a point of interest both with general and literary reviewers and with scientific reviewers. The same can be said for the discussion in online and social media, which sets in only with the growing popularization of these media around 2009. In the academic reception, in which the issue of plausibility and social critique is rarely the main focus, there is a growing tendency after 2009 to dismiss the power of Atwood's critique as insufficient, because it is misdirected, imprecise, and simplistic.

In the following section we will provide a more detailed account of the discussion of *Oryx and Crake* in the various contexts of reception (general and literary, academic, scientific, and online media). We will then focus on one of the most frequently discussed elements of the novel in relation to the potential critique of current and future technological developments, the artificial meat product ChickieNobs.

Public Attention to Oryx and Crake: *A Survey*

Discussions of a novel's topical relevance are a customary element of reviews of fiction in general and literary media, as are the author's overall oeuvre and the literary traditions to which she might belong. Reviewers give a significant amount of space to the social and economic contexts for scientific practice, taking the plausibility of the world depicted in *Oryx and Crake* as a central criterion. In most cases, they praise the novel for this reason (see Hensher 2003; Wagner 2003). Other reviewers, however, criticize what they see as the novel's lack of plausibility (e.g., Kakutani 2003).[9] The early reviewers often also focus on the topic of "technology and genetic manipulation gone . . . horribly awry" (Richards 2003; see also Kemp 2003b; *Times* 2003), and they tend to do so in connection with the issue of sociostructural contexts for biotechnology.[10]

In terms of literary precedents, most reviewers compare *Oryx and Crake* to Atwood's earlier novel set in a potential future, *The Handmaid's Tale* (1985). Some reviewers draw a clear distinction between the two novels by linking *The Handmaid's Tale* to political critique and *Oryx and Crake* to a critique of developments in science (e.g., Kemp 2003a; Kipen 2003; *Economist* 2003). Others consider both to be critiques of social conditions and tendencies (see N. Walter 2003), a position shared by reviewers who place *Oryx and Crake* in the dystopian literary tradition (with, for example, *Brave New World*; see Disch 2003).

Whereas *The Handmaid's Tale* is still occasionally invoked (see Scurr 2013) in reviews of Atwood's subsequent works (*The Year of the Flood* [2009b]; *In Other Worlds* [2011a]; *MaddAddam* [2013a]), *Oryx and Crake* itself becomes part of the background of discussion. Characterizations of "the pre-catastrophe world" in the novel as "a Caligulan nightmare of pornography, fast food and science-for-profit" (Martin 2013) and as "a world in which profit has outstripped any desire for medicine to heal" (Freeman 2009) still occur, but these observations tend to no longer be coupled with any critical application to current social tendencies. It appears that the critical edge associated with the notion of "speculative fiction," as initially propagated by Atwood, tends to wear off the longer the novel remains under discussion.

How is the novel reviewed in the field of academic criticism? The issue of plausibility, whether in relation to the concept of speculative fiction or in relation to representation of the socioeconomic context of scientific practice, does not play a prominent role in the extensive academic discussion of *Oryx and Crake*, at least initially. A large proportion of research contributions focuses on aspects of the novel that form part of the traditional critical canon of Atwood studies. These include gender (Löchel 2008; Evans 2010; Labudová 2011; Banerjee 2013), memory and myth (Appleton 2008 and Osborne 2008 on myth; Snyder 2013 on memory), narrative and writing (Mohr 2007; Wilson 2013), nation (see Sutherland and Swan 2009; Spiegel 2010), and nature (S. Mayer 2006; Glover 2009; Trauvitch 2013; Copley 2013; Mohr 2015). Frequently, these aspects are treated in connection with one another (see, for example, dystopia and gender in Snyder 2013 and Lapointe 2014; ecocriticism and gender, or ecofeminism, in S. Mayer 2006; Copley 2013; and Dunlap 2013).

But a substantial part of the recent research on *Oryx and Crake* focuses on new topics that were not widely debated in relation to Atwood's earlier novels and that we may understand as variously addressing the problem we have described as dystopian science. These topics are science (see Ferreira 2011 and Arias 2011 on eugenics; see also McHugh 2010), economy (McHugh 2010; Hall 2010; Appleton 2011; Malewitz 2012; Kaufman 2013; Vials 2015), and the posthuman (Engélibert 2009; Arias 2011; J. Mayer 2011; Grace 2012; Mosca 2013; Hoepker 2014). These articles discuss the ways in which the novel engages with the subjection of science to purely economic rationales and with the current and future developments in biotechnology and genetic engineering. Appleton, for instance, shows how greed and a capitalism that is "manipulative at best, totalitarian at worst" (2011, 71) create a framework for scientific practice that allows Crake simply to appropriate its institutions in order to destroy all of humanity. According to Kaufman, *Oryx and Crake* debunks the notion that "free market capitalism is permanently sustainable and self-regulating" (2013, 12), showing that it leads instead to "a new feudalism governed by a corporate-government hybrid" (11). Hoepker reads *Oryx and Crake* against the background of a recent discussion on "risk narratives" (2014; see also Heise 2008), pointing out that the preapocalyptic society in the novel is endangered by its misguided risk management, which goes along with its exclusive economization and profit-maximization goals. Academic criticism includes instances in which the societal issues are dealt with in depth. As our survey has briefly indicated, however, broader socioeconomic issues are by no means considered in all cases. One reason for this, certainly, is that specific disciplinary interests are a crucial factor in guiding critical attention.

The reception of *Oryx and Crake* in science journals is substantial but far from extensive. Reviews appear sometimes after a considerable delay and are often prompted by the appearance of subsequent related publications (see Atwood 2009b, 2011a, 2013a). *Science* magazine reads *Oryx and Crake* as a plausible representation of scientific-technological progress with critical potential, describing it as "an entertaining and only slightly exaggerated satire of commercial biotechnology" (Squier 2003) and "a fascinating, sometimes nauseating, picture of biotechnology gone awry" (Gebel 2009).

Despite depicting the novel as a "cautionary tale" (Gebel 2009), however, reviewers tend to be somewhat vague about the phenomena that Atwood's critique targets. In a late review of the whole trilogy, any critical potential contained in Atwood's description appears to have vanished and given way to a sense of the inevitability of disastrous developments: "Will our technologies swallow us? The book's palindromic title [*MaddAddam*] suggests as much: disastrous ends yoked to new beginnings, with one flowing into the other in a never-ending cycle" (McEuen 2013). At the same time, any positive perspectives are tied not to the avoidance of disaster but to an anthropological notion of resilience. According to McEuen, the trilogy "is a warning but also . . . a hopeful meditation on the cycle of life, death and the possibility of life anew" (2013). The fact that reviewers in science journals less and less explicitly place sociocultural conditions for the dystopian fictional world at the center of the critical diagnosis can be read as a tendency to deproblematize its specific critical potential in relation to the societal contexts for scientific practice.

No doubt helped by Atwood's own remarkable online presence, there has been widespread attention to Atwood and specifically to *Oryx and Crake* in online media. Atwood's online activities include several websites, social media, and blogs (e.g., Facebook, Flipboard, and Wattpad). As one critic put it, "'Margaret Atwood' on the Web is less a single site than a network of electronic connections and interfaces" (York 2013, 142).

The platform she has used most extensively is Twitter. Registered since July 2009, Atwood has enjoyed a continuously growing number of followers.[11] She tweets about her book tours and presentations, provides links to newspaper articles, rallies to support certain political campaigns (most of ecological concern), and responds to her followers' questions.[12] But the main reason she has embraced this platform so much is that it "created the opportunity for this kind of horizontal relationship between readers, rather than that traditional model of a writer's work fanning outward to readers" (Atwood 2013b).[13]

In addition to sending tweets to Atwood herself, users tweet general media articles about topics from *Oryx and Crake* and tie them to certain names and concepts from the novel, especially Atwood's neologisms. People utilize hashtags such as #oryxandcrake, #pigoons, and #chickienobs in order to tag news about certain technological and scientific developments. In this way, a continuous perspective on such developments is constructed.[14] The reading of Atwood's novel variously affects the tone of comments relating to, for example, innovations in genetics. Often, users directly address Atwood as an author who, in their eyes, strikingly anticipated certain developments: "@margaretatwood saw it coming! #oryxandcrake | Could Autoluminescent Trees Be The Streetlights Of The Future? http://t.co/5BN2kWHZJO" (G [MissInformd], July 17, 2014, 23:28 UTC). In another case, a report from *The Atlantic* about plans to release genetically modified mosquitoes in Florida in order to contain the spread of infectious diseases comes with a sarcastic reference to Atwood's dystopia: "What could possibly go wrong? #OryxandCrake [A few million mutant insects could slow the spread of dengue and . . .] http://t.co/qMbMo1hWgv" (hyung nam [hyungknam], January 28, 2015, 21:32 UTC). Thus, these neologisms turned hashtags operate like other hashtags that are often employed "to express sarcasm or parenthetical comment" (Halavais 2014, 37).

Considering what we said earlier about speculative fiction, however, it is striking that such tweets mainly concern the question, How close are we *technologically* to the future outlined in *Oryx and Crake*? In contrast to general media reviewers, Twitter users relate the novel's speculations to real-world technological outcomes of scientific research, but they rarely consider the social framework of economization within which it operates. Consequently, the constant focus on technology comes at the price of a reduction of the critical potential that the novel initially offers. Furthermore, the repeated appraisal of Atwood herself for the (supposed) accuracy of her literary speculation tends to deflect attention from the scientific innovations in question. Finally, the condensed form of communication that Twitter provides seems to foster a somewhat reductive and one-sided discourse about science and its possible ramifications.

Although the increasingly exclusive focus on the technological dimensions of Atwood's scenario appears strongest on Twitter, it can also be observed during the same period as a growing tendency in the science journals as well as in the general review media. Only in the earliest stage of the novel's reception is the focus on the relationship between plausibility and socioeconomic critique strong in general and literary media and partially present in the science journals. Our survey of the reception of *Oryx and Crake* across the various media therefore shows a shift toward a growing concentration on technological plausibility and an accompanying loss of critical edge regarding socioeconomic questions.

ChickieNobs

Responses to ChickieNobs, the fictional artificial meat product featured in *Oryx and Crake*, provide a striking example of the shift we have just described. From the earliest reviews, this product is frequently mentioned in connection with the issues of plausibility, speculative fiction, and dystopian science. In the subsequent reception, it still forms part of the discussion of the novel's plausibility, but its critical potential appears to give way to a tentative acceptance of commercially driven technoscience. In the following discussion we will therefore focus on two phases of reception: one immediately following the novel's publication (2003–6) and a renewed phase of attention lasting from 2009 to the present.

Across the range of media attention to *Oryx and Crake* in the first years after publication, references to ChickieNobs are frequent and used emblematically to suggest a typical and representative element, even a symptom, of the condition of the fictional world; these references are possibly also linked to a critical perspective on the conditions that led to this future situation.

This is true for the general review media, in which ChickieNobs are described as indicators of plausibility and of how close we are already to this development (see the reference to KFC in *Times* 2003; see also the reference to "George W. Bush's call for genetically modified crops" in Miller 2003). In many cases, reviewers specifically link ChickieNobs and similar products to the novel's representation of the sociostructural aspect of scientific practice, either praising the novel as showing a scenario in which "scientists [are] constrained by nothing except the profit motive" (N. Walter 2003) or expressing doubt about whether such critical potential is displayed successfully in the novel. (Barnacle, for example, speaks of "Atwood's quaint notion that research scientists would be involved in marketing" as evidence of her "scant understanding of, or interest in, the way big business works" [2003].)

Remarkably, many of the early references in academic criticism resemble those in literary and general reviews in that ChickieNobs are seen as "emblematic" of the fictional world (see, for example, Cooke 2006), but these references rarely address the socioeconomic context. By contrast, references in science journals regularly couple this emblematic function of ChickieNobs with what we are describing as dystopian science. On one hand, ChickieNobs are taken to stand for a future world and society that are clearly undesirable to the implied reader; on the other hand, because they are seen as plausible and indeed as already partly real, they also stand for the uncomfortable suggestion that our current world and society may be closer to the dystopian future than we would like to admit. References to ChickieNobs as "only slightly exaggerated satire of commercial biotechnology" (Squier 2003) serve to link the fictional dystopian future to the reviewer's present by way of references to current research that will very likely lead to similar results. In this sense, ChickieNobs function as indicators of the scientific or technological plausibility of the novel as a whole. Only one response, in an author profile in *Nature Biotechnology*, describes *Oryx and Crake* as "a kind of cultural critique" and the production of ChickieNobs as an example of the exploitation of "biotech . . . on the basis of commercial imperatives" (Louët 2005).

In this first phase, then, the discussion of Atwood's ChickieNobs proved to be rather homogenous. Like other biotechnological creations in the novel, they are emblematic of an unchecked scientific practice that pervades the preapocalyptic world of *Oryx and Crake*. Although the sociostructural context of this practice comes into focus on occasion, ChickieNobs were nevertheless more frequently mentioned to draw attention to the plausibility of the book's account of biotechnological research. At the same time, such mentions hardly led to any prolonged or controversial attention to the phenomenon—and indeed, from around 2006 until the publication of the second novel in the trilogy in 2009, they no longer appeared to be part of discussions of *Oryx and Crake*.

Reception Phase II: 2009–Present

The renewed critical and media attention to ChickieNobs since 2009 may be related to several factors: the publication of the second part of the trilogy, the new developments in the production of artificial meat, and Atwood's own participation in online media. In connection with Atwood's online media activities, ChickieNobs immediately has gained a remarkable prominence. Among all the neologisms picked up from Atwood's novel and utilized on Twitter, #chickienobs is the most frequent.[15] Users relate ChickieNobs to recent debates about the pros and cons of artificially grown flesh, or "lab meat," and Atwood takes note of this on Twitter: "In the course of writing my little tech piece for @NYTimes, I searched #ChickieNobs. Hmm. They have entered the language. :>} #maddaddam" (Margaret E. Atwood [MargaretAtwood], September 17, 2013, 12:54 UTC). Most Twitter users express unease about the possibility of being confronted with such products one day. In a tweet to Atwood about reports that the fast-food company Kentucky Fried Chicken would serve a greater amount of boneless chicken in response to consumer demand for more convenient food, one user explicitly makes a connection to the literary genre of *Oryx and Crake*: "@margaretatwood #chickieNobs SpecFic not so SpecFic. KFC chicken going boneless http://cbc.sh/Kfj48uf" (Dr. Shelley Turner [TheShelleyT], April 6, 2013, 13:42 UTC). But in some instances ChickieNobs are deemed a positive innovation—for example, when contrasted with the customary mass killing of male chicks in conventional food production: "OMFG. Male chicks are thrown into grinders ALIVE. This is common practice??? http://bit.ly/10FGbU Case for #chickie nobs" (Shannon Esposito [soesposito], September 1, 2009, 21:13 UTC). Again, continued tweets regarding the development of lab meat allow for reconstructing the dynamics and normalization of the discourse surrounding it.

Nevertheless, the majority of such comments boil down to "look how close this is."[16] Although this amounts to an effective decontextualization of ChickieNobs in relation to dystopian science, we do not attribute this to an inadequate reception of the novels by readers. Instead, we can take the references to ChickieNobs on Twitter as an indication of the normalization of certain genetic innovations in the production of meat. Consequently, the corpus of tweets reads like a protocol of the supposedly inevitable coming-into-existence of lab meat. This does not mean that artificial meat has become generally accepted and is no longer controversial but that in the face of its de facto realization, critique on Twitter seems to take the form of individual expressions of unease without any consideration of larger discourses about economized science.

We can notice very similar tendencies across almost the entire range of public and critical attention. This does not mean that the commercialization of science in *Oryx and Crake* completely disappears from the set of critical concerns. But it does mean that such concerns are no longer connected with the discussion of the role of ChickieNobs in the novel. This disconnection becomes visible even when a reviewer states that "some elements of it will undoubtedly happen. Bioengineered meats are a staple in Atwood's pre-flood world, and earlier this month a bovine stem-cell hamburger created by Mark Post, a tissue engineer at Maastricht University . . . , was cooked and eaten" (McEuen 2013, 399). References to ChickieNobs in science journals after 2009 lead not so much to a critique of for-profit science as to an observation of the techniques of producing artificial meat in laboratories. Atwood's fictional ChickieNobs are referenced to show that the cultural imagination has anticipated current progress.

In general and literary reviews, reference to ChickieNobs is made above all in connection with an ongoing debate about artificially engineered meat. In comparison to the first phase of reception, normative perspectives on lab meat turn out to be more ambivalent, giving rise to a plurality of assessments of ChickieNobs. Along with expressions of "disgust" (Gold 2013; Bittman

2012), there are more neutral or positive perspectives, motivated by an interest in, for example, animal welfare, regenerative medicine, or solving the environmental crisis (see Specter 2011). The pluralization of evaluative perspectives that comes with the new focus on ethical and practical aspects of genetically engineered meat is accompanied by a detachment of ChickieNobs from the sociocritical aspect of the economization of scientific practice.

In the academic criticism, a different development leads to a similar detachment: if they are mentioned at all, ChickieNobs now tend to be discussed in relation to other topics (posthuman species relations in the case of McHugh [2010] and a submerged antivegetarian, meat-eating definition of the human attributed to *Oryx and Crake* by Parry [2009]). The novel's "dystopian vision of consumer capitalism run rampant" (Parry 2009, 242) and its critique of "corporate greed run amok" (McHugh 2010, 192), however, are largely dismissed as lacking in complexity. This is even more striking if we consider that what we have called dystopian science is prominent among the problems discussed in academic criticism from 2009 on. Evidently, the issue of artificially generated meat, which could serve as a point of indictment after 2003, could no longer perform this function starting around 2009—even in the eyes of those who are alert to the dangers posed by an excessive economization of science.

What the references to ChickieNobs in the second phase of the reception of *Oryx and Crake* have in common is a shift in attention from the social conditions of artificial meat production to the observation of its current state of realization. As we have seen, the early interest in a more substantial critique of the general social conditions for scientific practice has not disappeared but now shows up chiefly in the specialized academic discussion. Interestingly, the option to connect the textual element of ChickieNobs with this critique appears to exist only in the first phase.

What are we to make of the fact that the critical distance relating to products such as ChickieNobs, which we encountered in the first phase, gives way to the recognition of a drive toward technological realization that can no longer be fundamentally rejected? The development moves away from its original connection to the vision of a science "gone awry" and toward a pluralization of evaluative perspectives on genetic engineering: although originally perceived as an emblem of dystopian science, ChickieNobs undergo a partial reevaluation when connected to concerns of animal and environmental ethics. Nevertheless, it is remarkable how quickly the critique of socioeconomic frameworks for science can disappear from the debate about this novel.

Conclusion

After looking back at our selective survey of the exceptionally sustained and diversified media presence of *Oryx and Crake*, we may return to the questions we formulated at the beginning. Our focus was on the relation between science and society as depicted in the novel and as discussed in its reception. We asked what aspects of the novel are addressed in the various forms of reception and how they reflect the critical potential of Atwood's concept of speculative fiction.

By taking Atwood's claim that *Oryx and Crake* is speculative fiction as a point of departure, the novel appears as a critical reflection on the social conditions of biogenetic research and technology. According to our reading, it offers a disturbing picture of a world in which scientific research is a central instrument for promoting and maintaining corporate interests, and in which all other social spheres, from education to law and politics, have been deformed or even dissipated under the pressure of economic imperatives. In other words, to read *Oryx and Crake* as a work of speculative fiction is to insist that the dynamics of this dystopian-world science can be properly understood only in reference to the underlying social developments. The self-proclaimed plausibility of Atwood's fictional near-future dystopia hinges on the identification of contemporary developments—technological *and* social. In this sense, *Oryx and Crake* is a novel critically concerned with what we have called dystopian science as an outcome of the entanglement of technological potentials and general societal tendencies toward economization.

In our reception analysis, we distinguished different media contexts as well as two phases of reception and asked whether critics, interviewers, and readers relate to the critique of dystopian science offered by Atwood's speculative novel. We have found that the interest in *Oryx and Crake* as a critique of the economically motivated excesses of scientific activity was strongest in the years immediately following the appearance of the novel. A look at various media contexts suggests that despite differences in extent and depth, concern for social critique was generally present in the first phase of the reception. Although *Oryx and Crake* continues to be discussed across the media spectrum (frequently in association with Atwood's subsequent publications), the connection between scientific practice and its socioeconomic conditions seems to have disappeared rather quickly from the list of topical concerns. With some exceptions in academic criticism, this absence of social critique holds for all media contexts in the second phase of the reception and is most sharply exemplified by the technocentric comments on Twitter.

Remarkably, Atwood's own statements have never been very extensive or detailed when it comes to the social conditions of scientific practice and have come, quite soon, to neglect such issues altogether. Although her initially emphatic insistence on the generic label of speculative fiction implied social critique, she has tended more recently to privilege moral and humanistic concerns over social, economic, or political factors. The fact that, all in all, the issue of plausibility in reference to social critique ends up in a rather marginalized position might be due in part to the fact that the reviewers and interviewers sometimes follow—or at least do not contest—Atwood's strategy of linking the plausibility of her technological extrapolations to very general notions about human morality (see Case and McDonald 2003; Louët 2005; Akbar 2009; Hoffman 2011; McEuen 2013). It is the moral rather than the social aspect that is thus foregrounded.[17]

In this shift from social to moral questions, the normative perspective on technological developments is both sustained and transformed: although critics, readers, and Atwood herself frequently marvel at the speed with which yesterday's speculative projections become today's technological realities, this process is always subject to evaluative sentiments. In the first phase of the reception, such sentiments were, at least occasionally, tied to a critique of commercialized science, but more recent accounts of *Oryx and Crake* articulate a moral ambivalence that desists from questions about the social conditions of scientific practice. As shown in our earlier analysis, this shift is quite palpable in the discussions pertaining to the artificial meat product ChickieNobs. Critics and readers continue to articulate discontent with such products, but later in the debate they also attempt to reevaluate this originally dystopian vision in the light of real-world biotech innovations. Moral concerns about animal welfare and sustainability enter the picture and diversify the normative perspectives on biotechnological developments.

How does this relate to our suggestion that the critical focus on the socioeconomic contexts of scientific practice seems to be contingent on and even subordinate to the interest in the genre debate itself? If we make this connection, it would follow that the controversies over "speculative fiction" and other genre labels are, above all, one among various optional elements in generating critical discussion and drawing public attention to the novel. Over time, and in the context of other media and settings, Atwood and her critics then seem to turn toward other options for generating attention.[18]

If, however, we take the critique implied in the term *speculative fiction* as a meaning structurally embedded in the text and thus in some sense prescribed by the text, the fact that this reading is not more widely accepted becomes an empirical observation in need of explanation. The lack of engagement with the critique of commercialized science in *Oryx and Crake* might correspond to circumstances in which, paradoxically, socioeconomic developments—such as the financial crisis that began in 2008—have led to a situation in which it becomes apparent that corporate capitalism is implicitly accepted as the only game in town. The reception of *Oryx and Crake* would then appear to exemplify how the logic of capitalism undermines efforts to effectively develop social alternatives already in the realm of cultural imagination, a cultural phenomenon (see Jameson 1991) that has recently been described as "'capitalist realism': the widespread sense that not only is capitalism the only viable political and economic system, but also that it is now impossible even to imagine a coherent alternative to it" (Fisher 2009, 2).

But what such a fatalistic interpretation, which reads the diminishing critical potential of the novel as a mere function of the socioeconomic condition, fails to account for is the pluralization of the normative perspectives on biotechnological innovations that we encountered in the second phase of the reception. After more than a decade of research and development that has brought more and more seemingly odd biotech inventions to the brink of the mass market, the discourse surrounding dystopian science has changed. As indicated, in the context of the reception of Atwood's novel, real-world genetically engineered food is now seen not solely as the overwhelming manifestation of scientific research efforts but also as an *uncanny yet possibly helpful* means of coping with the moral and environmental consequences of modern consumerist societies. The novel's depiction of dystopian science provides not only a vocabulary for naming new developments but also a speculative frame for discussing critique as well as coping strategies for dealing with potential social outcomes of technological progress in pluralistic societies.

Notes

1. See, for example, Gussow 2003 and Potts 2003. On utopia/dystopia, see Atwood 2003, 2005a.

2. For later versions, see Atwood (2011a; 2004, 515). Atwood has also written about related genres, such as the "metaphysical romance" (2004, 514), "scientific romance" (2006), and "slipstream" (2011b; 2011a, 7).

3. For a discussion of the speculative scope of all three novels, see Bouson 2015 and Harland 2016.

4. We use the term "economization" to describe the increasing attention to economic factors such as financial costs and profits, in accordance with Schimank's definition in chapter 7.

5. The publication of *Oryx and Crake* was accompanied by a number of interviews, author profiles, and Q&A sessions. See, for example, Kemp 2003b; Potts 2003; Gussow 2003; and Brockes 2004; see also Wagner 2009; Adams 2009; Akbar 2009; Lee 2009; Kellogg 2009; Hoby 2013; Brockes 2013; and Doherty 2013.

6. In this vein, *Oryx and Crake* is repeatedly referenced in Atwood's reflections on utopia and dystopia. Utopias as a description of an imagined perfect society and dystopias as imagined "bad places" are not "polar opposites," she claims. They are "more like a yin and yang pattern: within each utopia, a concealed dystopia, within each dystopia, a hidden utopia" (Atwood 2011a, 85). To capture this intermingling between utopian and dystopian elements she proposes the neologism "ustopia." Although the term is rarely taken up in literary scholarship, discussions around the concept of the "critical utopia/dystopia" demonstrate that scholars have recognized the phenomenon described by Atwood as ustopia: while classical utopias and dystopias describe nonexistent societies in great detail but leave out any ambivalent dynamics, critical utopias/dystopias contain elements of social change and of conflict or resistance (Moylan 2000, 74).

7. See also Kemp 2003b and Lee 2009.

8. For Atwood's rather combative insistence in earlier interviews and profiles that it is not, in fact, science fiction but speculative fiction, see, for example, Gussow (2003): "Had I written it 20 years ago, I would have called it science fiction, but now it's speculative fiction, believe me." After 2009, and not least as the result of a discussion about genre with science fiction author Ursula K. Le Guin, Atwood articulates a more conciliatory and encompassing position: "Is it science fiction or speculative fiction? Call it what you like. I don't give a damn. I just hate making false promises. Science fiction conjures images of flying saucers and monstrous squids and my books don't provide them" (2009a). On the debate with Le Guin, see Atwood (2011a), introduction.

9. A particular charge of implausibility is put forward by Canadian scientist Anthony Griffiths, who dismisses Atwood's representation of genetics in *Oryx and Crake* as based on "her reading of the popular media" rather than on objective data made available by "expert sources" (2004, 193).

10. For example, Hensher (2003) describes the representation of trends in the corporate world as "brilliantly plausible," even though he concludes that "bio-engineering is what the novel is about." Kipen (2003) praises the rendition of "rampant, all-devouring consumerism." Another critic discusses the actual US-American trend of gated communities and sees Atwood's depiction of the compounds as only "a step or two further" in comparison (Aaronovitch 2004).

11. 1.8 million as of November 2017.

12. What is significant about the topic of "Margaret Atwood Online" is that her literary standing and her online presence reinforce each other, which, besides resulting in continuously growing numbers of followers and thus potential readers, affects both the production and the reception of her literary work—for example, her latest novel *The Heart Goes Last* (2015) emerged from several chapters she had published on the online platform Byliner; see Alter (2015).

13. Atwood has not always been fond of new media. For a discussion of her changing and multifaceted attitude toward major shifts in media and information technology (which is also reflected in her fictional works), see York (2013, chaps. 4 and 5), and Wolframe (2008).

14. This is one sort of communication that makes Twitter an interesting object of study for the social sciences and the humanities, as the contributors to Weller et al. (2014) argue. In this vein, our look at tweets relating to Atwood's work is an effort "to document the utility of Twitter as a key many-to-many medium which complements, and sometimes even outperforms and supplants, conventional mass media" (Bruns and Moe 2014, 24).

15. Note that the topic of artificial meat also occurs frequently under #oryxandcrake and #maddaddam.

16. It is worth noting that hashtags constitute a specific level of communication on Twitter that is "more dynamic and ephemeral" than follower-followee networks but that "can also solidify into long-standing communities" (Bruns and Moe 2014, 18). Although one cannot speak of a "community" forming under #chickienobs—due to a lack of interaction among users and a rather low number of tweets—its continued employment from 2009 onward is striking. But it remains an open question whether the Twitter discussion will continue or eventually cease.

17. This focus on morality, however, might not be an arbitrary substitute for social critique but might be linked to the genre of postapocalypse itself. Such narratives typically invoke an "anthropology of catastrophe" (Horn 2018), that is, speculations about what remains of the human being after the collapse of its civilizational surroundings. Clearly, the scenario of human survivors of the pandemic living alongside the posthuman Crakers plays with such anthropological questions.

18. For example, by offering yet another genre label for the literary contextualization of *Oryx and Crake*. See Atwood's remarks on "ustopia" (note 6, this chapter).

References

Adams, Tim. 2009. "Margaret Atwood on a Voyage to the World's End." *Observer*, August 30, 2009.

Akbar, Arifa. 2009. "Margaret Atwood: People Should Live Joyfully." *Independent*, September 4, 2009.

Alter, Alexandra. 2015. "Margaret Atwood, Digital Deep-Diver, Writes 'The Heart Goes Last.'" *New York Times*, September 27, 2015.

Appleton, Sarah A. 2008. "Myths of Distinction; Myths of Extinction in Margaret Atwood's *Oryx and Crake*." In *Once upon a Time: Myth, Fairy Tales and Legends in Margaret Atwood's Writings*, edited by Sarah A. Appleton, 9–23. Newcastle upon Tyne, UK: Cambridge Scholars.

———. 2011. "Corp(Se)ocracy: Marketing Death in Margaret Atwood's *Oryx and Crake* and *The Year of the Flood*." *LATCH: A Journal for the Study of the Literary Artifact in Theory, Culture, or History* 4:63–73.

Arias, Rosario. 2011. "Life After Man? Posthumanity and Genetic Engineering in Margaret Atwood's *Oryx and Crake* and Kazuo Ishiguro's *Never Let Me Go*." In *Restoring the Mystery of the Rainbow: Literature's Refraction of Science*, edited by Valeria Tinkler-Villani and C. C. Barfoot, 379–94. Amsterdam: Rodopi.

Atwood, Margaret. 2003. *Oryx and Crake*. London: Virago.

———. 2004. "*The Handmaid's Tale* and *Oryx and Crake* 'in Context.'" In "Special Topic: Science Fiction and Literary Studies: The Next Millennium." Special issue, *PMLA* 119 (3): 513–17.

———. 2005a. "'Aliens Have Taken the Place of Angels.'" *Guardian*, June 17, 2005.

———. 2005b. *Writing with Intent: Essays, Reviews, Personal Prose, 1983–2005*. New York: Carroll and Graf.

———. 2006. "My Life in Science Fiction." *Cycnos* 22 (2): n.p.

———. 2009a. "My Week: Margaret Atwood." *Sunday Times*, September 6, 2009.

———. 2009b. *The Year of the Flood*. London: Bloomsbury.

———. 2011a. *In Other Worlds. SF and the Human Imagination*. New York: Anchor Books.

———. 2011b. "The Road to Ustopia." *Guardian*, October 14, 2011.

———. 2013a. *MaddAddam*. London: Bloomsbury.

———. 2013b. "On the Red Couch with Author Margaret Atwood." *Inside Flipboard* (blog). September 19, 2013. http://inside.flipboard.com/2013/09/19/on-the-red-couch-with-author-margaret-atwood.

Banerjee, Suparna. 2013. "Towards 'Feminist Mothering': Oppositional Maternal Practice in Margaret Atwood's *Oryx and Crake*." *Journal of International Women's Studies* 14 (1): 236–47.

Baranovichi, David. 2004. "Tear Down the Barriers." *Guardian*, September 25, 2004.

Barnacle, Hugo. 2003. "The End Is Nigh." *New Statesman*, May 19, 2003.

Bittman, Mark. 2012. "A Chicken Without Guilt." *New York Times*, March 11, 2012.

Booker, M. Keith, ed. 2013. *Contemporary Speculative Fiction*. Ipswich, MA: Salem.

Bouson, J. Brooks. 2015. "A 'Joke-Filled Romp' Through End Times: Radical Environmentalism, Deep Ecology, and Human Extinction in Margaret Atwood's Eco-Apocalyptic MaddAddam Trilogy." *Journal of Commonwealth Literature* 51 (3): 341–57.

Brockes, Emma. 2004. "The Monday Interview: Do Keep Up." *Guardian*, April 12, 2004.

———. 2013. "Margaret Atwood: 'I Have a Big Following Among the Biogeeks. "Finally! Someone Understands Us!"'" *Guardian*, August 24, 2013.

Bruns, Axel, and Hallvard Moe. 2014. "Structural Layers of Communication on Twitter." In *Twitter and Society*, edited by Katrin Weller, Axel Burns, Jean Burgess, Merja Mahrt, and Cornelius Puschmann, 15–28. New York: Peter Lang.

Case, Eleanor, and Maggie McDonald. 2003. "Life After Man." *New Scientist*, May 3, 2003.

Cooke, Grayson. 2006. "Technics and the Human at Zero-Hour: Margaret Atwood's *Oryx and Crake*." *Studies in Canadian Literature / Études en littérature canadienne* 31 (2): 105–25.

Copley, Soraya. 2013. "Rereading Marge Piercy and Margaret Atwood: Eco-Feminist Perspectives on Nature and Technology." *Critical Survey* 25 (2): 40–56.

Disch, Thomas M. 2003. "The Hot Zone." *Washington Post*, April 27, 2003.

Doherty, Mike. 2013. "Margaret Atwood on Books: 'Push Comes to Shove, They're Great Insulating Material.'" *Salon*, September 8, 2013.

Dunlap, Allison. 2013. "Eco-Dystopia: Reproduction and Destruction in Margaret Atwood's *Oryx and Crake*." *Journal of Ecocriticism* 5 (1): 1–15.

Economist. 2003. "Biting at the Future." May 1, 2003.

Engélibert, Jean-Paul. 2009. "L'éloge posthumain des humanités: *Oryx and Crake* de Margaret Atwood et les fictions de l'homme fabriqué depuis." *Revue de littérature comparée* 4 (332): 459–69.

Evans, Shari. 2010. "'Not Unmarked': From Themed Space to a Feminist Ethics of Engagement in Atwood's *Oryx and Crake*." *Femspec* 10 (2): 35–58.

Ferreira, Marie Aline. 2011. "'Toward a Science of Perfect Reproduction?' Visions of Eugenics in Contemporary Fiction." In *Restoring the Mystery of the Rainbow: Literature's Refraction of Science*, edited by Valeria Tinkler-Villani and C. C. Barfoot, 395–415. Amsterdam: Rodopi.

Fisher, Mark. 2009. *Capitalist Realism: Is There No Alternative?* Winchester, UK: Zero Books.

Flood, Alison. 2009. "Kim Stanley Robinson: Science Fiction's Realist." *Guardian*, November 11, 2009.

Freeman, John. 2009. Review of *The Year of the Flood*, by Margaret Atwood. *Los Angeles Times*, September 27, 2009.

Gebel, Erika. 2009. "Pages to Turn on a Lazy Day." Review of *Oryx and Crake*, by Margaret Atwood, *Science* 324 (5932): 1267.

Glover, Jayne. 2009. "Human/Nature: Ecological Philosophy in Margaret Atwood's *Oryx and Crake*." *English Studies in Africa: A Journal of the Humanities* 52 (2): 50–62.

Gold, Tanya. 2013. "Horse Burgers Should Have Us All Weeping in the Aisles." *Guardian*, January 18, 2013.

Grace, Daphne. 2012. "A Beast or a God? Margaret Atwood's Vision of Posthuman Consciousness." In *Consciousness, Theatre, Literature and the Arts, 2011*, edited by Daniel Meyer-Dinkgräfe, 40–49. Newcastle upon Tyne, UK: Cambridge Scholars.

Griffiths, Anthony. 2004. "Genetics According to *Oryx and Crake*." *Canadian Literature* 181:192–95.

Gussow, Mel. 2003. "Atwood's Dystopian Warning: Hand-Wringer's Tale of Tomorrow." *New York Times*, June 24, 2003.

Halavais, Alexander. 2014. "The Structure of Twitter: Social and Technical." In *Twitter and Society*, edited by Katrin Weller, Axel Burns, Jean Burgess, Merja Mahrt, and Cornelius Puschmann, 29–42. New York: Peter Lang.

Hall, Susan L. 2010. "The Last Laugh: A Critique of the Object Economy in Margaret Atwood's *Oryx and Crake*." *Contemporary Women's Writing* 4 (3): 179–96.

Harland, Paul W. 2016. "Ecological Grief and Therapeutic Storytelling in Margaret Atwood's Maddaddam Trilogy." *ISLE: Interdisciplinary Studies in Literature and Environment* 23 (3): 583–602.

Heinlein, Robert A. (1947) 1965. "On the Writing of Speculative Fiction." In *Of Worlds Beyond: The Science of Science Fiction Writing*, edited by Lloyd Arthur Eshbach, 11–19. London: Dennis Dobson.

Heise, Ursula K. 2008. *Sense of Place and Sense of Planet: The Environmental Imagination of the Global.* Oxford, UK: Oxford University Press.

Hensher, Philip. 2003. "Back to the Future." *Spectator*, April 25, 2003.

Hoby, Hermione. 2013. "Margaret Atwood: Interview." *Sunday Telegraph*, August 18, 2013.

Hoepker, Karin. 2014. "A Sense of an Ending: Risk, Catastrophe and Precarious Humanity in Margaret Atwood's *Oryx and Crake*." In *The Anticipation of Catastrophe: Environmental Risk in North American Literature and Culture*, edited by Sylvia Mayer, 161–80. Heidelberg, DE: Winter.

Hoffman, Jascha. 2011. "Q&A: Speculative Realist." *Nature* 478:35.

Horn, Eva. 2018. *The Future as Catastrophe: Imagining Disaster in the Modern Age.* New York: Columbia University Press.

Jameson, Fredric. 1991. *Postmodernism; or, The Cultural Logic of Late Capitalism.* Chapel Hill, NC: Duke University Press.

Kakutani, Michiko. 2003. "Lone Human in a Land Filled with Humanoids." *New York Times*, May 13, 2003.

Kaufman, Amy S. 2013. "Our Future Is Our Past: Corporate Medievalism in Dystopian Fiction." In *Corporate Medievalism II*, edited by Karl Fugelso, 11–19. Cambridge, UK: Brewer.

Kellogg, Carolyn. 2009. "Margaret Atwood on Green Rabbits, Writing Sex and Twitter." *Los Angeles Times*, October 9, 2009.

Kemp, Peter. 2003a. Review of *Oryx and Crake*, by Margaret Atwood. *Sunday Times*, April 27, 2003.

———. 2003b. "Visions of the Future's Darkness." *Sunday Times*, April 20, 2003.

Kipen, David. 2003. "It's the End of the World as He Knows It." *San Francisco Chronicle*, April 27, 2003.

Labudová, Katarína. 2011. "Hybrid Bodies—Ambiguous Identities: Margaret Atwood's *Oryx and Crake* (2003) and Angela Carter's *The Passion of New Eve* (1977)." In *Does It Really Mean That? Interpreting the Literary Ambiguous*, edited by Kathleen Dubs and Janka Kaščáková, 140–54. Newcastle upon Tyne, UK: Cambridge Scholars.

Lapointe, Annette. 2014. "Woman Gave Names to All the Animals: Food, Fauna, and Anorexia in Margaret Atwood's Dystopian Fiction." In *Blast, Corrupt, Dismantle, Erase: Contemporary North American Dystopian Literature*, edited by Brett Josef Grubisic, Gisèle M. Baxter, and Tara Lee, 131–48. Waterloo, ON: Wilfrid Laurier University Press.

Lee, Felicia R. 2009. "Back to the Scary Future and the Best-Seller List." *New York Times*, September 22, 2009.

Le Guin, Ursula K. 2007. "Head Cases." Review of *The Stone Gods*, by Jeanette Winterson. *Guardian*, September 22, 2007.

Löchel, Rolf. 2008. "Männer, Frauen, Neuters: Gender in C. I. Gilmans *Halfway Human*, M. Atwoods *Oryx und Crake* sowie in T. Sullivans *Maul*." In *Genderzukunft: Zur Transformation feministischer Visionen in der Science Fiction*, edited by Karola Maltry, Barbara Holland-Cunz, Nina Köllhofer, Rolf Löchel, and Susanne Maurer, 89–142. Königstein, DE: Helmer.

Louët, Sabine. 2005. "Margaret Atwood." *Nature Biotechnology* 23 (2): 163.

Malewitz, Raymond. 2012. "Regeneration Through Misuse: Rugged Consumerism in Contemporary American Culture." *PMLA* 127 (3): 526–41.

Martin, Tim. 2013. "*MaddAddam* by Margaret Atwood—Review." *Telegraph*, August 28, 2013.

Mayer, Jed. 2011. "A Darker Shade of Green: William Morris, Richard Jefferies, and Posthumanist Ecologies." *Journal of William Morris Studies* 19 (3): 79–92.

Mayer, Sylvia. 2006. "Literary Studies, Ecofeminism and Environmentalist Knowledge Production in the Humanities." In *Nature in Literary and Cultural Studies: Transatlantic Conversations on Ecocriticism*, edited by Catrin Gersdorf and Sylvia Mayer, 111–28. Amsterdam: Rodopi.

McEuen, Paul L. 2013. "Science Fiction: A Post-Pandemic Wilderness." *Nature* 500: 398–99.

McHugh, Susan. 2010. "Real Artificial: Tissue-Cultured Meat, Genetically Modified Farm Animals, and Fictions." *Configurations: A Journal of Literature, Science, and Technology* 18 (1–2): 181–97.

Miéville, China. 2009. "Cognition as Ideology: A Dialectic of SF Theory." In *Red Planets: Marxism and Science Fiction*, edited by Mark Boulder and China Miéville, 231–48. London: Pluto Press.

Miller, Peter. 2003. "Hot Holiday Reading." *Times*, July 12, 2003.

Mohr, Dunja M. 2007. "Transgressive Utopian Dystopias: The Postmodern Reappearance of Utopia in the Disguise of Dystopia." *Zeitschrift für Anglistik und Amerikanistik* 55 (1): 5–24.

———. 2015. "Eco-Dystopia and Biotechnology: Margaret Atwood, *Oryx and Crake* (2003), *The Year of the Flood* (2009), and *MaddAddam* (2013)." In *Dystopia, Science Fiction, Post-Apocalypse: Classics—New Tendencies—Model Interpretations*, edited by Eckart Voigts and Alessandra Boller, 283–302. Trier, DE: Wissenschaftlicher Verlag Trier.

Mosca, Valeria. 2013. "Crossing Human Boundaries: Apocalypse and Posthumanism in Margaret Atwood's *Oryx and Crake* and *The Year of the Flood*." *Altre Modernità* 9:38–52.

Moylan, Tom. 2000. *Scraps of the Untainted Sky: Science Fiction, Utopia, Dystopia*. Boulder, CO: Westview-Perseus Press.

Osborne, Carol. 2008. "Mythmaking in Margaret Atwood's *Oryx and Crake*." In *Once upon a Time: Myth, Fairy Tales and Legends in Margaret Atwood's Writings*, edited by Sarah A. Appleton, 25–46. Newcastle upon Tyne, UK: Cambridge Scholars.

Parry, Jovian. 2009. "*Oryx and Crake* and the New Nostalgia for Meat." *Society and Animals* 17 (3): 241–56.

Potts, Robert. 2003. "Light in the Wilderness." *Guardian*, April 20, 2003.

Richards, Linda L. 2003. "Cilantro Prose." *January Magazine*, June 2003.

Scurr, Ruth. 2013. "A Score for Voices." *Times Literary Supplement*, August 16, 2013.

Snyder, Katherine V. 2013. "Screen Memories: Maternal After-Images in Margaret Atwood's Dystopian Novels." In *Women's Utopian and Dystopian Fiction*, edited by Sharon R. Wilson, 186–203. Newcastle upon Tyne, UK: Cambridge Scholars.

Specter, Michael. 2011. "Test-Tube Burgers." *New Yorker*, May 23, 2011.

Spiegel, Michael. 2010. "Character in a Post-National World: Neomedievalism in Atwood's *Oryx and Crake*." *Mosaic: A Journal for the Interdisciplinary Study of Literature* 4 (3): 119–34.

Squier, Susan M. 2003. "A Tale Meant to Inform, Not to Amuse." *Science* 302 (5648): 1154–55.

Sutherland, Sharon, and Sarah Swan. 2009. "Margaret Atwood's *Oryx and Crake*: Canadian Post-9/11 Worries." In *From Solidarity to Schisms: 9/11 and After in Fiction and Film from Outside the United States*, edited by Cara Cilano, 219–35. Amsterdam: Rodopi.

Times. 2003. "In the End There Was the Word." April 23, 2003.

Trauvitch, Rhona. 2013. "The Bible's Paradise and *Oryx and Crake*'s Paradice: A Comparison of the Relationships Between Humans and Nature." In *Plants and Literature: Essays in Critical Plant Studies*, edited by Randy Laist, 165–80. Amsterdam: Rodopi.

Vials, Chris. 2015. "Margaret Atwood's Dystopic Fiction and the Contradictions of Neoliberal Freedom." *Textual Practice* 29 (2): 235–54.

Wagner, Erica. 2003. "Falling in Love with a Tree." *Times*, December 6, 2003.

———. 2009. "Margaret Atwood Interview." *Times*, August 15, 2009.

Walter, Damien G. 2011. "China Miéville Leads Radical SF's Invasion of the Mainstream." *Guardian*, February 2, 2011.

Walter, Natasha. 2003. "Pigoons Might Fly." *Guardian*, May 10, 2003.

Weller, Katrin, Axel Burns, Jean Burgess, Merja Mahrt, and Cornelius Puschmann, eds. 2014. *Twitter and Society*. New York: Peter Lang.

Wilson, Sharon R. 2013. "Storytelling in Lessing's *Mara and Dann* and Other Texts." In *Women's Utopian and Dystopian Fiction*, edited by Sharon R. Wilson, 23–29. Newcastle upon Tyne, UK: Cambridge Scholars.

Wolframe, PhebeAnn. 2008. "Invented Interventions: Atwood's Apparatuses of Self-Extension and Celebrity Control." *Margaret Atwood Studies* 2 (1): 13–28.

York, Lorraine. 2013. *Margaret Atwood and the Labour of Literary Celebrity*. Toronto: University of Toronto Press.

6.
When the Scientist Is a Woman
Novels and Feminist Science Studies

Carol Colatrella

Depictions of women scientists in selected contemporary realist novels about science stage many issues that feminist philosophers and social scientists have raised in scholarly research, including social interactions in science, technology, engineering, and mathematics (STEM) fields and epistemological claims associating scientific objectivity and method with masculinity (Rossiter 2012; Schiebinger 1999; Subramanian 2009). Since the 1970s, many governments have sought to diversify the STEM workforce. Organizations such as the US National Science Foundation and European national science councils developed initiatives to enhance the advancement of women professionals and academics. In the United States, the 1971 Comprehensive Health Manpower Act prohibited discrimination in university admissions, leading to increased numbers of female STEM graduates (Rossiter 2012, 42). But although women now obtain bachelor's degrees in some scientific fields at almost the same rate as men, fewer go on to graduate school or pursue careers as scientists, and women remain underrepresented at all levels in engineering, computer sciences, and physics (European Commission 2015; NSF 2017). Women exiting STEM career pathways report workplace discrimination, sexual harassment from peers and supervisors, and unequal opportunities for scientific collaboration (Branch 2016; Coil 2017; Ceci and Williams 2007).

Media stereotypes affect gendered perceptions of women in science, influencing viewers' ideas about who should work in science and what constitutes science (Steinke 1998; Kitzinger et al. 2008). For centuries, scientists have been represented in diverse media as stereotypically evil, greedy, mad, dangerous, and male (Haynes 2017; Frayling 2006). For example, the protagonists in Goethe's *Faust* and Mary Shelley's *Frankenstein* were driven by ambitions to control nature (Perkowitz 2007; Kirby 2011). As women scientists began to appear in popular fiction and film, they acquired their own stereotypes—as glamorous and feminine, quirky, or androgynous (Colatrella 2011, 8). Recent events indicate that such sexual stereotypes continue to present challenges for women scientists. In an informal toast at the 2015 World Conference of Science Journalists, Nobel laureate Sir Timothy Hunt commented that the problem with "girls in the lab" was that "you fall in love with them, they fall in love with you, and when you criticize them, they cry" (Telegraph Women 2015). His remarks went viral on social media, eliciting a barrage of photos of women scientists under the hashtag #DistractinglySexy, and Hunt resigned his positions at University College London and on the European Research Council.

A number of scholars have explored fiction's power to impart knowledge and stoke empathy for disparate individuals and social groups (Keen 2010; Zunshine 2006). In *Toys and Tools in Pink*, I examined how narrative settings, characters, and plots incorporate and reconfigure gender stereotypes about women in STEM fields (Colatrella 2011). Realist novels such as William Dean Howells's *Dr. Breen's Practice* (1881), Elizabeth Stuart Phelps's *Dr. Zay* ([1882] 1987), and Sarah Orne Jewett's *A Country Doctor* ([1884] 2008) depicted fictional female doctors whose medical ambitions conflicted with the nineteenth-century stereotype of women as caregivers and explored prejudices that historical women also faced (Noble 1992). Carl Sagan's *Contact* (1997) sympathetically explored the perspective of a talented woman radio astronomer who confronts gender-related barriers in the highly competitive, male-dominated field of physics.

The six novels considered in this essay explore gender-related biases and stereotypes that affect the work and careers of women scientists: *The Signature of All Things* by Elizabeth Gilbert (2013), *A Whistling Woman* by A. S. Byatt ([2002] 2004), *Brazzaville Beach* by William Boyd ([1990] 2010), *Carbon Dreams* by Susan M. Gaines (2001), *Intuition* by Allegra Goodman (2006), and *State of Wonder* by Ann Patchett (2011). Like many of the novels described elsewhere in this volume, they detail how institutional, economic, and societal constraints interact with personal ambition, romance, and integrity to influence scientists' lives and the development, dissemination, and reception of scientific theories. The novels discussed here cover a range of historical periods and scientific disciplines, and reference feminist critiques of science by describing "gender in the cultures of sciences" and "gender in the substance of science" (Schiebinger 1999).[1]

Feminist scholars have documented the accomplishments of exceptional women in the nineteenth and twentieth centuries, describing how women such as Marie Curie, Rosalind Franklin, and Barbara McClintock struggled to establish secure professional positions and relationships, often working in relative isolation to develop new knowledge based on careful observations and analyses (Rossiter 2012; Subramanian 2009). Curie enjoyed a successful collaboration and happy marriage with Pierre Curie until his early death, after which she was rejected by the French Academy of Sciences and criticized for her love affair with a married scientist (Quinn 1995). Without Franklin's knowledge, her colleague Maurice Wilkins shared her data and photographs of DNA with James Watson and Francis Crick, enabling them to identify the molecular structure of genes, but Franklin's contributions to the discovery of DNA were not well known until years after she died in 1958, at age thirty-seven, of ovarian cancer (Maddox 2002, 213). Geneticist McClintock was not able to secure professorships as easily as her mid-twentieth-century male peers and spent the majority of her working life researching the mobility of genes in relative isolation at the Cold Springs Harbor research lab—a job that apparently suited her temperament, as her "capacity to be alone began in the cradle," and she "discovered, if one looked hard enough and carefully enough, a single organism would reveal its secrets" (Keller 1983, 20, 180).

The protagonist of Gilbert's historical novel, *The Signature of All Things* (2013), is an unusual nineteenth-century woman whose excellent education, inherited wealth, and unhappy romantic life combine to encourage a devotion to scientific collection, observation, and analysis. At a time when women were not generally educated in the sciences, Alma Whittaker has been mentored by family members, educated in math and science by her botanist mother and by tutors her father hires. This brings to mind a number of accomplished women from the history of science, such as Margaret Cavendish, who was taught by her brothers; Caroline Herschel, who worked with her brother; and Maria Mitchell, who was educated by her father. And like many "gentleman scientists" of the time (see chapter 2), Alma does not have to worry about money or equipment.

Despite enjoying privileges enabled by family wealth, Alma realizes her gender constrains her work. "And the task of a naturalist, as Alma understood it, was to discover," but as a woman, she cannot travel on expeditions to make observations and discoveries like male naturalists of her time (Gilbert 2013, 159). Instead, she turns to the study of mosses, which no one has paid much attention to, and notices that the rocks around the estate contain "ancient, unexplored galaxies" (162). Twenty years of watching moss colonies grow and reading works by Charles Lyell and John Phillips enables Alma to develop a taxonomy of time—Human Time, Moss Time, Geological Time, and Divine Time (170–71). Released from domestic responsibilities by her father's death and hoping to solve the mystery of her husband's last days, Alma travels to Tahiti, where, inspired by the exotic landscape and her island experiences, she develops the "theory of competitive alteration," hypothesizing that "the struggle for existence—when played out over vast periods of time—did not merely *define* life on earth; it had *created* life on earth. It had certainly created the staggering variety of life on earth. Struggle was the mechanism" (441).

After her excursion to Tahiti, Alma joins her mother's family in Amsterdam, where she becomes curator of mosses at the botanical garden and further develops and writes up her evolutionary ideas. She never publishes the manuscript because she believes it is "not quite yet scientifically incontrovertible," and she is "a perfectionist" who is "not going to be caught publishing a theory with a hole in it, even a small hole" (464). Years later, she shows it to Alfred Russel Wallace and is pleased with his response—"This means there were three of us!"—but demurs when he urges her to publish, claiming it is not necessary (490). She tells him that her scientific "study of the world" (497) has made her "the most fortunate woman who ever lived," despite the lack of public recognition (496). Disadvantaged by nineteenth-century social conventions that discouraged women from participating in scientific circles, Alma nevertheless possesses autonomy and time, circumstances that allow her to monitor the undisturbed mosses on her estate, to observe their evolution over years, and to make a great discovery. Thus, *The Signature of All Things* rewrites the history of evolutionary biology with a story about a talented woman scientist who has managed to develop a theory, albeit unpublished, that is on par with the work of Charles Darwin and Alfred Russel Wallace.

Set a century later, A. S. Byatt's *A Whistling Woman* (2004) brings together more than fifty characters in entangled plots touching on university reforms, a religious cult, and television production and examining the social and intellectual preoccupations of 1960s England, including feminism, psychology, and sociobiology. One of several characters grappling with changing opportunities for women, Jacqueline Winwar is a biology student who becomes enthralled with studying Darwinian selection in snails: "She was beginning to recognize the inexorable force of her own curiosity, her desire to know the next thing, and then the next, and then the next. It lived in her like a bright dragon in a cave, it had to be fed, it must not be denied, it would destroy her if she did not feed it" (26). Determined to continue research after graduation, she approaches Professor Lyon Bowman and asks to be hired for a postdoctoral study of snail neurons and the physiology of memory. During the job interview, Jacqueline explains her "obsession" with scientific research to Bowman, who counters, "Obsessive women make bad members of teams, in my narrow experience" (56). He also asks if she has a boyfriend. Responding that she does not, Jacqueline says she has "tried to see her sex—with some success—as a problem and an obstacle, to be solved and surmounted" (56).

Despite Bowman's negative attitude about women in science, he hires Jacqueline and later propositions her. He has a reputation for pursuing women at conferences, and when he comes to her hotel room with a bottle of liquor during one such trip, she rapidly calculates her response: "What her mind said to her was, after all, why not? It was probably the quickest way of getting a good night's sleep, her body said. The line of least resistance, her brain mocked" (169). Bowman offers her backhanded "compliments," telling her that she looks *comfortable* and doesn't dress well or say much, but she decides to have sex with him anyway, finding him "at once repellent and irresistible" (169, 170). After sex, he calls her "a good girl," and his words haunt her: "At twenty-nine she is hardly any longer a girl, was indeed a woman who was heading beyond the natural age for easy child-bearing." Jacqueline does not want to repeat going to bed with Bowman, but "he created in her a kind of angry hunger for sex" (172).

After her colleague Luk notices she is upset and declares his love for her, she tells him that "I want to live, not just to think" (174). The two become lovers, Jacqueline accidentally becomes pregnant, and they decide to get engaged. But after she miscarries, she realizes she is relieved and decides to break off the romance, which she feels was a mistake, although Luk still wants to marry her. She invokes their shared history as colleagues: "We've always understood each other. You know I mean what I say. You must let me know what I want—and I do know. . . . There doesn't have to be a reason. As long as I know. And I know" (188). Despite having capitulated to Bowman's harassment, Jacqueline acts independently in refusing to marry Luk.

At a university conference, Jacqueline realizes that Bowman has absorbed her research data in his presentation without crediting her contribution; she "sat there and heard her results described, and so to speak, claimed, without acknowledgement. It was her work—her months of trial and error, failure and triumph, smoothly taken over as part of the Lab's generally excellent performance.... She was a see-through implement, that was all" (367). Nevertheless, Jacqueline wants to remain in science. Her friend Daniel, the local pastor, later informs her that their mutual friend Ruth "bequeathed"[2] her baby to Jacqueline, who says she wants "to do what's right" (420). Daniel reminds her that she is committed to science and doesn't want a child. Jacqueline tells him that what she really wants is to "go to Paris and work with French neuroscientists on the electricity and chemistry of memory" and that "she had also got to get away from Lyon Bowman. Who treated his lab like—like a harem." Daniel advises her to be true to herself. "I like you as you are," he says, and then he kisses her (420). Readers must guess whether Jacqueline will continue in science or pursue a new romance rather than adopt the baby, although the limited textual evidence leaves all options open.

Two of the same topics—romance for scientists and recognition for scientific discoveries—also inform *Brazzaville Beach* (2010), in which author William Boyd tracks scientist Hope Dunbar Clearwater's graduate education, her problematic marriage in England, and her love affair in Africa. Hope has come of age in 1960s Britain and does graduate work in botany before shifting to write a dissertation in ethology. Before completing her doctoral exam, she marries mathematician John Clearwater, whose income offers her a brief, happy "hiatus" during which she "read and shopped, visited friends and went to films in the afternoon, repainted their bedroom and looked vaguely for a larger flat" (58). Hope's faculty mentor advises her that her paper on a botanical subject is unpublishable but that he nevertheless incorporated her data into his symposium talk: "All his pupils knew this was part of the quid pro quo for his patronage" (59). After receiving her doctorate, Hope delays applying for jobs: "She had published one article [in *Nature*] and done some reading, but little more" (87). Her mentor presses her to accept a scientific position, and, irritated with her marriage, Hope takes a job studying the ecology of hedgerows in Dorset, although John remains in

London. Their relationship becomes rockier, and he commits adultery with a colleague's wife before succumbing to mental illness. After John commits suicide, Hope joins a team doing fieldwork on primates in Africa.

Hope studies chimpanzee behavior in Africa, joining a project at the Grosso Arvore wildlife preserve, a research station run by famous primatologist Eugene Mallabar. A latecomer and the only single woman on the team, she is treated as a third-class citizen by the others. Allocated the most uncomfortable, least private tent, she is propositioned by several male members of the research team and treated coldly by their wives, who despite their scientific education and expertise are limited to secondary roles as assistants. Troubled by memories of her dead husband, Hope finds comfort in a casual love affair with Usman, an Egyptian pilot who is working as a mercenary out of the city in which the researchers obtain their supplies. Her professional problems begin when her observations of chimpanzees challenge ideas developed by Mallabar during his twenty years of research at Grosso Arvore.

Historian Londa Schiebinger has explained that women primatologists developed "new methods that encouraged the inclusion of formerly ignored research subjects—both females and low-status males" (1999, 7). Thelma Rowell, Jane Goodall, and Jeanne Altmann have been credited with "canceling out" the bias of their male counterparts by focusing on female primates, "but arguably their more profound contribution was to prompt a significant reorientation in both methods and understanding. Whereas previously the emphasis was primarily on theory, and observation was done mostly at a distance (from a jeep), the women entrants went to extraordinary lengths, virtually living amongst the apes or monkeys, to get to know and observe the individual animals at close quarters" (Faulkner and Kerr 2003, 68). In *Brazzaville Beach*, Hope employs similar observational methods. While Mallabar oversees chimps attracted to the generous supply of bananas in a human-made enclosure, Hope endures the discomforts of working in the bush as she tracks the breakaway southern chimpanzees assigned to her. After the northern chimps attack her group, she begins to follow their movements as well. She observes chimpanzees committing cruel, violent acts, including murder and cannibalism, and she realizes the two groups are fighting over a female. Hope's persistent curiosity and her sensitivity to the chimps' personalities and to the changing dynamics of their interactions inspire her new theory of chimp infanticide and cannibalism.

If published, Hope's theory of chimp violence would overturn decades of Grosso Arvore research. Mallabar, who is completing a book about the chimpanzees' peaceful, cooperative behavior, refuses to believe her observations because he and the rest of his team are deeply invested in their ideas about chimp sociability and fear losing funding and prestige. They go so far as to manufacture evidence to convince Hope that predators have killed the chimps, and someone sets fire to her tent, where her research notes are stored. Realizing her discovery could make her famous, Hope retrieves copies of her notes kept by her local assistant and secretly submits a paper based on her observations of chimp violence to a journal for publication: *"What was taking place at Grosso Arvore was unparalleled, revelatory—no matter what explanation might be offered up later. And Hope was aware, from very early days, that there was every chance that it would be her name forever associated with this new knowledge and understanding"* (Boyd 2010, 196–97, italics in original). Hope is concerned about the northern chimps' attacks on the southern group, and she wonders if the researchers should intervene to end the violence. She finally convinces Mallabar to accompany her in the field to observe the chimps for himself, but he is so shocked by the violence he witnesses that he becomes irrationally angry, accusing her of having done something to affect the chimps' behavior. In his rage, he physically attacks and injures Hope; she escapes, however, by joining a colleague who happens to be leaving the reserve on a supply run.

Near the beginning of their journey, Hope and her colleague are kidnapped by rebel fighters. She eventually escapes and makes her way to the city, only to learn that her lover Usman has disappeared during one of his flying missions and left her his belongings, including a gun. Back at Grosso Arvore, Mallabar has suffered a nervous breakdown, and his colleagues have revised his book manuscript to incorporate Hope's insights, mentioning her only in a footnote. She is banned from the research station and prevented from publishing her article by her contract, which assigned all publication rights to the project. She nevertheless returns to the reserve to track down her southern chimps, arriving as they are being massacred by invading northerners. The southern alpha male, Conrad, is dying a slow, painful death, so Hope uses Usman's gun to put him out of his misery and kill the marauding northern males, ending violence between the two groups. In "About the Book: The Chimpanzee Wars," an appendix to the 2010 reprint edition of the novel, Boyd comments that "everything Hope does at the end of the novel is ... the morally right thing to do. She is both human and humane. She carries out, with a clear conscience, a small act of redemption for our species" (appendix, 13).

Feminist philosopher Hilary Rose describes how science as a system depends on its relationship with "other forms of power: cultural, economic, and military" (1994, 114). Her manifesto for love applies to Hope's empathy for the chimps: "We see feminism bringing love to knowledge and power. It is love, as caring respect for both people and nature, that offers an ethic to reshape knowledge and, with it, society" (238). At the end of *Brazzaville Beach,* Hope is living in a beach bungalow inherited from Usman. She is no longer a scientist but instead works as a driver for the researchers at Grosso Arvore. She has abandoned ideas of professional recognition and happiness in romantic love and spends her days wondering whether Usman survived and meditating on what she calls "my indecision, my moral limbo" (Boyd 2010, 315). Others take credit for her scientific research, and her personal losses leave her isolated, but she is philosophical. Readers understand that, as a scientist, Hope acted with integrity and compassion.

Set in the early 1980s, Susan M. Gaines's *Carbon Dreams* (2001) tells the story of a young geochemist who is studying climates of the distant geologic past and is thrust into the growing controversy over contemporary global warming. Tina Arenas forms intimate relationships and develops her scientific reputation, managing the same challenges that Jacqueline and Hope confronted in the 1960s. A postdoctoral researcher at the Brayton Institute of Oceanography (BIO) in Northern California, Tina occupies the lab of a senior researcher who is away on sabbatical. Obsessed with research, she works long hours and has little social life. *Carbon Dreams* exposes a creative, intuitive dimension of the scientific process, revealing how Tina's dreams, speculations, and casual conversations merge with hard data and analysis to influence her insights and form her experimental designs and theories. Her friendly, helpful mentor and professional role model is a famous but marginalized older male professor who works at a neighboring university and collaborates with Tina. He offers steady scientific advice and helps her stay true to her own vision of science, although he has little knowledge of the social issues that affect women pursuing scientific careers.

Young women began to enter science in large numbers in the 1980s, but they did not always find research positions. There are few women with PhDs on the BIO research staff, as Tina's friend Katharine, a doctoral student, points out: "I wonder what [these old guys] think happens to all those students.... Are we supposed to fade away into domestic bliss with our PhDs? Spend six years of our lives as indentured servants subject to miscellaneous forms of psychological torture so that we'll make better wives and technicians?" (7). Tina and Katharine's friendship exemplifies the kind of female camaraderie that helps women scientists navigate minority status, making up for a lack of female role models and advisors. Katharine works for Sylvia Orloff—the only female full professor at BIO—who is successful, famous, and deeply flawed as a mentor, particularly for young women scientists: "She just believes that the way to prepare a young woman for a life in science is to work her to death, encourage cutthroat competition and tell anyone who isn't ten times better than the best of the men that she will never amount to a heap of beans.... Sylvia actually believes it herself, that there's no such thing as a good woman scientist, only a brilliant one. Just because that's how *she* made it" (9).

Katharine supplements her advice about work with efforts to find a suitable scientist boyfriend for her friend, but Tina by chance meets and later becomes involved with an environmentally conscious organic farmer, who has a side job landscaping a garden at her rented house. Tina considers her relationship with Chip a "vacation love affair.... It was as if he were a large sponge sopping up her anxiety and doubt in one quick swipe" (126). He is also supportive of her work. Chip discovers that Tina's research has been misrepresented in a *New York Times* article about climate change, and he convinces her she has a responsibility not only to get the science right but also to clarify climate issues for the public. Like Jacqueline in *A Whistling Woman*, Tina accidentally becomes pregnant. She tells Chip she doesn't want a baby, and although he supports her decision to terminate the pregnancy, he hopes for a future with their children, telling her, "You're just getting your career off the ground. It won't always be that way.... Famous scientists have kids too, right?" (Gaines 2001, 264). Tina's abortion is physically and emotionally traumatic, but the next day she goes back to work and meets with the only famous female scientist she knows, a woman who most definitely does not have children. Sylvia Orloff flies into "a fury" when Katharine decides to marry and accept an inferior job in a navy lab so she can follow her husband (276). As Katharine explains, "Sylvia sees herself as the creator of superwoman scientists—meaning tenure-track academic scientists publishing in

Nature and *Science*.... It adds to her power, having us scattered throughout the country's finest research labs.... But now we're betraying her right and left. First Janice decides that having a baby is more important than a Ph.D. from BIO, and now I'm going off to work for the Navy and publish who knows what kind of drivel, if I even publish at all'" (276–77).

Motivated by her intense curiosity and desire to create new knowledge, Tina lands a coveted tenure-track research position. She achieves a good deal more than many peers because of her excellent analysis, hard work, and willingness to make sacrifices in her personal life. Offered a job at an East Coast institute, she asks Chip to accompany her, but he refuses to give up his farm and begs her to look for a position in California. In the end, Tina leaves him for the job, although there is a wistful, ambivalent note in the novel's last pages, where she reflects on her "profound loneliness" even as she thrills at the prospect of her new position, which, ironically, has her pursuing the socially responsible climate change research that Chip encouraged (351). A male scientist might also have chosen work over romance, but he would have done so in accordance with traditional heterosexual domestic arrangements—perhaps with a female partner who didn't have a job or whose career was more accommodating than that of a scientist: "Being a scientist and a wife and mother is a burden in a society that expects women more often than men to put family ahead of career" (Schiebinger 1999, 93). Although Tina's future is not sketched in the novel, she might find a partner who is willing to build his life and work around the demanding constraints of her scientific appointment.

Allegra Goodman's *Intuition* describes just such a man: Jacob Mendelssohn is a former child prodigy who is a competent but not creative postdoc when he encounters college freshman Marion, who, he recognizes, will be a successful scientist: "When they were twenty he asked her to marry him. She was only a girl, but he believed she would make radical discoveries. This was why Jacob dedicated himself to Marion" (2006, 30). When the novel opens, in the mid-1980s, Marion Mendelssohn is the codirector of a Massachusetts cancer research institute. She and physician Sandy Glass supervise a number of technicians and postdocs, including Cliff and Robin, who are romantically entangled and not closely monitored. After Cliff's R-7 tumor-reducing experiments show promise and become the focus of the lab's work, Robin, the senior postdoc who has struggled for years on an impossible assignment, resents being directed to assist Cliff in his R-7 research, which she is unable replicate, and she and Cliff break off their romantic involvement. Robin later follows up on Jacob's remark that "the results seem almost too good to be true" (144); she looks closely at Cliff's results and accuses him of manipulating his data. The two women scientists, Marion and Robin, had begun as mentor and mentee, but they become antagonists disagreeing over the value of Cliff's R-7 experiments.

Echoing Jacqueline's and Hope's experiences, *Intuition* points to two ways in which sexism affects scientific research practice—employment inequities and men's appropriation of women's results—and thus creates disadvantages for women that fit what Margaret Rossiter has called the "Matilda effect" (1993). Robin's PhD advisor made her wait "almost a year to file her dissertation, because the whole lab was concentrating on pushing another [male] student out the door.... His case was more urgent. The techniques were new, the genetic manipulations cutting-edge, but the psychology was utterly traditional" (Goodman 2006, 89). Robin's resentment of Cliff builds on her recognizing disparities between how they were treated in the Mendelssohn-Glass lab: "He had come in as heir apparent to the lab.... He'd usurped Robin's position, beating her out for money, space, time, attention. From the first day he'd had special treatment, and it infuriated her that he would not acknowledge that" (64). Marion has also suffered career disadvantages and lacks adequate recognition. Harvard professor Art Ginsburg had "stolen Marion's ideas in the past. Years ago, hearing of her metabolic work with mice, he'd pursued a similar line himself and then presented his results first at a major conference, effectively stealing her thunder" (199). Marion's temperamental caution ensures the high quality of her science; however, realizing that she is sometimes too slow in the race to publish, she lets the overconfident Sandy Glass persuade her to act assertively in publishing Cliff's results before others confirm them.

Intuition describes the complex intermingling of scientific, political, and social issues surrounding Robin's examination of Cliff's "too good to be true" results. During an informal inquiry at the institute, Robin produces a graph of Cliff's published results, which "cluster beautifully," alongside one of his unpublished results—including data from pages he had torn out of his lab notebook—which "scatter" (201). But Marion and Sandy disagree with Robin's conclusion that Cliff distorts the data; when Robin persists with her complaints, she and her supervisors end up on opposite sides of a congressional hearing into lab misconduct. Cliff may have thrown out data that didn't fit his hypothesis: "He had sifted out what was significant, and the rest had floated off like chaff" (322). No one can replicate Cliff's results with R-7, tumors start recurring in the mice treated with it, and his records are messy—all of which throws his results into doubt. Although Cliff and the lab directors are, in the end, not sanctioned for scientific fraud, Marion ultimately acknowledges Cliff's offense and tells Sandy, "I think he may in fact have suppressed some data" (316). She dismisses Cliff from the lab and insists on withdrawing from publication the paper featuring his data. She is sad but relieved when Sandy becomes head of a private cancer facility, as this decision ends their collaboration. Celebrated as "a whistle-blower," Robin is nevertheless embarrassed that her only discovery is of cheating; she persists in science, however, and finds a job with Art Ginsburg, who comforts her by telling her that "sometimes . . . the truth has to be enough" (302, 330).

The novel ends with Marion's presentation at the annual cancer meeting, where she notices Ginsburg and Robin sitting together in the audience: "Ginsburg had deeper pockets than Marion, the more formidable reputation, the more aggressive approach. Still, he was not above competing with her" (342). Her talk is initially marred by "trouble with her transparencies" and speaking too quietly and too fast (343). To Robin, Marion looks "fussy and nervous" (343–44), but when she presents her new data "her quiet voice grew stronger; her detailed disquisition resolved itself into three main points. She was not charismatic, but her ideas were. And when she launched her propositions, she was the archer, shooting arrows into the audience; each of her statements incisive, brilliant, and characteristically self-critical" (344). Pleased that many attendees want to ask questions or comment, Marion realizes she can remedy her previous neglect of Robin, whose hand is raised with the others: "What did she need? In that calm, clear, nearly joyous moment after her talk, the answer began to come to Marion. Ah, yes, of course, she thought with some surprise. And she called on Robin" (344). The conclusion redeems both Robin and Marion. Robin has navigated various hurdles, including neglectful mentors and a competitive, unsupportive boyfriend, to become a peer scientist able to discuss Marion's paper. Although Nanette, Robin's only loyal friend from the lab, claimed that "women are always meanest to other women . . . especially women scientists," Marion acts to help her former postdoc (104). Thus, the novel suggests that practices routinely available to men (having role models, equitable mentoring, respect, and support from peers) ought to also be available to women, as these are critical, necessary resources enabling scientists' satisfaction and career prospects.

Thematically similar to Joseph Conrad's *Heart of Darkness* and focusing on a woman scientist thrust into a foreign adventure, Ann Patchett's *State of Wonder* (2011) follows former medical doctor turned pharmacologist Marina Singh, whose boss, Mr. Fox—the company CEO who is also her lover—sends her to the Amazon to investigate the Vogel company's project studying a plant-derived fertility drug. Marina's colleague Anders Eckman reportedly died of a fever during his journey to report on the project, which is directed by the uncommunicative Dr. Annick Swenson. Mr. Fox asks Marina to look into the project, but she has misgivings about doing so because she quit her medical residency, which Swenson supervised. Marina nevertheless responds to a plea from Anders's wife and goes to Brazil to find out what happened to Anders.

Despite encountering various impediments, Marina makes her way to Swenson's research station in the Lakashi tribe's remote village, where she is befriended by locals and project scientists. Many Lakashi women are pregnant, including women over sixty, and even seventy-three-year-old Dr. Swenson reveals her own seven-month pregnancy. Swenson has discovered that the bark of the Martin trees, which the women chew regularly, keeps them fertile and protects them against malaria, "the greatest discovery to be made in relation to the Lakashi tribe" (Patchett 2011, 264), but she insists on crediting the discovery to her deceased mentor and lover, Martin Rapp (231). Swenson claims that Dr. Rapp "saw no limitations for women," and she regards her successful career as owing to his guidance (166). Yet Rapp's summer research expeditions with his male college students and his love affair with Annick Swenson raise ethical questions. Nancy Saturn, "a botanist with a degree in public health" who works on Swenson's project (224), disapproves of Dr. Rapp's extramarital intimacy with his subordinate and tells Marina that "he wasn't a good man" (232).

The scientists also confront other ethical dilemmas concerning experimentation and medical practice. Marina questioned her own behavior during her long-ago residency: she operated then without Dr. Swenson's required approval, and the baby Marina delivered by caesarean section was blinded in one eye. Recognizing her former resident, Dr. Swenson requested that Marina operate on a Lakashi mother even though "interference in the medical needs of an indigenous people suddenly struck Marina as the worst possible idea" (272). Marina worries about keeping her intimate relationship with Mr. Fox secret from Swenson, while she conceals from Fox the fact that Swenson is actually using her Vogel funding to develop a vaccine against malaria rather than the fertility drug that the company wants. Marina has qualms about hiding information from her employer, even after Swenson tells Marina that it is the same drug under development: "I don't see the harm in making an American pharmaceutical company pay for a vaccination that will have enormous benefits to world health and no financial benefits for company shareholders" (288). Whereas women in the West will pay enormous sums for a fertility drug, a malaria vaccine is useful only in places where people cannot afford it.

The malaria research has been conducted in an ethically questionable manner. The scientists infect the Lakashi men with malaria to test the vaccination, supplying cokes as an incentive to volunteers but failing to warn them of dangers. When Marina questions this conduct, Dr. Alan Saturn, one of Dr. Rapp's "awestruck" male students, who still admires his mentor, responds by telling her not to "make this out to be the Tuskegee Institute," because the subjects probably already had malaria anyway, and the potential benefits of finding a vaccine justified cutting corners (294–95). He claims "it's good to get out of the American medical system from time to time. . . . It frees a person up, makes them think about what's possible" (295); he fails, however, to convince Marina to become a vaccine subject.

After Mr. Fox arrives at the Lakashi field site looking for Marina and wanting answers about the fertility drug, Swenson points to her own pregnancy as proof of the drug's efficacy, but she conceals the fact that the fetus has died and makes no mention of the malaria vaccine. She then persuades Marina to deliver the stillbirth and after surgery asks her former student to remain at the research station as project director. Although Marina is honored by the offer, she turns it down, only to find that Mr. Fox, who is pleased that the fertility drug is effective, orders her to remain with the Lakashi after he returns to the United States. Marina unexpectedly learns that Anders is alive with another tribe and, surprising even herself, manages to bargain for her colleague's release, enabling him to return to his family.

By the time Marina returns to Minnesota, she has accomplished many things she had not thought herself capable of, including performing obstetric surgery and rescuing Anders. Dr. Swenson has finally addressed the error Marina made as a medical resident and relieved Marina's guilt about blinding the baby: "You made a very common mistake that night at the General. You rushed, nothing more than that. . . . In retrospect the real loss was your quitting the program" (322). Marina realizes that Dr. Swenson's career has not been as perfect as Marina imagined and that Swenson regretted not having children. The orphan Swenson has adopted from another tribe also arouses Marina's maternal instincts. Newly fertile from chewing the bark of Martin trees, she begins to imagine herself raising children, returning to Mr. Fox or finding another lover. Marina realizes that Fox thinks of her more as his employee than as his girlfriend and understands that he manipulated her into going to Brazil to protect the company, but her heroism in the Amazon has made her more confident and earned her the respect of Dr. Swenson and the scientists on the Lakashi site.

Feminist studies of science include historical scholarship describing the lives of women scientists, sociological and anthropological analyses of women scientists and their workplaces, and philosophical accounts of the gendered dimensions of knowledge and its creation. Feminist philosopher of science Sandra Harding notes that "modern science has again been reconstructed by a set of interests and values—distinctively Western, bourgeois, and patriarchal" (1991, 145). Feminist scholars point to a number of interrelated issues that have affected women's progress in science: limited access to educational and professional opportunities; discriminatory practices and processes in scientific settings; scientists' masculinist constructions of science, nature, and gender; and a discourse that identifies objectivity, rationality, power, and privilege as implicitly or explicitly masculine. Feminist critiques recognize the constraints that affect women's place in science and consider how gender has influenced the substance of science. The novels discussed here describe the lives of female scientist characters, identifying social conditions that affect women's careers while speculating to a lesser degree about masculinist bias in creating scientific knowledge.

The novels incorporate plots about women scientists navigating barriers and facilitators along professional pathways. Set in different historical eras and referencing concepts elucidated in feminist studies of science, the narratives describe cultural conventions and workplace conditions that affect professional outcomes for women scientists. In *The Signature of All Things*, public recognition of Alma's research is hampered during the nineteenth century, when women did not generally engage in professional activity. A

Whistling Woman describes Jacqueline's struggle to establish a scientific career during the late 1960s, when women were beginning to gain access to male-dominated professions. Like her male colleagues, Hope in *Brazzaville Beach* has her own ambitions to achieve recognition for her discovery about chimpanzee behavior, but her employer subsumes her discovery. *Carbon Dreams* depicts Tina's day-to-day work and professional interactions as a research scientist and her simultaneous struggle to overcome barriers to her advancement and resist the attractions of marriage and family that sideline her friend Katherine. Scientific fraud and social attitudes and behaviors that disadvantage women in science are intertwined themes in *Intuition*, which explains how Marion's temperamental caution and social deference to her aggressive male collaborator constrain her research and limit her effectiveness as a mentor. *State of Wonder* explores the professional and personal choices of women scientists from different generations as they face the physical and ethical challenges of conducting science in an age of globalization.

The cultural belief that women should limit themselves to marriage and children rather than look for professional success persisted well into the twentieth century and affected the treatment of women who opted for scientific careers. Limitations may have benefits; for example, Alma's mostly celibate existence allowed her time and independence to pursue science. By the 1960s, ideas about gender roles were changing, and women in science began to pursue new professional opportunities. Jacqueline's drive to pursue a scientific career is in tension with her need for intimacy and romantic fulfillment. Relationships for other female scientists vary—they are frustrating (Alma's and Marina's), don't last (Tina's, Robin's, and Hope's), or result in marriage with children (Marion's). Annick Swenson's affair with the married Dr. Rapp apparently satisfied her, although the younger Nancy Saturn deems Dr. Rapp's behavior unfair to his wife. Women's choices represent their diverse responses to material circumstances and social expectations regarding appropriate professional pursuits and personal relationships.

Each of these novels details the conditions of scientific work, referencing women's ways of pursuing knowledge and developing results. Taken as a group, they illustrate the ways that talented women scientists manage challenging social conditions with varying degrees of professional success. Alma cannot travel until later in life, and Tina competes for equipment, materials, and research funding. Limited, bad, or selfish advice affects the protagonists, all of whom would have benefited from more supportive mentoring during their careers. Some women suffer because of gender stereotypes, notably the assumption that men's careers matter more than women's do. Jacqueline, Hope, and Marion have their research results appropriated by male employers, and Robin's career was delayed when her male PhD supervisor gave precedence to a male student's project. Social scientists Diana Bilimoria and Abigail Stewart use the term *relative isolation* to describe conditions for LGBT minorities and women in STEM academic departments: "This isolation has been commonly found for racial-ethnic minorities, and even for heterosexual white women, in science and engineering . . . , suggesting that these environments are experienced as powerfully monolithic by people who are not straight white men" (2009, 92).

In exploring women's scientific approaches and judgment, these narratives also reflect and refract cultural assumptions about feminine emotions. Jacqueline, Hope, Tina, and Robin allow intuition to combine with scientific method and analysis. Evelyn Fox Keller, who earned her Harvard PhD in physics in the early 1960s, called attention to the "deeply rooted popular mythology that casts objectivity, reason, and mind as male, and subjectivity, feeling, and nature as female. In this division of emotional and intellectual labor, women have been the guarantors and protectors of the personal, the emotional, the particular, whereas science—the province par excellence of the impersonal, the rational, and the general—has been the preserve of men" (1985, 6–7). According to this mythology, men are predisposed to be scientists, actively unveiling nature's truths, whereas women's emotionality and closeness to nature colors their observations and judgment.

Tracing this thinking from the roots of modern Western science through contemporary developments in evolutionary biology, Keller asks two questions: "How is it that the scientific mind can be *seen* at one and the same time as both male and disembodied? How is it that thinking 'objectively,' that is, thinking that is defined as self-detached, impersonal, and transcendent, is also understood as 'thinking like a man'?" (1985, 19). If scientific knowledge is objective, and we associate objectivity with masculinity, should we assume that only women who resist feminine stereotypes are competent scientists? For example, Jacqueline's disinterest in feminine fashion and her tendency to be quiet are, in Bowman's eyes, signs that she might make a good researcher. Feminine characteristics appear to disqualify women from being taken seriously as scientists. Mallabar paints Hope as hysterical when she reports chimp infanticide and violence, and Mr. Fox makes decisions for Marina because he thinks she overreacts.

The epistemological questions Keller raises, and to which she and other feminist critics of science respond, suggest how scientific knowledge itself might be characterized as gendered. Faulkner and Kerr posed this question: "If there were more women in science, would this in any way alter either the way science is practiced or the knowledge produced?" (2003, 59). That science practiced by women might turn out differently from that practiced by men has prompted some to consider the related notion that scientific analyses created by feminists might constitute "feminist science." Both *Brazzaville Beach* and *Carbon Dreams* feature fictional women scientists whose intuition contributes in significant ways to their scientific practices and methods, suggesting that they may have developed different approaches to studying nature than have their male counterparts. These novels exemplify Donna Haraway's argument that science is situated knowledge, developed by embodied individuals with cultural predispositions who act in particular ways according to contingent circumstances: "Feminism is about a critical vision consequent upon a critical positioning in unhomogeneous gendered social space. . . . That is because feminist embodiment resists fixation and is insatiably curious about the webs of differential positioning. There is no single feminist standpoint because our maps require too many dimensions for that metaphor to ground our visions" (1988, 589–90). Tina's dreams combine with her careful data collection and rigorous analysis to produce ingenious results. Hope's chimp interactions and observations inspire her new theory about the species. Such "alternative methods are not directly related to sex or presumed womanly traits," but marginalization and other aspects of women's socialization may well contribute to their developing different perspectives that reveal new information (Schiebinger 1999, 7).

In an ethnography comparing physicists in the United States and Japan, Sharon Traweek concludes that the "heroic" challenges of the discipline of high-energy physics mean that in each culture "the virtues of success, whatever their content, are associated with men" (1992, 105). The female protagonists of the novels considered here work in environments dominated by male scientists, where cultural ideals of masculinity are pervasive: scientific practice and publication appear as intellectual activities that are largely initiated and controlled by men with resources, who compete to make discoveries or to incorporate women's discoveries into their own research without crediting the women. Women work with and for men, who may nurture and mentor them, manipulate them, or engage with them in unwelcome or ambivalent sexual relationships. In these fictions, gender-related advantages and disadvantages in material resources and the influences of colleagues, family, and friends hinder or facilitate professional outcomes. The narratives depict the patriarchy, sexism, and bias that feminist analyses of science have found to be pervasive in scientific practice: Jacqueline, Hope, Robin, Marion, and Marina all negotiate their professional responsibilities while being subjected to sexist harassment, discrimination, bias, and intimidation not directed toward male scientists.

In sum, women's scientific practice, their application of the scientific method, and their insights are represented in these novels as associated in certain ways with gender, although to describe the female scientists as exhibiting a "feminine" way of doing science would be mistaken. Women scientists engage in various ways in science: some are more interested in acquiring scientific knowledge for its own sake and less focused than their male peers on achieving extrinsic rewards, while others seek professional recognition of their achievements. Because women generally have fewer resources and allies than their male counterparts, they often resort to doing science differently, looking at a problem from a different angle, as Alma, Tina, and Hope do, or adapting their scientific work to the social conventions and constraints associated with gender, as Jacqueline, Marina, and Marion do.

Hewing closely to the archetype of a woman scientist whose gender sets her apart, the female scientists in these novels are members of an isolated, plucky breed. They find the study and practice of science intellectually interesting, intrinsically rewarding, and socially relevant. The novels delineate scientific practices and circumstances and ideological biases that affect women's working conditions, rebutting stereotypical views of women as less able than men to perform scientific research and contributing to the debate over the continuing underrepresentation of women in scientific fields. Offering personalized stories of how women persist in or exit from career pathways in science, the novels provide popular images of women scientists that complement and reinforce feminist studies of women in science and of scientific theories and practices.

Notes

1. These are the section headings employed by Schiebinger in *Has Feminism Changed Science?* (1999).
2. Ruth gives her baby to Daniel to offer to Jacqueline. Two days later Ruth dies in a fire that also kills the cult's leader and another member.

References

Bilimoria, Diana, and Abigail J. Stewart. 2009. "'Don't Ask, Don't Tell': The Academic Climate for Lesbian, Gay, Bisexual, and Transgender Faculty in Science and Engineering." *NWSA Journal* 21 (2): 85–103.

Boyd, William. (1990) 2010. *Brazzaville Beach*. New York: Harper Perennial.

Branch, Enobong Hannah, ed. 2016. *Pathways, Potholes, and the Persistence of Women in Science: Reconsidering the Pipeline*. Lanham, MD: Rowman and Littlefield.

Byatt, A. S. (2002) 2004. *A Whistling Woman*. New York: Random House.

Ceci, Stephen J., and Wendy M. Williams, eds. 2007. *Why Aren't There More Women in Science? Top Researchers Debate the Evidence*. Washington, DC: American Psychological Association.

Coil, Alison. 2017. "Why Men Don't Believe the Data on Gender Bias in Science." *Wired*, August 25, 2017.

Colatrella, Carol. 2011. *Toys and Tools in Pink: Cultural Narratives of Gender, Science, and Technology*. Columbus: The Ohio State University Press.

European Commission. 2015. *She-Figures 2015*. http://ec.europa.eu/research/swafs/pdf/pub_gender_equality/she_figures_2015-final.pdf.

Faulkner, W., and E. A. Kerr. 2003. "On Seeing Brockenspectres: Sex and Gender in Twentieth-Century Science." In *Companion to Science in the Twentieth Century*, edited by Dominique Pestre and John Krige, 59–72. New York: Routledge.

Frayling, Christopher. 2006. *Mad, Bad, and Dangerous: The Scientist and Cinema*. London: Reaktion Books.

Gaines, Susan M. 2001. *Carbon Dreams*. Berkeley, CA: Creative Arts Books.

Gilbert, Elizabeth. 2013. *The Signature of All Things*. New York: Penguin.

Goodman, Allegra. 2006. *Intuition*. New York: Random House.

Haraway, Donna. 1988. "Situated Knowledges: The Science Question in Feminism and the Partial Perspective." *Feminist Studies* 14 (3): 575–99.

Harding, Sandra. 1991. *Whose Science? Whose Knowledge?* Ithaca, NY: Cornell University Press.

Haynes, Roslynn D. 2017. *From Madman to Crime Fighter: The Scientist in Western Culture*. Baltimore: Johns Hopkins University Press.

Howells, William Dean. 1881. *Dr. Breen's Practice*. Project Gutenberg. http://www.gutenberg.org/ebooks/3364.

Jewett, Sarah Orne. (1884) 2008. *A Country Doctor*. New York: Random House/Bantam.

Keen, Suzanne. 2010. *Empathy and the Novel*. New York: Oxford University Press.

Keller, Evelyn Fox. 1983. *A Feeling for the Organism: The Life and Work of Barbara McClintock*. New York: W. H. Freeman.

———. 1985. *Reflections on Gender and Science*. New Haven, CT: Yale University Press.

———. 2001. "Gender and Science: An Update." In *Women, Science, and Technology: A Reader in Feminist Science*

Studies, edited by Mary Wyer, Donna Cookmeyer, Donna Giesman, Mary Barbercheck, Hatice Ozturk, and Marta Wayne, 132–42. Hove, UK: Psychology Press.

Kirby, David. 2011. *Lab Coats in Hollywood: Science, Scientists, and the Cinema.* Cambridge, MA: MIT Press.

Kitzinger, Jenny, Joan Haran, Mwenya Chimba, and Tammy Boyce. 2008. *Role Models in the Media: An Exploration of the Views and Experiences of Women in Science, Engineering, and Technology.* UK Resource Centre for Women in Science, Engineering, and Technology. https://pdfs.semanticscholar.org/9ad7/d330616863a237c5e6fa2a28b6f2b3ee1ab3.pdf.

Maddox, Brenda. 2002. *Rosalind Franklin: The Dark Lady of DNA.* New York: HarperCollins.

Noble, David. 1992. *A World Without Women: The Christian Clerical Culture of Western Science.* New York: Alfred A. Knopf.

NSF (National Science Foundation) National Center for Science and Engineering Statistics. 2017. *Women, Minorities, and Persons with Disabilities in Science and Engineering: 2017.* Special Report NSF 17–310. https://www.nsf.gov/statistics/wmpd.

Patchett, Ann. 2011. *State of Wonder.* New York: HarperCollins.

Perkowitz, Sidney. 2007. *Hollywood Science: Movies, Science, and the End of the World.* New York: Columbia University Press.

Phelps, Elizabeth Stuart. (1882) 1987. *Dr. Zay.* New York: Feminist Press.

Quinn, Susan. 1995. *Marie Curie: A Life.* New York: Simon and Schuster.

Rose, Hilary. 1994. *Love, Power and Knowledge: Towards a Feminist Transformation of the Sciences.* Cambridge, UK: Polity Press.

Rossiter, Margaret W. 1993. "The Matthew/Matilda Effect in Science." *Social Studies of Science* 23 (2): 325–41.

———. 2012. *Women Scientists in America: Forging a New World Since 1972.* Vol. 3. Baltimore: Johns Hopkins University Press.

Sagan, Carl. 1997. *Contact.* New York: Pocket Books.

Schiebinger, Londa. 1999. *Has Feminism Changed Science?* Cambridge, MA: Harvard University Press.

Steinke, Jocelyn. 1998. "Connecting Theory and Practice: Women Scientist Role Models in Television Programming." *Journal of Broadcasting and Electronic Media* 42:142–51.

Subramanian, Banu. 2009. "Moored Metamorphoses: A Retrospective Essay on Feminist Science Studies." *Signs: Journal of Women in Culture and Society* 34 (4): 951–980.

Telegraph Women. 2015. "#Distractingly Sexy: Female Scientists Mock Sir Tim Hunt on Twitter." *Telegraph*, June 11, 2015. http://www.telegraph.co.uk/women/womens-life/11667981/Tim-Hunt-Distractinglysexy-female-scientists-post-photos-on-Twitter.html.

Traweek, Sharon. 1992. *Beamtimes and Lifetimes: The World of High Energy Physicists.* Cambridge, MA: Harvard University Press.

Zunshine, Lisa. 2006. *Why We Read Fiction: Theory of Mind and the Novel.* Columbus: The Ohio State University Press.

7.

Economization of Science
Insights from Science Novels

Uwe Schimank

The economization of contemporary society, especially of noneconomic societal spheres such as health care, education, the arts, and science, has been a topic of public debate since the 1980s as well as the subject of many empirical studies. Political buzzwords such as "liberalization," "deregulation," "privatization," "managerialism," "new public management," "entrepreneurialism," "marketization," and, above all, "neoliberalism" (Mudge 2008) all share a common denominator that I call economization: the increasing importance of explicitly articulated economic considerations for financial costs and profits (Schimank and Volkmann 2008, 2012, 2017). Such considerations clash with the guiding values of noneconomic spheres, and the individuals and organizations that provide services in these spheres often lament the ways in which money rules their operations.

Here I will take a closer look at the economization of science as it is presented in the following science novels: *Carbon Dreams* by Susan M. Gaines (2001); *Oryx and Crake* by Margaret Atwood ([2004] 2009); the Science in the Capital trilogy—*Forty Signs of Rain* ([2004] 2005), *Fifty Degrees Below* ([2005] 2007), and *Sixty Days and Counting* (2007)—by Kim Stanley Robinson; *Intuition* by Allegra Goodman ([2006] 2010); *Generosity* by Richard Powers ([2009] 2010); *The Honest Look* by Jennifer Rohn (2010a); *Solar* by Ian McEwan ([2010] 2011); *State of Wonder* by Ann Patchett ([2011] 2012); *Ein tiefer Fall* by Bernhard Kegel ([2012] 2013);[1] and *The Falling Sky* by Pippa Goldschmidt (2013). I will use these works of fiction to exemplify five facets of economization that are discussed widely in social science investigations as well as public debates (Schimank 2007, 2008; Jones 2009):

1. The underfinancing of universities and research institutes, which leads to pressure to acquire soft money from funding agencies or industry
2. Pressures to economize on research expenses, which leads to increased competition for scarce funding
3. Increased compliance with business interests in the thematic agenda of science
4. Commodification of academic research so as to generate financial profits
5. The transformation of traditional *homo academicus* into what Lothar Peter has called the "*homo academicus-oeconomicus*" (2010, 214–17)

As my discussion of these novels will reveal, these facets are not unrelated to each other: pressures from underfinancing can lead to increased competition or increased compliance with business interests. And although the commodification of research and compliance with business interests can result from a variety of motives and pressures, the cumulative effect of these tendencies may be to produce a gradual "corrosion of character"—to adopt sociologist Richard Sennett's (1998) well-known phrase—such that the fifth facet may, in the extreme, culminate in an overall conversion of the prevalent social character of the scientist.

Underfinancing and Dependence on Soft Money

Since the mid-1970s, tax revenues in most Western industrialized nations have increasingly lagged behind the financial needs of the public sector, and university systems have suffered from funding shortages. This underfinancing has led to a general deterioration of teaching and research conditions. Academic staffing at universities has not been able to keep pace with steadily rising student enrollments—in some countries, there has been little increase or even a decline in university personnel. Teaching loads have increased markedly, leaving less and less time for research activities, even with the de facto extension of weekly working hours that many academics have undertaken in their attempts to keep up. This has been accompanied by the decreasing availability of funds and shrinking budgets for buildings, laboratory equipment, libraries, and other important elements of university infrastructure. Academics have tried to compensate for such shortfalls by finding alternative ways of financing their research projects with third-party funding from government agencies, nonprofit foundations, and industrial partners—what is known in academic circles as soft money. Today, soft money is a prerequisite for doing research in most disciplines: when a scientist's project proposals are unsuccessful, his or her research generally comes to a standstill.

The pressures generated by these aspects of economization are dramatized in Allegra Goodman's *Intuition* (2010). The initial descriptions of its setting portray an institution in dire financial straits: "In 1985, the Philpott was famous, but it was full of old instruments. Dials and needle indicators looked like stereo components from the early sixties. The centrifuge, designed for spinning down cells in solution, was clunky as an ancient washing machine. There wasn't enough money to buy new equipment. There was scarcely enough to pay the postdocs" (4). The Philpott, as the reader learns later, is "an institute that has run a deficit for the past three years" (290). The reason for this critical state of affairs is that the institute's grant applications to the National Institutes of Health (NIH)—the most important funding agency for medical research in the United States—have been unsuccessful. When Cliff, one of the Philpott's PhD students, gets some promising experimental results, the two directors are divided about how to proceed. Marion Mendelssohn considers the results preliminary and wants to confirm them before making them public, whereas Sandy Glass wants to use them immediately as the basis for a new grant proposal:

> The grant proposal for NIH would be a knockout, an utter masterpiece. How could he be sure of this? He'd already written it. Marion didn't know. She would have been scandalized, but Sandy had drafted the whole thing. He'd left out the numbers, of course, the actual tables and figures. The data were still to come, but secretly, Sandy had crafted all the filigree for the proposal. He'd extrapolated from Cliff's preliminary results, and discussed their significance at length. The data would come; Marion would come around. Craftily, Sandy did his work in the meantime, forecasting the future. Language was important when it came to winning large sums of money; style was essential. By April first, Sandy's statements of purpose and declarations of intent would be polished to such a sheen the reviewers would see themselves reflected there. He was a poet of the NIH form. (59)

Two things are striking about this reasoning. First, we see the director of a scientific institution under such pressure to procure funds that he is willing to gamble on a postdoc's unverified preliminary results, investing his time and energy in a premature grant proposal and, in the process, putting himself in a position in which he is likely to overinterpret any new, possibly ambivalent data. Second, strategic impression management, rather than data or ideas, has become the most important attribute of the proposal. We see how underfinancing might lead to a betrayal of trust among peers and endanger scientific objectivity, forcing a transfer of intellectual energy from the tasks of asking questions and establishing facts to those of fabricating certainty and creating attractive stories.

When Sandy announces the success of the new grant at the institute's annual picnic event, the emotional tolls of economization on the lab's postdocs and doctoral students are apparent: "'Phew,' said Pritwish [one of the postdocs] amid applause and laughter. They could joke now. Funding after such a long drought was like coming back from the dead" (170). In the institute's hierarchy, the postdocs, whose salaries eat up much of the institute's scarce money, are just one step above the doctoral students, whose situation is even more precarious: "Like scientific sharecroppers, they slaved all day. They were too highly trained to stop. Overeducated for other work, they kept repeating their experiments. They kept trying to live on their seventeen-thousand-dollar salaries" (20). The protagonist of Susan M. Gaines's *Carbon Dreams*, Tina Arenas, experiences an even more drastic version of this situation: "Her funding would run out in six months, and she had wasted the last two days in the instrument lab repairing a pump. She really shouldn't be wasting this Friday afternoon at yet another interesting-but-irrelevant talk" (2001, 2). When Tina mentions to a younger colleague that she had turned down a teaching position at a state college, the colleague replies, "Well, but it's got to be better than soft money. . . . BIO doesn't exactly have a reputation for treating its soft-money researchers nicely when they run out of grant money. They don't care if you end up unemployed and homeless" (8). For the postdoc in Pippa Goldschmidt's *The Falling Sky*, a similar situation means a literal loss of sleep: "She's answerable to herself when she wakes up at three o'clock in the morning and lies in bed working out how many more months, weeks, and days she has left on her grant" (2013, 12).

Robin, one of the doctoral students in *Intuition*, articulates the longings of young researchers in a conversation with Marion Mendelssohn: "'I would like,' she said slowly, 'to make some progress—and to feel as though my work actually made a difference. I would like to be part of a community where resources aren't so scarce, and it doesn't have to be a choice between my work or his, or now or later'" (Goodman 2010, 101). It is a longing that is echoed in one form or another by many of the scientist characters in these novels, a part of their scientific ethos that they see threatened by financial pressures. Indeed, the science novel author Jennifer Rohn, a practicing scientist concerned with the portrayal of scientists and their ethos in popular culture, mobilized a campaign against cuts in the British science budget, not so much to protect her job but in service to this ethos. "You don't go into science to get rich," she writes in an opinion piece in the *Guardian*, passing on the advice of her mentors. She goes on to describe her reasons for doing science, sounding not unlike Goodman's fictional Robin: "I am in love with science. . . . I love the mind-bending problems, the euphoria of seeing something that no one else in the world ever has before. I love the thought that, despite the bad pay and the poor prospects, the work that I do might actually help people" (2010b). But if PhD students are to continue in academic careers, they need to produce original results for their dissertations before their stipendiums end, while institutes and principal investigators need soft money to continue their work and build their reputations—and apply successfully for more soft money. In *Intuition*, the institutional structure and scarce resources combine to encourage bad scientific practice that borders on scientific fraud: Cliff had adopted dubious experimental practices in a desperate attempt to get tangible results for his dissertation, and those results are immediately picked up by an institute director who is willing to clutch at any straw.

Bernhard Kegel's *Ein tiefer Fall* (2013) describes a similar case at a German university. But in Kegel's scenario, scientific fraud originates not from a doctoral student's desperate situation but from a constellation in which any leading tenured scientist could easily become enmeshed. In a conversation with a colleague, a highly esteemed professor tries to justify having manipulated his data: "Really, I didn't want to do it, that much you can believe. If I could have concentrated on my work, things would probably—no, surely!— have been different. But I'm only human. The move [to the new job] and everything else was a lot more demanding than I expected. The cells started dying and I couldn't hinder it—couldn't be in two places at once, couldn't deal with it and unpack and write proposals and conduct job interviews and prepare my lectures and write. . . . And so it happened" (310–11). Here we get a vivid picture of a dedicated researcher working under time limitations, conditions of intense multitasking, and pressures to acquire financial resources for further research—no excuse for individual misconduct, but a sociological explanation for the growing number of cases.

The problematic effects of underfinancing and the dependency on soft money discussed up to this point have nothing to do with the content of the research. Funding agencies such as the NIH, the Deutsche Forschungsgemeinschaft (German Research Foundation), and the British Research Councils routinely support basic research according to its scientific quality and do not require that results have applicability to any extrascientific use. These agencies may also, however, set up special programs to support research with applications to problems of particular societal concern, such as disease control or climate change. And since they are dependent on government allocations, such funding is not always free of political undertones. In Kim Stanley Robinson's *Forty Signs of Rain* (2005), the main protagonists work for the National Science Foundation (NSF), the other large funding agency in the US science system, which asks Congress to earmark funding for a special research program on climate change. The NSF's congressional liaison officer explains to her new colleague that "science sets its own agenda. To tell the truth, that's why the appropriation committees don't like us very much." When the colleague wonders why the senators would mind, the liaison officer goes on to explain: "Because they hold the purse strings, honey. And they're very jealous of that power. I've had senators who believe the Earth is flat say to me, 'Are you trying to tell me that you know what's good for science better than I do?'. . . That's the kind of person we sometimes have to deal with. Even with the best of committees, there's a basic dislike for science's autonomy" (121–22). The need to please politicians who are not just ignorant in scientific matters but, much more dangerously, ignorant about their own ignorance might have even more dire consequences for scientific integrity than the need to devote one's intellectual energies to impression management in proposal writing and PR.

Regime of Competition

One feature of contemporary economization that distinguishes it from earlier phases of public sector cutbacks is that rather than treating the shortage of funds—in regular budgets and in sources of soft money—as an inherent difficulty of service provision, the financiers of hospitals, museums, and universities are taking advantage of it to establish a veritable regime of competition called New Public Management (NPM).[2] NPM is based on the neoliberal premise that unless service providers are under competitive pressure and threatened with losing their funding if they underperform, they will do the minimum possible and betray their customers and financiers.[3] Competition is expected to improve performance, and providers who do not measure up are likely to be shut down. In other words, the regime of competition works on the principle of survival of the fittest and serves as a mechanism of evolutionary selection. In many national university systems, budget distribution and professors' salaries are now based on performance. Furthermore, rating and ranking systems for universities, institutes, and individual researchers have proliferated at both the national and global levels. Of course, what counts as good performance depends on who defines the criteria: peers, administrators, or politicians. The big change here is that all researchers who need funding for their work must now conform to mainstream standards that render unconventional new approaches to certain research topics infeasible.

Again, Goodman's *Intuition* is a fitting anchor example for a reflection of these tendencies. In a conversation between Sandy Glass and Marion Mendelssohn at the beginning of the story, Glass wants to push ahead with writing a grant proposal, while Marion hesitates: "'We'll have to scrape something together,' he tells Marion. 'We don't have the results,' she replies." But then she reflects on what Sandy has said:

> She knew as well as he that their old grant from the National Institutes of Health was ending, that last year's research gambit had failed, and that they desperately needed funding. She knew they had to pull together a resoundingly good grant proposal for NIH by April first or contemplate folding. The Philpott Institute was governed by strict Darwinian principles. Investigators broke even or went bankrupt, losing staff and space and equipment to their rivals. . . . Lab directors without funding had little recourse; they took desperate measures: they switched fields, or retired, or sometimes left science altogether. (2010, 17)

Marion's observations express the regime of competition in a nutshell. Later, one of the institute's former postdocs goes even further in his assessment: "It's feudal, actually. There are the lords and ladies like Glass and Mendelssohn, and then the postdocs are the vassals paying tribute every year in the form of publications, blood, sweat, tears, et cetera" (211). The doctoral students are the first to be sacrificed in such a regime, as we see when Sandy and Marion are struggling over what to do about Cliff at the beginning of the story, before he gets his promising results: Cliff had been deemed a "star in the making" but has failed to deliver, and Sandy insists that he "has to go," though Marion wants to continue to nurture his "talent" (18–19).

No one has explicitly threatened to expel him from the lab, but Cliff is only too aware that his time is running out when he resorts to the dubious experimental practices that raise Robin's suspicions. When Robin, who is Cliff's ex-girlfriend, airs her suspicions to some scientist friends from another institute, they are incredulous:

> "Well, what are you suggesting? You're telling us Cliff is actually hiding data?"
> "Why would he try to hide his data?" asked Wendy.
> ". . . I think the data didn't conform to his ideas," Robin spluttered, "and so he suppressed the results that didn't fit."
> "No scientist would do something like that," Larry declared. (182)

Larry goes on to argue that what Robin alleges Cliff did would be "crazy" because there was no chance of getting away with such fraud. Of course, no one knows how much scientific misconduct goes undetected or, for that matter, whether the reported cases deter those who are trapped in survival-of-the-fittest struggles for their careers and futures. Larry and Wendy are unwilling to confront this possibility, but Robin becomes obsessed by it and takes on the role of whistle-blower:

> Her doubts had grown into weather systems of their own, her single intuition now transformed into a conspiracy theory implicating not only Cliff but nearly everyone who worked around him. After working so closely with him for so long, why hadn't Feng spoken up about Cliff's unorthodox record keeping? How could Marion, famous for overseeing every detail, have allowed Cliff to work virtually unsupervised? Had they not seized rapaciously on the promise of Cliff's work? Starved for results, they'd conjured up a banquet. Cliff had begun, and then the others followed, and the entire scientific community began to partake. Weren't they all, then, eating air? (251)

At a congressional hearing on the alleged fraud, organized by the NIH's Office of Research Integrity in Science (ORIS), a congressman known for despising scientists mounts an attack on Sandy Glass that, ironically, gets to the heart of the matter:

> Your laboratory is the oppressive regime. You are the dictator there in a totalitarian system. Yours is a culture of accepted truths corrupted by your desire for more and still more funding, and a lust for quick results. Your lab is but one example in a long line ORIS is just now bringing to light. . . . I fault the senior scientists in each case. I fault the principal investigators who nurture quick fixes and engineer the fast track from a whiff of success to pharmaceutical riches or academic glory. . . . You reward intellectual dishonesty. (269)

The accused scientists have difficulties in countering such an attack because they know it contains a kernel of truth. But the politician's demagogic language obscures the fact that the situation he describes was not created by scientists such as Sandy Glass—it is instead a result of the science policies installed by politicians enamored of NPM.

Competition is nothing new. The race to be the first to publish a new scientific finding is inherent in modern science. But with the escalating competition for scarce and indispensable funds, the inclination to sacrifice standards of reliability and validity for speed has reached a new level. Marion's husband, Jacob, compares her old-fashioned scientist's mind-set to Sandy's:

> "That's Sandy's sport—thinking about science as a competition."
> "It is a competition," she said.
> "You never thought that before."
> "But don't you see?" Marion said. "I was never in the running."
> "Right, because you were working," Jacob said. "Why don't you let Sandy place his bets and go off to the races?" (141)

Jacob wants his wife "to develop her ideas at her own pace. To earn recognition without Sandy" (140). His distinction between working and competing is somewhat naive—as in sports, it has never been possible to earn a reputation in science without entering the race. But he is right that the new era of competition in science bears a disturbing resemblance to contemporary athletics, where competition has led to widespread doping.

In Kegel's *Ein tiefer Fall*, Professor Hermann Pauli struggles with a German science system that is just as infected with NPM as the American one is in *Intuition* and in which the so-called incentives for better performance lead an established star into self-delusion and misconduct. Like Robin, Pauli is surprised to find that his scientific community lacks both the will and the wherewithal to cope with the fallout. Pauli recaps what the university ombudsman told him when he asked what he should do about his famous colleague's misconduct: "We are all in the same boat. [Do you], in [your] furor, really [want] to run the risk that all of science and its institutions will be discredited? The case will surely turn out to be more complicated than envisaged. . . . Punishing scientific misconduct, provided it really exists, would require a well-grounded, dedicated scientific court—or [are you] of the view that the state should interfere in research even more than it already has? What happens then to the freedom and autonomy of science?" Pauli worries about what it means when the very entities tasked with safeguarding ethical scientific practice express such laissez-faire cynicism: "Don't these bureaucrats understand what's at stake? Had they even listened to him? One of the most spectacular discoveries in biology in the last decade turns out to be the fabrication of a prestige-addicted careerist. . . . They'd all, without exception, fallen for his crap. Not a single critical or skeptical voice was raised when Frank's fairy tale of the shadow biosphere took the world by storm. A system that produced such blunders with ever increasing frequency was completely sick—only frank, unsparing candor and clarification could help" (2013, 461–63).

Kegel's novel demonstrates a level of cynical resignation that cannot be topped: representatives of the scientific community call on the autonomy of science to cover up dysfunctions and ethical disasters that stem from heteronomy. And those who are pressured into committing scientific misconduct deny that they are victims, for fear of being victimized even more if they speak out about it. This perversion is the ultimate result of the regime of competition.

Business Interests

In modern society, the capitalist economy dominates all other societal spheres (Schimank 2015). Business interests are politically powerful, and when economic growth rates slow, political decision-makers become obsessed with helping the economy to recover. But the business sector is not the only one to feel the effects of a weak economy: when business profits decline, so too does the tax revenue collected on those profits, and the societal services that depend on taxes—including education and scientific research—experience shortfalls. Attempts to bolster the economy may include pressure to lower taxes, which further exacerbates financial shortfalls for services dependent on these taxes. Moreover, state-financed research organizations may come under pressure to focus on applied research that supports industry and economic growth while avoiding research that might hurt industry (e.g., studies of the health or environmental repercussions of industrial products or waste). Government funding programs may even specify industry-relevant research topics or prescribe partnerships with industry.

The protagonist of Gaines's *Carbon Dreams* (2001) works in the field of organic geochemistry, which evolved hand in hand with the oil industry. But though she knows that petroleum is her field's "bread and butter," she is determined to do basic research: "She had the vague idea that she could address oceanographers' questions—big sprawling questions about the dynamic history of oceans and continents, the evolution of climate and global chemical cycles—using an organic geochemist's techniques" (16). Public funding for such basic research is limited, however, and competition is high; when Tina's application to the NSF fails, her friend Garrett, an experienced older professor, advises her to emphasize the "use value" of her research for the oil industry and apply to an industry-endowed fund of the American Chemical Society. At first, Tina protests: "Damn it, Garrett, I don't want to do petroleum geochemistry. . . ." But Garrett urges her to dress up her real research interest so that it looks sexy to industry: "'You can still do your paleoclimate work,' Garrett said patiently. '. . . You write it into the proposal, same as before. You have to move this hydrocarbon work to the fore, develop it more—but that doesn't mean you have to eliminate the paleoclimate work. . . . Petroleum is just the buzzword, a front for some very solid, even eloquent, geochemistry'" (72–73). But Tina is uneasy and resentful:

> There was something infuriating about this sort of talk from Garrett. The cynicism in his voice didn't belong there, seemed foreign, unnatural. Tina met his gaze. "I bet you've never done that. Tossed around buzzwords. . . ."

"I never had to. You know that. . . . And things were different. I wasn't vying with the most respected researchers in my field for a slice of a shrinking basic research pie. There was plenty to go around for a young researcher." (73)

What Tina resists is "an idea with no depth. No soul. Not an idea to be married to" (100). Later, as her unease comes into focus, she distinguishes between "the compulsion to *know* the universe and technology's compulsion to *use* it" (217).[4] For want of other alternatives, she ends up following Garrett's advice, though she feels guilty about it. At the end of the novel, having been drawn into debates about anthropogenic climate change, she wonders whether it would not have suited her better to have become an astronomer, observing nature beyond Earth, where humans could not use or affect it—but even then, she realizes, science might eventually allow them access.

Ann Patchett's *State of Wonder* (2012) portrays a scientist doing pharmaceutical research in the Amazonian jungle, where she uses volunteers from a small local tribe as her experimental subjects. Like Tina, Dr. Swenson is driven largely by curiosity in her practice of science, and she has moral principles concerning the application of her findings. She was a professor at a medical school who found a pharmaceutical company to fund her research: "The first three years I pieced together grants but the constant search for funding was more time consuming than flying back and forth to teach. There wasn't a major pharmaceutical company in the world that wouldn't have been willing to foot the bill for this but in the end Vogel won. I give credit where credit's due" (169). Unable to accomplish her research goals as a regular professor with teaching duties and only a trickle of public money from grants, she promised to develop a profitable fertility drug and struck a deal with industry that allowed her a surprising amount of autonomy. The novel, however, is interested in other moral issues and does not consider the feasibility or limitations of such a double game.

As noted, economization may drive research organizations to focus on applied science that supports industry while avoiding research that might prove detrimental to business interests. In Robinson's *Forty Signs of Rain*, scientists have elucidated the progress of anthropogenic climate change, which has dire consequences for many industries, at least on the short-term time scale that matters for economic projections (2005). The novel is set in the near future, and Anne Quibler, an NSF science administrator, describes the events of the recent past this way: "The battle for control of science went on. Many administrations and Congresses hadn't wanted technology or the environment assessed at all, as far as Anne could see. It might get in the way of business. They didn't want to know" (123). Her husband, Charlie, who works for a minority party congressman concerned with environmental issues, remembers

> when the administration's first science advisor had been sent packing for saying that global warming might be real and not only that, amenable to human mitigation. . . . [This administration's] line was that no one knew for sure and it would be much too expensive to do anything about it even if they were certain it was coming—everything would have to change, the power generation system, cars, a shift from hydrocarbons to helium or something. . . . They were going to punt and let the next generation solve their own problems in their own time. . . . Easier to destroy the world than to change capitalism even one little bit. (155–56)

Forty Signs of Rain is the first in Robinson's Science in the Capital trilogy, which eventually presents a utopian resolution in which heroic scientists confront economization and are able to harness business interests to save society and the planet it depends on. But in most of the novels discussed here, scientists are powerless in the face of business interests—unable to ignore them but at the same time unable to put them to use in the pursuit of any research that is not linked to economic interests.

Academic Capitalism

So far, I have dealt with only one side of the economization of science: that in which there is pressure to adapt to a funding shortfall. On the other side is pressure, or an opportunity, to earn money by doing research—that is, the direct commodification of scientific knowledge as a means of profit-making. In academic capitalism the lines between the basic research that was traditionally the purview of the academic sector and the applied research of for-profit companies have blurred. Investments in research generate profits for academic research institutions as well as for associated industrial labs, with patents being the most common, though not the only, profit-earning mechanism (Slaughter and Leslie 1997). Traditional limits on how much professors at universities and state-financed institutes can earn for outside work have partly eroded, and large companies may pay fees or extra salaries to those who do certain kinds of research and concede exclusive rights to the results. The university itself may offer bonuses as an incentive for scientists whose research produces patentable results. The potential dangers of this are articulated by a resentful former Philpott student in *Intuition*: "There's just too much money involved. . . . I'm talking about the pharmaceutical companies. Don't you think academics are all tangled up with corporations. Don't you think Sandy Glass is in the pocket of a drug company—or would be, if he could? There's big bucks out there, and where there's money like that there is no such thing as academic freedom, or independent inquiry" (Goodman 2010, 211; ellipses in original).

The economic attractions are such that some academics are tempted to leave academia and start their own firms, though as we see in *Forty Signs of Rain*, they may run into difficulties: "Torrey Pines Generique, like most biotech start-ups, was undercapitalized, and could only afford a few rolls of the dice. One of them had to look promising enough to attract the capital that would allow it to grow further" (Robinson 2005, 37). Only investors willing to gamble will be attracted by such start-ups: "This was not a kind of investment that banks would make, nor anyone else in the loaning world. The risks were too great, the returns too distant. Only venture capitalists would do it" (216–17).

The scientific norm of "communalism"—an essential element of the traditional ethos of science in which "the fruits of academic science should be regarded as 'public knowledge'" (Ziman 2000, 33)—does not apply to such profit-driven research. Until the knowledge has been patented, secrecy is an omnipresent imperative, and publication is prohibited. At Torrey Pines Generique, the legal department blocks its researchers from publishing an interesting research result. Some of them have internalized the scientific ethos and find this hard to accept:

> "It's good work, it's interesting! It could help make a big breakthrough!"
> "That's what they don't want," Brian said. "They don't want a big breakthrough unless it's our big breakthrough."
> "Shit." This had happened before, but Leo had never gotten used to it. Sitting on results, doing private science, secret science—it went against the grain. It wasn't science as he understood it. (Robinson 2005, 98–99)

The scientist in Richard Powers's *Generosity* is annoyed about this consequence of the "capitalization of life sciences" within the university system: "Even colleagues in his own university department, funded by corporate grants, can no longer talk freely to one another" (2010, 131). As one reviewer observes, "Powers lays out economic and ethical implications that are already playing out in life science labs throughout the US" (Zipp 2009).

Another way that profit-driven scientific work may deviate from the traditional scientific ethos is exemplified by the problem that Claire Cyrus, the heroine of Jennifer Rohn's *The Honest Look*, confronts (2010a). Claire is a new employee at the biotech start-up NeuroSys when her research results indicate that the firm's "lead drug compound ... is going to be useless" (141)—it worked in mice, but it would not be the hoped-for great advance in the treatment of human beings (240, 322). In a conversation with a colleague, Claire begins to understand the repercussions: "The company is doomed, isn't it? My God, how can I tell them now?" (141). She later goes on to reflect, "It was one thing to react reasonably about a potential flaw that might make necessary a minor chemical adjustment in an established drug. . . . But it would be quite another to be faced with the destruction of a life work, a cherished theory and the entire reason for NeuroSys's existence" (190–91). Under this pressure, Claire commits an act of serious scientific misconduct that she eventually confesses to colleagues: "I was terrified, and covered up the finding" (314). This reveals how academic capitalism can also undermine the requisite self-critique and skepticism about theories and empirical data (Ziman 2000, 42–44): if scientific success becomes a matter of economic survival, errors are not acknowledged but covered up to maintain an image of success and progress—even when this could, as in the case described in Rohn's novel, cost patients their lives.

An episode in Margaret Atwood's dystopian novel *Oryx and Crake* carries academic capitalism to its extreme (2009).[5] Crake explains to his friend Jimmy (the novel's narrator, sometimes known as "Snowman") how the pharmaceutical company HelthWyzer makes money "out of drugs and procedures that cure sick people, or else—better—that make it impossible for them to get sick in the first place." He asks the rhetorical question, "So, what are you going to need, sooner or later? . . . After you've cured everything going." And then he answers it himself: "So, you'd need more sick people. Or else—and it might be the same thing—more diseases." He goes on to uncover the ugly secret that this is exactly what the firm has been up to:

"There's a whole secret unit working on nothing else. . . . Listen, this is brilliant. They put the hostile bioforms into their vitamin pills. . . . Naturally, they develop the antidotes at the same time as they're customizing the bugs, but they hold those in reserve, they practice the economy of scarcity, so they're guaranteed high profits. . . . The best diseases, from a business point of view . . . would be those that cause lingering illnesses. Ideally—that is, for maximum profit—the patient should either get well or die just before all of his or her money runs out. It's a fine calculation." (246–48)

The ultimate cynicism of this business model is apparent in Crake's observation that once the patient runs out of money and there is no chance of further profit, it makes no difference to the company whether the patient dies or lives on.

Culmination: *Homo academicus-oeconomicus*

My discussion of the four facets of economization up to this point has shown that there are distinct paths of economization. Most research units at universities have to cope with underfinancing and NPM without the help of business or profits from commodified research products. How can an institute of theoretical physics make money with its research? In many fields of science, opportunities for profit-making are still rare. In others, such as the engineering sciences or certain fields of chemistry or the life sciences, profit-making has always been possible: the question there is whether a professor or institute director chooses to be an academic capitalist. Generally, this is—or has been—a conscious choice. But it can also happen that an institution or an individual academic is driven involuntarily into profit-making in order to avoid the calamities of underfinancing. As more and more individuals, institutes, and universities move along one of these economization paths, a distinctive kind of social character emerges that differs from that of the traditional academic scientist. Lothar Peter coined the term *homo academicus-oeconomicus* to describe a scientist for whom scientific interests and research have become subordinated to financial ones—someone who is preoccupied with financial shortfalls, whose self-esteem depends on financial indicators of success such as funding acquisitions, or who strives to get rich from the commercialization of research (2010). This new social character may work in academia, in industry, or in both.

Intuition's Sandy Glass is an example of a homo academicus-oeconomicus. He is so fixated on acquiring funding for his institute that he has neglected all scientific concerns—including his responsibility to educate and mentor young researchers. When he finally takes a position as director of a private cancer clinic, it is unclear whether he does so because he thinks the clinic will be able to make inroads into a cure for cancer or because it offers him "untold sums of money" (Goodman 2010, 331). Marion, his old friend and codirector, accuses him of being corruptible: "'You did not hold out against them. You never hold out against anything,' she said. He shrugged: 'They made me an offer I couldn't refuse'" (31). In this new job, the "entrepreneurial self" (Bröckling 2016) that had long been the core of Sandy's academic identity would finally find its complete expression.

Another interesting variation of homo academicus-oeconomicus can be found in the protagonist of Ian McEwan's satirical novel *Solar* (2011). Nobel physicist Michael Beard has not had any interesting scientific ideas for decades, but he can still use his reputation for financial gain: "Beard was always on the lookout for an official role with a stipend attached. A couple of long-running sinecures had recently come to an end, and his university salary, lecture fees and media appearances were never quite sufficient. Fortunately . . . the Blair government wished to be, or appear to be, practically rather than merely rhetorically engaged with climate change and announced a number of initiatives, one of which was the Centre, a facility for basic research in need of a mortal at its head sprinkled with Stockholm's magic dust" (22).

Using a scientific theory he has stolen from a young researcher at the Centre, Beard founds a new company that is designed to profit from patents based on a new method of producing renewable energy. In a speech to venture capitalists, he declares that "the planet . . . is sick. . . . Curing the patient is a matter of urgency and is going to be expensive. . . . I am convinced, and I have come here to tell you, that anyone who wishes to help with the therapy, to be a part of the process and invest in it, is going to make very large sums of money, staggering sums." Rather than appeal to any moral imperative, he tells them that the only way to save the planet is "not by being virtuous, not by going to the bottle bank and turning down the thermostat and buying a smaller car. That merely delays the catastrophe by a year or two. . . . For humanity en masse, greed trumps virtue. So we have to welcome into our solutions the ordinary compulsions of self-interest. . . . You, the market, either rise to this, and get rich along the way, or you sink with all the rest" (204–7).

With Beard, McEwan reminds us of an old topos of early modern social philosophy from Bernard Mandeville's famous *Fable of the Bees* that "private vices" can produce "public virtues" ([1714] 1924). Beard considers whether one can then assume that "private virtues" produce "public virtues." On an expedition ship to the North Pole, Beard is confronted with the growing chaos of the boot room and notes how much easier it is to be careless about keeping order when confronted with the disorder produced by others—how powerless "private virtue" is in the face of "public vice." The problems of climate change, Beard reasons, are much too big for the limited range of weak "private virtues": "How were they to save the earth . . . when it was so much larger than the boot room?" (McEwan 2011, 207). Instead, it seems more likely that human-made climate change can be averted by the greed for profit—a "private vice"—that Beard shares with the investors in his firm. Seen in this light, homo academicus-oeconomicus, even in its most extreme incarnation, may not be as dangerous to science and society as one might think.

The geneticist in Powers's *Generosity* is a somewhat more ambivalent personification of the homo academicus-oeconomicus who has "simply accepted science's latest survival adaptation—salesmanship" (2010, 145). Thomas Kurton "has founded seven companies and advises fifteen more. He serves on the editorial board of six scientific journals while holding positions with three different universities." Unlike Beard, however, Kurton is a dedicated scientist for whom profit-making is not the main motive: "The love he really lived for was *knowing*" (46). He feels it is his mission to contribute with his research to perfecting human life. His specific aim is "to discover the genetic causes of joy" (198). In an interview, he sketches his general agenda in a broad historical frame: "Six hundred generations ago, we were scratching on the walls of caves. Now we're sequencing genomes. Three billion years of accident is about to become something truly meaningful" (275). In another presentation, he formulates this ambition more boldly: "I don't believe in God, but I do believe that it's humanity's job to bring God about" (206).

Although the hyperbole of these public statements is partly due to the scientific "salesmanship" that Kurton has resigned himself to, he is earnest about his research goals. But when those turn out to be overly ambitious, one of his biotech companies gets into trouble, and amid rising public doubts fueled by the media, his board of directors requests him to "get back to more practical research," which means, as Kurton realizes, making a profit soon:

> So long as he produced the prizes, so long as he was *profitable*, the tribe let him mate with everything in sight. Now, at the first sign of weakness, they launch this inevitable takedown.
>
> He remembers the thousand beautiful implications of his association study, and a parent's panic seizes him. The genetic screen for well-being will be shelved in favor of more practical, portable projects. (295)

Had he been interested *only* in money he would also have come to this conclusion. It is not that he is uninterested in money. But to him, profit-making is more of a long-term gamble than a directed effort, as he notes when an interviewer asks him how his companies make profit: "Forget about bookkeeping. You can't bookkeep what's coming. . . . The coming market is endless. Think about the five years just before the internet. . . . Only those companies that free themselves of preconceptions will take advantage of the biggest structural change in society since . . . " (189). Moreover, he sets some ethical limits to profit-making, agreeing wholeheartedly when the media challenges him to respond to a British ethicist's criticism of overstepping biotech companies: "'These people want royalties for tests that used to be free. They're prosecuting others for mentioning patented scientific discoveries in public. They own entire organisms. . . . ' He [Kurton] nods in sympathy. 'I agree; no patent should be allowed to prevent progress. The only thing profit is good for is reinvesting in research'" (108–9). This last sentence turns capitalism upside down: instead of products generating profits for investors, profits become the means to make better and more useful products. And again, such wishful thinking raises the question of how realistic it is to think that capitalism can be harnessed to serve the public good.

The advent of the homo academicus-oeconomicus marks a decisive point in the economization of science that goes far beyond changes in the budgets and financial incentive structures of scientific institutions: economization is no longer just an external feature of scientists' social contexts but has been internalized by individual scientists who remember only faintly, if at all, the traditional scientific ethos. They have, to use a well-known psychoanalytic concept, identified with the aggressor. In *Oryx and Crake*, Jimmy's father is a scientist at NooSkins, a company that aims to sell new skin to older people so that they can look young and sexy again. When Jimmy's father started to work there, his ambition was to help people who had skin problems from diseases or accidents, but this has changed radically, as we see when his wife reproaches him:

> "It's wrong, the whole organization is wrong, it's a moral cesspool and you know it. . . . Don't you remember the way we used to talk, everything we wanted to do? Making life better for people—not just people with money. You used to be so. . . . You had ideals, then."
> "Sure," said Jimmy's father in a tired voice. "I've still got them. I just can't afford them." (64)

The culmination of economization may well be reflected in such internalization: if more and more universities, institutes, research groups, and individual academics in more and more fields of science are drawn into the processes of economization, and homo academicus-oeconomicus becomes the norm rather than the exception, the very ethos of science comes under siege.

Conclusion

Most of the novels I examined portray economization as a serious but containable problem that can and should be handled by measures taken within the science system or by its political regulation and funding. To be sure, Gaines, Goldschmidt, Goodman, Kegel, Powers, and Rohn diagnose economization as a serious problem, but they do not see a fundamental threat to the autonomy of science ending in a totally economized homo academicus-oeconomicus whose sole interest in doing science is money-making. *Solar* goes further, registering a deep cynicism about the human ability to care for the common good and portraying an out-of-control homo academicus-oeconomicus, which, ironically, hints that our only hope of salvation from human-made climate change may actually lie in the random, fickle realm of profit-driven innovation. Atwood and Robinson, however, place their work within the nuanced utopian tradition and use imagined future societies to warn about the potentially extreme consequences of the economization of science (Atwood 2011; Robinson and Feder 2018).[6]

In Atwood's *Oryx and Crake* (2009) we get the impression that humankind is no more than one step away from the abyss. What makes it so disturbing is its utter plausibility, the resemblance that so many phenomena in the book have to real-life phenomena. Atwood herself insists that the novel is simply an extrapolation of the dystopian tendencies inherent in the utopian hopes that scientific progress and capitalism encourage, such as eternal health and growing wealth—tendencies that are "all too easy to recognise in the lineaments of the present day" (Phillips 2017, 152).[7] So the imminent future Atwood presents to us is perhaps not totally doomed but instead leaves open the possibility of counteraction. The novelist's hopeless cynicism is meant to be a self-destroying prophecy: a vision of the future the author does not want to come true and communicates precisely for this reason, as a cautionary tale (Clausen and Dombrowsky 1984).

Robinson, in some senses, goes further. Like the MaddAddam trilogy, the Science in the Capital trilogy takes readers to the edge of the abyss and then plays out a retreat. But in this case, Robinson provides an actual scenario of counteractions within the dystopian setting of a world threatened by abrupt climate change (Johns-Putra 2010, 750–51). Like the novels discussed here that are set in the near past or present, Robinson's trilogy begins with many of the moderate facets of economization and their political and bureaucratic influence on scientific research. But then Frank Vanderwal, an NSF science administrator who has struggled with many of the same issues as Anne Quibler, comes to the conclusion that science has an obligation to disregard short-sighted and narrow-minded business and political interests: "The world is in big trouble and NSF is one of the few organizations on Earth that could actually help get it out of trouble" (Robinson 2005, 211). Science, Vanderwal maintains, "has to *insist on itself*" (325). Courageously, he takes action, demanding far-reaching legislative authority for the NSF and a makeover of the federal budget that shifts the emphasis from defense to research policy: if they are to halt the capitalist dynamics that have had such disastrous consequences for society, science must assume power.

In *Fifty Degrees Below* (2007) and *Sixty Days and Counting* (2007), Robinson continues his apocalyptic story of a US society driven by business interests and going to hell. The NSF manages to forge a coalition between crucial industries, regulatory agencies, and the four biggest international reinsurance companies—which, as insurers of insurance companies against major risks, are especially interested in avoiding the costs of huge weather catastrophes. The charismatic congressman Phil Chase runs for president and convinces the public that climate change is not only a matter of life and death for humanity but also "an incredible opportunity for new industries" (Robinson 2005, 535–36). Charlie is incredulous and asks his boss if this makes "saving the world a capitalist project . . . with a great six-month rate of return" (Robinson 2007, 373). Taking capitalism as a given, the president's answer is simple: "It's sustainability that works as the next big investment opportunity. . . . We the people can aim capitalism in any direction we want . . . , creating the new regions of maximum profitability" (378–79). Whereas *Solar* portrays a society incapable of caring for the common good and, rather cynically, leaves us to hope that the greed and chance exploitation inherent in capitalism will somehow breed the necessary innovations, Robinson creates a scenario in which capitalism is harnessed for the common good. In the hopeful utopian turnaround of the final volume of Robinson's trilogy, it is easy to get rid of capitalism's economizing pressure on science and on society at large: "We the people" just have to stand united and force business interests to adhere to our preferences, which are in accordance with the agenda of responsible science. Even if we believe this age-old ideology of a free-market society in which we as consumers are the ultimate decision-makers about products and methods of production, it is difficult to ignore the well-known fact that consumers often prefer ecologically harmful products simply because they are less expensive.

Still, Robinson draws an idealistic picture of science as it *ought* to be, that is, "an integral part of an ethical and spiritual—rather than a purely instrumental—solution to environmental crisis . . . : Throughout the trilogy, scientific procedures—collecting data, testing hypotheses, and rewarding successful pilot projects—offer a utopian model of the ways in which politics should work" (Markley 2012, 11). This kind of "science that is to come" (15) will fight back against economization and turn out to be stronger. It will not only banish the pressures of economization from the "republic of science" (Polanyi 1962) but also overcome the evil forces of capitalism in society at large. Science as the rescuer of modern society from capitalism: this is truly an original story—but probably too good to be true! In the end Robinson offers a utopian silver lining on the horizon of his realistic appraisal of polytonal societal interest and power constellations. His trilogy provides a radical alternative to both the moderate and the extreme versions of the economization narrative. His nuanced portrayal of science's societal entanglements offers no clear-cut utopian recipe for the therapy of economization but leaves room for contradiction and openness without giving up all hope for a collective solution.

Taken together, these science novels not only dramatize and play out the contemporary dynamics of economization but also provide a commentary that ranges from cynical to idealistic. The speculative novels go so far as to offer what Tom Moylan calls critical utopias and dystopias that allow us to imagine various futures as "recognizable and dynamic alternatives" (1986, 11). As works of art, the novels are able to go further than sociological studies or journalistic accounts in the direction of what Robinson, adopting a term coined by Charles Sanders Peirce, calls "projective realism" (2010, 215). As I have shown, with their "scenario-building and talking about various futures that might come to pass" (Heise 2016, 30), novels can articulate dystopian warnings as well as utopian hopes and encouragements. Both might be needed in a society that seems to have difficulties finding a way out of a future—a future we are already entering—of deep economization.

Notes

1. This novel is available only in German; translations of quoted segments are by volume editor Susan M. Gaines.

2. For a general discussion, see Schimank and Volkmann (2017, 75–95). On the implementation of NPM in western European university systems, see de Boer, Enders, and Schimank (2007).

3. On the principal-agent theory in management studies, see Ebers and Gotsch 1993.

4. This brings to mind Hannah Arendt's distinction between "*vita contemplativa*" and "*vita activa*," with the latter displacing the former as the signum of modernity ([1958] 1998).

5. This is the first novel in the *MaddAddam* trilogy, which generally explores the disastrous effects of the combined "forces of free-market capitalism and biotechnology" (Narkunas 2015, 2). On humanity and ecology, see also DeFalco 2017.

6. For a detailed discussion of the subgenres of utopian writing, see Moylan 2000.

7. For a detailed discussion of the novel's perceived plausibility and Atwood's own understanding of her utopian writing, see chapter 5.

References

Arendt, Hannah. (1958) 1998. *The Human Condition*. Chicago: University of Chicago Press.

Atwood, Margaret. (2004) 2009. *Oryx and Crake*. London: Virago.

———. 2011. *In Other Worlds: SF and the Human Imagination*. New York: Anchor Books.

Bröckling, Ulrich. (2006) 2016. *The Entrepreneurial Self: Fabricating a New Kind of Subject*. Translated by Steven Black. London: Sage.

Clausen, Lars, and Wolf R. Dombrowsky. 1984. "Warnpraxis und Warnlogik." *Zeitschrift für Soziologie* 13:293–307.

De Boer, Harry, Jürgen Enders, and Uwe Schimank. 2007. "On the Way Towards New Public Management? The Governance of University Systems in England, the Netherlands, Austria, and Germany." In *New Forms of Governance in Research Organizations: Disciplinary Approaches, Interfaces and Integration*, edited by Dorothea Jansen, 137–52. Dordrecht: Springer.

DeFalco, Amelia. 2017. "MaddAddam, Biocapitalism, and Affective Things." *Contemporary Women's Writing* 11 (3): 432–51.

Ebers, Mark, and Wilfried Gotsch. 1993. "Institutionenökonomische Theorien der Organisation." In *Organisationstheorien*, edited by Albrecht Kieser, 193–242. Stuttgart: Kohlhammer.

Gaines, Susan M. 2001. *Carbon Dreams*. Berkeley, CA: Creative Arts Books.

Goldschmidt, Pippa. 2013. *The Falling Sky*. Glasgow: Freight Books.

Goodman, Allegra. (2006) 2010. *Intuition*. London: Atlantic Books.

Heise, Ursula K. "Kim Stanley Robinson. 2016: Realism, Modernism, and the Future. An Interview with Kim Stanley Robinson." *ASAP Journal* 1 (1): 17–33.

Johns-Putra, Adeline. 2010. "Ecocriticism, Genre, and Climate Change: Reading the Utopian Vision of Kim Stanley Robinson's Science in the Capital Trilogy," *English Studies* 91:744–60.

Jones, Mark Peter. 2009. "Entrepreneurial Science: The Rules of the Game." *Social Studies of Science* 39:821–51.

Kegel, Bernhard. (2012) 2013. *Ein tiefer Fall*. Frankfurt am Main, DE: Fischer Taschenbuch.

Mandeville, Bernard. (1714) 1924. *The Fable of the Bees: or, Private Vices, Public Benefits*. Oxford: Clarendon Press.

Markley, Robert. 2012. "'How to Go Forward': Catastrophe and Comedy in Kim Stanley Robinson's Science in the Capital Trilogy." *Configurations* 20 (1–2): 7–27.

McEwan, Ian. (2010) 2011. *Solar*. London: Vintage.

Moylan, Tom. 1986. *Demand the Impossible: Science Fiction and the Utopian Imagination*. London: Methuen.

———. 2000. *Scraps of the Untainted Sky: Science Fiction, Utopia, Dystopia*. Boulder, CO: Westview-Perseus Press.

Mudge, Stephanie Lee. 2008. "What Is Neo-Liberalism?" *Socio-Economic Review* 6 (4): 703–31.

Narkunas, J. Paul. 2015. "Between Words, Numbers, and Things: Transgenics and Other Objects of Life in Margaret Atwood's *MaddAddams*." *Critique* 56 (1): 1–25.

Patchett, Ann (2011) 2012. *State of Wonder*. New York: HarperCollins.

Peter, Lothar. 2010. "Der Homo academicus." In *Diven, Hacker, Spekulanten: Sozialfiguren der Gegenwart*, edited by Stefan Moebius and Markus Schroer, 206–18. Frankfurt am Main: Suhrkamp.

Phillips, Dana. 2017. "Collapse, Resilience, Stability and Sustainability in Margaret Atwood's MaddAddam Trilogy." In *Literature and Sustainability: Concept, Text and Culture*, edited by Adeline Johns-Putra, John Parham, and Louise Squire, 139–58. Manchester, UK: Manchester University Press.

Polanyi, Michael. 1962. "The Republic of Science: Its Political and Economic Theory." *Minerva* 1:54–73.

Powers, Richard. (2009) 2010. *Generosity*. New York: Picador.

Robinson, Kim Stanley. (2004) 2005. *Forty Signs of Rain*. New York: Bantam Spectra.

———. (2005) 2007. *Fifty Degrees Below*. New York: Bantam Spectra.

———. 2007. *Sixty Days and Counting*. New York: Bantam Spectra.

———. 2010. "Science, Justice, Science Fiction: A Conversation with Kim Stanley Robinson." *Polygraph* 22:201–17.

Robinson, Kim Stanley, and Helena Feder. 2018. "The Realism of Our Time. Interview with Kim Stanley Robinson." *Radical Philosophy*, ser. 2 (201): 87–98.

Rohn, Jennifer L. 2010a. *The Honest Look*. Cold Spring Harbor, NY: Cold Spring Harbor Laboratory Press.

———. 2010b. "Science: It Beats Living in Caves." *Guardian*, October 4, 2010. https://www.theguardian.com/science/the-lay-scientist/2010/oct/03/science-funding-crisis.

Schimank, Uwe. 2007. "Market Unbound—and Everything Went Well . . . ?" In *Looking Back to Look Forward—Analyses of Higher Education After the Turn of the Millennium*, edited by Barbara M. Kehm, 61–71. Kassel, DE: INCHER-Kassel.

———. 2008. "Ökonomisierung der Hochschulen—eine Makro-Meso-Mikro-Perspektive." In *Die Natur der Gesellschaft: Verhandlungen des 33. Kongresses der Deutschen Gesellschaft für Soziologie in Kassel*, edited by Karl-Siegberg Rehberg, 622–35. Frankfurt am Main: Campus.

———. 2015. "Modernity as a Functionally Differentiated Capitalist Society: A General Theoretical Model." *European Journal of Social Theory* 18 (4): 413–30.

Schimank, Uwe, and Ute Volkmann. 2008. "Ökonomisierung der Gesellschaft." In *Handbuch der Wirtschaftssoziologie*, edited by Andrea Maurer, 382–93. Wiesbaden, DE: VS.

———. 2012. "Economizing and Marketization in a Functionally Differentiated Capitalist Society—A Theoretical Conceptualization." In *The Marketization of Society: Economizing the Non-Economic*, edited by Uwe Schimank and Ute Volkmann, 37–63. Bremen: Forschungsverbund "Welfare Societies."

———. 2017. *Das Regime der Konkurrenz: Gesellschaftliche Ökonomisierungsdynamiken heute*. Weinheim, DE: Beltz Juventa.

Sennett, Richard. 1998. *The Corrosion of Character: The Personal Consequences of Work in the New Capitalism*. New York: Norton.

Slaughter, Sheila, and Larry L. Leslie. 1997. *Academic Capitalism: Politics, Policies and the Entrepreneurial University*. Baltimore: Johns Hopkins University Press.

Ziman, John. 2000. *Real Science: What It Is, and What It Means*. Cambridge, UK: Cambridge University Press.

Zipp, Yvonne. 2009. "Generosity: An Enhancement." *Christian Science Monitor*, October 23, 2009. http://www.csmonitor.com/layout/set/print/Books/Book-Reviews/2009/1023/generosity-an-enhancement.

Part 3
Cause and Effect?
Science and Its Societal Outcomes

8.
The Science Fiction of Technological Modernity
Images of Science in Recent Science Fiction

Sherryl Vint

As the name implies, science fiction (SF) is a genre that engages with science, although precisely what "science" means in this context has been a topic of considerable debate. The influential pulp magazine editor Hugo Gernsback named the genre in the 1920s, but much of the fiction he called SF—and much of what is still published under this label—might be better understood as futuristic or surrealistic rather than scientific. Gernsback did not invent the genre but coined a term that united several kinds of speculative writing—future war stories, scientific romances such as those by H. G. Wells, extrapolations from science such as works by Jules Verne, and utopian fables—that had been in circulation since at least the mid-nineteenth century and were subsequently understood as part of the same genre.[1] SF is perhaps best described as a literature that responds to how science and technology change human culture. In this chapter, I review how the historical relationship between science and SF has changed, providing analyses from three of the genre's most prevalent twenty-first-century preoccupations: artificial intelligence, genomics, and climate change.

Science and Science Fiction in Historical Perspective

Gernsback promoted *Amazing Stories* as a "new sort of magazine" that collected stories that were "interwoven with a scientific thread" and recognized the "entirely new world" produced by science and technology (1926, 3). "Our entire mode of living has changed with the present progress," he opined, "and it is little wonder, therefore, that many fantastic situations—impossible 100 years ago—are brought about today" (3). His editorials—often prefaced with "Extravagant Fiction Today . . . Cold Fact Tomorrow"—conveyed a sense of excitement about the new world that science was making possible. He touted a pedagogical role for SF, which he claimed would "supply knowledge that we might not otherwise obtain" and do so "in a very palatable form . . . without once making us aware that we are being taught" (3).

Although extrapolating about the future remains central to SF, the emphasis on science was never as essential as Gernsback proclaimed. Writers repeatedly rejected the idea that the genre had only a narrow and instrumental role of "science education," even if they agreed that artistic responses to ways that science was reshaping society could also convey scientific literacy. With the ascent of influential editor John W. Campbell at rival magazine *Astounding Science Fiction* in 1937, SF writers became more concerned with writing style. Although there were and remain examples of weak prose in SF—as in mainstream publishing—the primary characteristics that distinguished SF from literary fiction at the time were venue and audience. SF attracted readers educated for emerging scientific careers and interested in learning more about science and technology, while mainstream fiction remained the province of those with a liberal humanist education. Mainstream fiction continued to enjoy more prestige than did SF, but the humanities were rapidly losing ground to the sciences in academic and social domains. Thus, while C. P. Snow's "two cultures" divide (see chapter 1) prevailed for aficionados of mainstream fiction, the SF community considered science a worthy topic for literature.

During the 1950s and into the 1960s, several publishers developed SF imprints, and novels supplanted short fiction as the genre's dominant form. Writers of the 1950s responded to contemporary social crises, especially the threat of nuclear war, but they also responded to (and inspired) the space race, creating optimistic visions of a space-faring and harmonious future. SF increasingly became a genre of extrapolation beyond the scientific. Robert Heinlein coined the term "speculative fiction" in an essay first published in 1947, noting that one could either "write about people, or write about gadgets" (2011, 221) but insisting that any extrapolation from science was also about producing "a new framework for human action" (224).[2] The genre became a tool for imaginative extrapolation that ranged from dystopian fables warning of the consequences of current trends, such as George Orwell's

Nineteen Eighty-Four (1949); to feminist thought experiments envisioning alternate worlds in which women had not been deformed by misogyny, such as Joanna Russ's *The Female Man* (1975); and indictments of colonial and capitalist ideologies, such as the ironic deflations of Space Age techno-optimism in J. G. Ballard's *Vermillion Sands* (1971).

Although this terminology is fading, early critics sometimes distinguished between "hard" and "soft" science fiction: the former was used starting in the late 1950s to describe fiction extrapolating from the physical sciences, whereas the latter was coined in the mid-1970s to describe work drawing on the social sciences and biology. Fan and writer communities argued over these terms throughout the 1970s and into the 1980s—disagreements that were tinged with the politics of gender and race, as an old guard of white male writers sought to exclude work that was sociological rather than "rational" in its orientation. These categories were never central to shaping SF criticism—for example, cyberpunk is hard to define as either hard or soft. Although I will narrow my focus to *hard SF* in the rest of this chapter, the term itself has fuzzy boundaries and describes only a small subset of the field. Most fiction does not fall cleanly into one camp or another: these labels are applied retroactively and unevenly, and their relevance changes as the status of certain sciences also changes (for example, few would now doubt that biology is a "real" science). For most writers, both SF and mainstream, the point is that changes in science and technology will change the human social world, and so the hard and the soft are coproduced.

SF and mainstream literature began to move toward one another in the 1980s, in both the literature and the critical responses to it; this shift was informed by the self-reflexive stance of postmodernist writing and by a poststructuralist decentering of the subject that produced a generation of literary scholars for whom SF captured contemporary preoccupations better than realism did. Larry McCaffery's foundational *Storming the Reality Studio* (1992) vitalized academic interest in SF, a genre that exhibited the same fragmented subjectivity and unstable ontology central to contemporary literary theory. Such scholars and the cyberpunk fiction they embraced—set among the ruins of deregulated capitalism and in near-future worlds in which IT fuses with its users—changed SF, offering a vision in which technology got better but humanity (or its circumstances) got worse.

Science fiction today is a diverse genre that increasingly overlaps with mainstream fiction. There are, and have always been, SF writers who are also scientists—Joan Slonczewski and Peter Watts are important contemporary examples—but such writers have never been numerically dominant. Indeed, an SF writer is more like a historian, sociologist, or anthropologist of science—sufficiently educated about science to study its culture and draw conclusions from it but still external to its practice. The contemporary stories classified as SF may be unabashedly optimistic or may be technophobic, and they may or may not engage the minutiae of scientific concepts or research practices, as is true of the realist novels discussed in this volume. Some writers offer scientifically plausible details for their extrapolations, whereas others simply explore what such innovations might mean for the social world. For example, Neal Stephenson's cyberpunk novel *Snow Crash* (1992) invents a virtual space called the Metaverse, which was carefully extrapolated from his own coding experience and was later an inspiration for coders of the online virtual world Second Life. William Gibson's far more influential *Neuromancer* (1984), however, popularized the word *cyberspace* and became a touchstone for a generation of computer enthusiasts, but it was written on a typewriter and contains no details regarding how its virtual world was coded.

With contemporary science and technology so much a part of daily experience, from smartphones to GMO foods to self-driving cars, it is no surprise that mainstream fiction now exhibits many of the themes and subjects that were once the sole province of SF. Writers who work in SF genre traditions, such as Jonathan Lethem, China Miéville, William Gibson, and Neal Stephenson, are increasingly embraced by the literary mainstream, while authors regarded as mainstream novelists, such as Charles Yu, Karen Tei Yamashita, Colson Whitehead, Margaret Atwood, and Cormac McCarthy, to name a few, turn their attention to future settings and speculative narratives.

SF imagines a wider range of possible settings for its stories—the future, alien planets, and distant galaxies—than have typically been embraced by mainstream fiction, and thus *worldbuilding* reflects a still-distinctive SF sensibility. The genre tends to be more focused on the world in which its stories take place—on that world's unfamiliar details, how it came to be, and how it changes—than on the emotions or psychology of its characters. This different focus means that SF may be unsatisfying to readers accustomed to canonical literary texts, with their emphasis on how characters change, but it makes the genre well suited to addressing systemic questions of social change. SF's capacity to focus such attention on how alternative worlds might come into being seems particularly necessary in a cultural moment in which human activity—often informed by science—has irrevocably changed the physical world. Scientists and scholars have started to refer to this period as the Anthropocene to reflect the impacts that such activities—CO_2 production, in particular—have had on Earth's geology and ecology. McKenzie Wark singles out SF as a genre capable of conceptualizing and responding to this reality, arguing that work by ecologically committed writers such as Kim Stanley Robinson is a "kind of realism of the possible" (2005, loc 205). Although often set in the future or some other estranged place, SF is fundamentally about the world contemporaneous to its publication, and its focus on worldbuilding allows it to reveal the mechanisms of social choice from which any social world is made.

The genre has changed in step with changing preoccupations in science. Early twentieth-century SF envisioned new communication technologies, extrapolating from the rise of radio and the telephone; authors of the 1940s and 1950s (known as the Golden Age of SF) extrapolated technologies of the Cold War—space exploration and the nuclear bomb—into imagined futures; in the 1980s SF was obsessed with computers and emerging network culture; and in the 1990s the obsession shifted to genetic engineering. The recent texts I focus on here similarly take as their starting point prominent areas of recent research—artificial intelligence, genomics, and climate change.[3]

Case Study 1: Artificial Intelligence and Robotics

One of the most active areas of current research is the quest to create or simulate artificial intelligence. Whereas inquiry once focused on the perfection of logic and fast calculation (e.g., IBM's chess-playing Deep Blue), researchers are now more interested in creating entities that interact conversationally with humans, responding to social cues and putting people at ease. We see the results of this kind of research in the (often female) personalities created for interactive systems designed to help us with daily tasks or encourage particular patterns of consumption, such as Apple's Siri, Microsoft's Cortana, and Amazon's Alexa. Jia Jia, a humanoid robot developed at the University of Science and Technology in China, for example, has been programmed to use microexpressions and make eye contact as she speaks, and researchers plan to increase her range of emotional expression in future work. Jia Jia is clearly designed to be more than a source of labor: she combines the interactivity of systems such as Siri with a body that resembles an attractive and demure young woman. What does it mean that these interactive AI assistants are increasingly imagined as female, especially given that an earlier generation of AIs used in weapons systems were imagined as male? How might humans change if their primary relationships were with such technologies? What would happen if entities such as Jia Jia begin to articulate their own desires, goals, and subjectivities?

Two popular SF films have taken on such questions recently. *Ex Machina* (Garland 2014) asks what it means for its AI protagonist to be out in the world and how we can assess her as an ethical being, given that the human who made her treated her as a thing. In *Her*, the AI protagonist, Samantha, seeks intellectual pleasures and experiences beyond human comprehension, but the film's focus is on the human protagonists who are left behind by an apotheosis that sees such AIs evolve to inhabit a space beyond the physical world (Jonze 2013). We might say that *Her* is more interested in the human experience of loving an AI, whereas *Ex Machina* is more interested in the world as changed by the invention of an AI. Although it might thus be tempting to see *Her* as a mainstream narrative about AI and to see *Ex Machina* as SF, the films actually demonstrate how difficult it is to differentiate SF and mainstream fiction about science in the twenty-first century: what they share is more central to their themes and modes than that which might differentiate them.

We see such a convergence in Rachel Swirsky's story "Eros, Philia, Agape" (2009). The story opens with a couple breaking up. "Lucian had always loved beauty," we read, as he packs his things, "beautiful scenes, beautiful tastes, beautiful melodies. He especially loved beautiful objects because he could hold them in his hands and transform the abstraction of beauty into something tangible" (2013, 85). Gradually, we learn that Lucian is a robot in a relationship with a human woman and an adopted child: the story is about what it means to transform the abstract words of love into something tangible and how—or if—such love might be possible for a humanoid AI. The story continually asks us to think about what constitutes love, what we can love, and what can love us. Adriana purchases Lucian in response to her sense of isolation. Her closest relationship was with a designer pet bird named Fuoco—a gift from her recently deceased father who, it is hinted, sexually abused her. Fuoco, whose DNA splices make him especially beautiful, "loved Adriana with frantic, obsessive jealousy" (87), and although systems in the house mimic Adriana's scent and voice for Fuoco when she is away, the bird can tell human from machine and is never fooled.

Adriana loves Fuoco, but he is a possession, not an equal, and once she begins to sleep with Lucian, the bird is increasingly confined to his cage to prevent his attacks of jealousy. Fuoco eventually attacks the baby Lucian and Adriana adopt, and the couple take the bird to be euthanized. Lucian recognizes the last "poignant, regretful look" Adriana gives the bird and is troubled by the realization that the feeling of loving someone or something is so similar to the feeling of possessing someone or something: "He'd never before realized how slender the difference was between her love for him and her love for Fuoco. He'd never before realized how slender the difference was between his love for her and his love for an unfolding rose" (105). This realization prompts Lucian to leave and to throw all of his beautiful possessions into the ocean. He reflects that "ownership is a relationship" and until he can work through what this means, he cannot "possess or be possessed" (92).

Lucian's neural pathways are designed to mimic the development of human neuronal connections and yet retain the plasticity of youth throughout his life. Thus, Lucian takes on his personality in response to subtle cues of what Adriana does or does not desire. Within their intimacy, Adriana comes to regard Lucian as a person, not a thing, although she also recognizes he is alien in the sense that he is not organic and mortal. When they decide to wed, a choice that scandalizes her family, she has Lucian's manufacturer develop "a procedure that would allow Lucian to have conscious control of his brain plasticity." This is her gift to him as they say their vows: "You are your own person now. You always have been, of course, but now you have full agency too" (99). This gift of love is what ultimately divides them, however. In his goodbye letter, Lucian says, "You gave me life as a human, but I am not a human. You shaped my thoughts with human words, but human words were created for human brains. I need to discover the shape of the thoughts that are my own. I need to know what I am" (108). He also expresses hope that he might one day return to Adriana and Rose, to love outside of or beyond the complicated entanglement of ownership.

Both Lucian and Adriana emerge as complex and sympathetic characters. We learn and understand more of Adriana's experience than of Lucian's, but this difference is tied to the story's concern with the subjectivity of nonhuman agents such as Lucian. As the story of Lucian's choice makes clear, he is an entity who has thoughts and feelings and is someone with whom a human might be in relation, yet his thoughts are not human or even organic. Thus, the story creates a space in which we are led to understand that an entity such as Lucian is a complex subject, yet we are not given direct access to his subjectivity, as we are with Adriana, because to fully narrate it would be to narrate it *as human consciousness*. The story is after something both more subtle and more profound, the presentation of nonhuman sentience that simultaneously acknowledges its reality and concedes that a human can never fully understand it. Lucian's silence thus speaks volumes, not only to Adriana in the story but also beyond: it prompts readers to think through what it might mean to share our world with AIs that are as complex as we are and yet fundamentally different in their mentation, with forms of thought not created by and for a human brain. It is a deeply affective story that prompts readers—through their identification with Adriana—to experience rather than just contemplate the emotional dilemmas that relationships with AI might entail.

Like Swirsky's story, Ken Liu's "The Algorithms for Love" extrapolates from ongoing AI and robotics research, but here the focus is on what it might imply about human life if love can be simulated by nonsentient machines ([2004] 2013). Told in first person by Elena, a robotics researcher, the story opens with her in despair, unable to connect to her husband, Brad, and contemplating suicide. When he seeks connection, she dutifully recites "I love you too," and she notes that for him this was enough to signify that "the routines are back in place, that he is talking to the same woman he has known all these years." But instead of being comforted, she comes to this conclusion: "It's an algorithm for love. I want to scream" (302). Like Swirsky's story, this one begins in medias res with an emotional disruption and then takes us back in time to explain it. Elena works for Not Just Your Average Toy Company, which makes interactive dolls. Brad is the CEO, and they meet when she is doing promotion for her first doll, Clever Laura™, which appears to understand questions addressed to it, makes eye contact when it speaks to people, and learns new words through interaction. As Elena explains in multiple interviews, Laura is not actually sapient: it is simply a matter of careful coding and rigorous if/then algorithms that enable Laura to respond to multiple situations seemingly spontaneously.

Elena and Brad marry, and Elena's research progresses, with the creation of ever-more-complex dolls. Eventually she and Brad fall into the predictable rhythms of a shared life. They have a baby, but she dies as an infant. To process her grief, Elena designs and markets a doll for grieving mothers and names it Aimee, after her lost baby. Her next research project, Tara, resembles a five-year-old child and is so successful at imitating human emotion and behavior that Brad at first thinks it is a real child. This success plants the seeds of Elena's depression. Understanding neural nets as well as she does, she can never be surprised by anything the doll does: "I could predict everything she would say before she said it. I'd coded everything in her, after all, and I knew exactly how her neural nets changed with each interaction" (309). She realizes that her fellow humans are equally predictable, that all her interactions—including saying "I love you" to Brad—are just the iterations of algorithms that run on brain cells instead of circuitry. Elena's once comforting and familiar routines are transformed into a torturous revelation that human consciousness is no more meaningful or transcendent than the automated responses of her dolls. The story ends on a sinister note: as Brad once again tells Elena he loves her, all she can feel is the gulf between them, "so wide that I can't feel his pain. Nor he mine" (312). Nonetheless, she tells us, "My algorithms are still running. I scan for the right thing to say. 'I love you.'" Brad does not reply, but Clever Laura responds by rote with "I love you too" (313).

Like Swirsky, Liu asks what developments in AI and robotics research imply about taken-for-granted ideas in human culture. Can we still think of love in the same way if we know how human neurons work and how they can be simulated? The world Liu builds is not that different from the quotidian one in which the reader lives, but the story puts some of our ideas about this world into an estranged perspective, one that emerges not only from ongoing AI research but also from concurrent research in cognition and brain mapping. It shows how our brain chemistry is at odds with philosophical concepts we have inherited from an era that emphasized agency, choice, and conscious decision-making as central to what it means to be human.

Swirsky's story asks us to think about what it might mean to love and to be loved by intelligent machines. Liu's story asks us to think about what it might mean for human relationships if research in brain function belies our long-standing cultural assumptions about how humans operate. The stories do not privilege scientific over humanistic concepts but rather suggest the importance of putting them in dialogue—that is, they function as science fiction.

One of the most prolific topics in SF since the 1990s has been the implications of the discovery and mapping of the human genome and, in particular, of genetic engineering. Such topics were explored in SF long before segments of microbial DNA were first demonstrated in 2012 to be a useful tool for genome editing. Even before the human genome was fully mapped, and long before the IVF industry took off, Nancy Kress's Beggars trilogy—*Beggars in Spain* (1993), *Beggars and Choosers* (1994), and *Beggar's Ride* (1996)—examined the consequences of a future in which the privileged can engineer even more advantage into their offspring. Kress imagines a world in which the wealthy can engineer their children so as not to need sleep. This additional waking time can be devoted to education and development, and it initiates a decisive split between regular humans and the sleepless, resulting in an unbridgeable class gap. It is not merely that the sleepless can outperform regular humans; they also use their intellectual advantages to create technology that makes the labor and other contributions of the baseline humans obsolete. The central question the trilogy asks is what, if any, social bond of obligation ties together the genetically enhanced and unenhanced populations, a question that is relevant for class-based societies in general.

Gwyneth Jones's *Life* makes this dialectic between science and the social especially clear (2004). The novel follows the experiences of genomics researcher Anna Senoz, who discovers Transferred Y, an ongoing mutation in the human genome wherein segments of DNA have been exchanged between X and Y chromosomes. This transposition[4] presages a future in which they become mirrored pairs, like most paired chromosomes (human Y chromosomes are much shorter than X chromosomes). Yet the X and Y chromosome are not just like any other pair, of course, since the distinction between XX pairs and XY pairs marks not just the difference between female and male individuals but also the "reality" of presumed gender difference that has long been central to human culture. This is precisely Jones's point, and Anna's research is evaluated based on the ideological panic it creates about the implied death of "the male" rather than on the merits of the data she offers to support her thesis of Transferred Y. The hysteria with which the publication of Anna's results on Transferred Y is greeted leads one newspaper editor to write, "Already the social boundaries of gender have become thoroughly uncertain, and we see the repercussions everywhere. So much of our philosophy, of our

Cause and Effect?

humanity itself, rests on this most vital opposition. I seriously wonder if we can be human without it" (334). Notably, as we see later in the novel, the social elements of so-called masculine and feminine tendencies persist and are unrelated to chromosomal gender.

Anna strives to separate science from daily political struggles; she wants to conduct her personal life on the basis of abstract reason alone, ignoring all the messy human desires, instincts, insecurities, and fears that shape so much of what we do. In contrast, her activist friend Ramone insists that "the most significant thing in your entire social and cultural life is your assigned gender" (24) and sees in Anna's research a chance to eliminate the second-class status of women. Anna's own career is thwarted by institutional sexism and the psychological consequences of being raped by a fellow graduate student, yet it is her own internalized feelings of guilt and shame that limit her prospects as much as the predatory attitude of male colleagues. She hopes that she and her husband have found an accommodation beyond the limitations of dominant gender roles but finds nonetheless that he is having an affair with a more traditionally feminine woman; rational beliefs cannot explain all of life, and gender identities are not created—and cannot be banished—by science alone. As the novel makes clear, although Transferred Y might eliminate notions of science-based sexual difference, the category "woman" is really about the allocation of power in a world rooted in inequality: "This leftover we call the liberal world is irrelevant, the war zones are the shape of things to come, and the one thing you don't want to be in a war zone or an armed camp is any kind of woman" (362).

Although Anna's discovery of Transferred Y is speculative, the novel is set in a world not so different from our own. It shows how genetics and the social entwine in often counterintuitive ways: Anna's rival, and rapist, Charles, whose name means "the manly" (62), is deeply invested in patriarchal dominance and traditional gender identities, yet he is a male with Transferred Y, that is, two X chromosomes. Anna's husband, Spence, is a stay-at-home dad, characterized in ways we typically think of as feminine, yet his chromosomes remain XY. The novel exhibits a knowledge of genomics and includes many scenes with Anna at work—as a PhD student, in an IVF clinic, in her research lab—but its themes stress that gender is not merely a matter of biology. Jones, a well-established SF writer, explores similar themes in more overtly science-fictional works, such as the *Aleutian* trilogy (1991–97) about an invasion of hermaphroditic aliens. *Life*, with its focus on character over worldbuilding, shows how some SF writers are adopting narrative techniques from mainstream literature, even as mainstream literature increasingly takes its topics and themes from SF.

The implications of Anna's work lead us to think about the boundaries and future of the human species. The idea of the posthuman has long been a theme in SF, but it proliferated with the advent of genetic engineering and the actual possibility of modifying future generations of humanity.[5] Like *Life*, many of the novels concerned with these themes base their narratives on actual genomic research, although they are less concerned with the details and processes of the science than with the cultural implications of a biological change in the human or, increasingly, with the potential environmental necessity of engineering another kind of human embodiment. Originally, such tales of posthuman transformation in SF were linked to space travel and imagined as a way that humanity might make itself viable in new environments. Bruce Sterling's *Schismatrix* (1989), for example, explored a future split between two groups of space-faring humans, one whose members use genetics to alter their embodiments (the shapers) and another whose members use technology (the mechanists). As risks of environmental collapse have become more pressing, however, posthuman tales have portrayed the future earth as a place where humans will need a new kind of embodiment to survive.

Nancy Kress's *Nothing Human* (2003) tells one such story, which is interwoven with other SF motifs of alien encounter and survival in a post-apocalyptic landscape. The novel begins in a world contemporaneous to its publication. Keith, a lawyer specializing in technology, explains his work to his niece, Lillie. He tells her that his cases inevitably involve weighing the relative benefits and costs of certain innovations—for example, genetically engineered soybeans will increase crop yields and the range of cultivable land types, but the inclusion of genes from other plant species may trigger allergies in some consumers. Can one apply a mathematical and utilitarian rubric to balance the few people the technology would kill against the many more it would save? Can one justify some deaths to improve life overall? As a lawyer, Keith must focus on assessing liability rather than asking such questions, but he acknowledges to Lillie that "new technologies always seem to cost lives at first" (loc 342–43), including technologies we now take for granted as worth the risk, such as air travel and heart transplants.

This opening section sets the stage for the more consequential technological innovations that come when an alien species called the Pribir arrive and seek to modify the human genome. The Pribir represent another long-standing SF motif: the superior alien species whose advanced technology will save humanity from the risks we have created for ourselves, often through our own technology. Kress's Pribir address the ecological crisis caused by human choices; they believe that changing political structures and values will not enable sufficient change in time, and thus humans must change their physical embodiment. Lillie and several other children prove to be the results of a secret Pribir intervention in IVF clinics: the children have been engineered such that, when they reach puberty, they develop, among other things, a chemical olfactory system that allows them to communicate with the Pribir, who then remove them to a spaceship. Much of the novel is taken up with discussions about the ethics of Pribir intervention into human morphology and behavior; some humans resist and others agree with the Pribir's plan, but the question of agency is complicated by the fact that they can use their chemical language to influence how humans think and feel.

When the engineered children reach their teens, the Pribir compel them to breed with one another, creating a race of modified humans better able to survive in the damaged earth environment. The Pribir eventually reveal that they are not aliens at all but a version of humanity many generations evolved beyond its current morphology. All Pribir technology is made of living tissue, including clothing and furnishings, and their detailed control of DNA means that they can easily offer cures for disease. Yet because they make changes to human behavior without seeking human consent, and especially because their interventions mean a changed human morphology in the future, the Pribir are regarded with suspicion.

The last section of the novel recounts the experiences of the impregnated teenagers after they have been returned to Earth. Due to the relativity effects of faster-than-light travel, only a few months have passed on the ship while forty years have passed on Earth. During this time, climate change and biological warfare have led to the apocalyptic collapse of civilization, but Lillie and the other abducted teenagers give birth to children who have extra genes in their chromosomes that enable them to adapt to "whatever we do to fuck up the planet" (Kress 2003, loc 3718). These children still appear human, but when one of them is lost in a dust storm, he survives by growing a hard shell that protects him from the elements and sending a kind of tap root deep into the soil that keeps him hydrated. An unmodified human out in the same storm dies. When this new generation attains puberty, the Pribir return and, shocked to find the ecological devastation worse than they had estimated, demand even more radical changes to the next generation, insisting it is the only way to enable survival on such a rapidly changing planet. Most humans recoil from the idea of giving birth to and nurturing a nonhuman generation, leading to extensive discussions of what constitutes "the human" and whether there is an ethical duty to preserve the human in a familiar configuration. The Pribir do not understand the humans' concerns, arguing, "How could they [the fetuses] not be human? They'll have mostly human genes" (loc 5079). The resulting offspring, however, are three feet tall, with leathery, almost reptilian skin, long snoutlike noses, and no mouths. They are disturbing to most remaining humans, but they are also able to thrive in the late-Anthropocene world.

Kress's novel takes the possible genetic engineering of the human much further than does Jones's novel, but it probes a similar philosophical question: How much can our species change and still remain human? Jones tells her story about a world that remains realistic, not that different from the world readers inhabit. Kress, in contrast, exemplifies the use of SF worldbuilding to depict not only a world whose ecology is radically changed by environmental destruction but also the radically different species we must become to survive in such a world. Both texts address themes that center on how we understand and explain what it means to be human, but the more overt SF motifs Kress uses—especially the "aliens" that prove to be humans changed beyond recognition—work to intensify the reader's sense of how thoroughly a changed environment might affect human futures. Both novels also reflect the capacity of SF to explore themes that exceed frameworks of individual emotional change since their narratives consider the future of the human species—either morphologically or in terms of social relationships—and not just the change in specific characters such as Jones's Anna or Kress's first generation of genetically changed children.

Case Study 3: Climate Change

The more-than-human time scales that SF embraces allow for a geologic perspective on the evolution of the earth and its life-forms. This time frame is similar to the one in Kress's and Jones's posthumanist exploration of the future of the species, but the thematic emphasis here is on the transformation of humans in interaction with earth systems rather than on the transformation of the humans per se. SF has been exploring this perspective since at least the late nineteenth century, when H. G. Wells's *The Time Machine* (1895) appeared. Ecological SF gained popularity in the 1970s, as environmental awareness was on the rise in the West. One of the most important contemporary SF writers, Kim Stanley Robinson, whose first novel was issued in the early 1980s, has focused on ecological themes over his entire body of work. He is joined by more recent authors such as Paolo Bacigalupi, whose near-future thriller *The Water Knife* (2015) draws on a history of water diversions for fundamentally unsustainable cities in the southwestern United States to provide a grim vision of a future in which crucial but dwindling water resources fall under corporate control.

The Water Knife tells three entwined stories held together by a conspiracy plot about a hidden water-rights document and the race among many factions to either claim the rights it specifies or destroy it to keep the status quo intact. Water rights are based on the seniority of documented ownership—the current configuration traces back to Californian control, but the hidden document reveals an earlier designation of indigenous ownership that would give Phoenix a prior claim. Since the seniority of rights determines who has first access, possessing this deed would enable a new ranking order and fundamentally shift local politics. Lucy is a journalist who holds high ideals about investigative journalism but fears that her reporting is simply a kind of "collapse porn" documenting the erosion of the liberal world (Bacigalupi 2015, 26). She meets and becomes involved with Angel, an orphaned Mexican street kid who has become a "water knife"—a corporate thug who manipulates water claims to privilege his employer, using violent means when legal ones fail. Maria is a climate refugee who accidentally gains access to the document denoting indigenous ownership while working as a prostitute. Although she has seen the suffering of those displaced by lack of water and might be expected to identify with the underdog city of Phoenix, she decides instead to sell the document to a corporate bidder in Las Vegas, who promises her escape from the hardships of this world by granting her access to its privileged compound.

In the climax, as all three physically struggle to possess the document, Maria shoots Lucy to prevent her from releasing it to the public; notably, the more mercenary Angel had willingly capitulated to Lucy rather than resort to even more violence to regain control of the document. All three are complex characters, and the novel takes pains to remind us that they are what their world has made them: "When people lost hope, they sometimes lost their humanity, too. Desperate people did desperate things, became avatars of unexpected tragedy" (156). The characters' ethical and emotional dilemmas drive the narrative, as in literary fiction, but the novel also fuses character and world in typical SF fashion: it foreshadows both the physical world to come if we continue to deplete water reserves and the kinds of people we might become in such a future world. Angel started out as a middle-class child, the son of a police officer, before his entire life was destroyed by gang violence and climate change. His world is like the Stanford prison experiment, in which his ethics emerge from his circumstances, as he himself observes: "You live in a nice house, you're one kind of person. You live in the barrio, you run with a gang. You go to prison, you think like a con. You join up with the guardies, you play soldier" (282).

Bacigalupi's future is split between the privilege of corporate-owned arcologies—gated communities with water recycling systems and air conditioning—and the world beyond, in which thousands of displaced migrants struggle daily with brutal violence to secure a single day's water ration. In the background, we are given glimpses of a new kind of even-more-innovative arcology being built by the Chinese, who offer water handouts to the poor, an image clearly meant to offer an alternative model to the collapsing American system of desperate struggle between a privileged few and an immiserated many. The novel articulates the need for more sustainable development by focusing on political and corporate structures and the history of water diversion that created them rather than on the science of climate change and its possible amelioration. The technology of the arcologies—built from sustainable materials shaped by 3-D printers, with walls that turn sunlight into electricity—is mere background here. Kim Stanley Robinson, however, combines a similar interest in how social organization can create barriers for change—or directly exploit negative conditions—with a more intensive focus on technologies that might help us to overcome the damage done by climate change and live in a way that halts or even reverses the Anthropocene.

For Robinson, these environmental concerns have always been linked to a socialist commitment to more equitable political and economic systems, and in his most celebrated work, the Mars trilogy (1993–97), they are linked to a detailed vision of how humans might terraform Mars to create a better society.[6] His Science in the Capital trilogy—*Forty Signs of Rain* (2004), *Fifty*

Degrees Below (2005), and *Sixty Days and Counting* (2007)—explores these ideas in the near future and most directly depicts the struggles scientists face in dealing with political intervention and funding agencies. It models technological solutions that he suggests might be tried in the present, such as using clean-energy pumps to divert ocean waters back toward the poles, where it might refreeze, to mitigate the rising sea levels caused by the erosion of polar ice caps.

Like *The Water Knife*, Robinson's *2312* (2012) shows how environmental destruction and inequalities generated by capitalism are entwined. It is set in a world that might have followed the one portrayed in the *Mars* trilogy, in which Earth fell into economic and ecological ruin while the socialist organization of governance on Mars led to enhanced ecological policies. Robinson's masterful worldbuilding showcases the distinctive capacity of SF to help us comprehend the Anthropocene. Such fiction can use devices such as faster-than-light travel or life-extension technologies to narrate change over many generations. In *2312*, Robinson has created protagonists who live two centuries or more, which allows the novel to portray change over an extended period from an individual's point of view. SF that focuses on periods of time beyond the normal human life-span—extending for hundreds or thousands of years by imagining AI characters, or extremely advanced medical technologies—can bring geological and human temporalities closer together, enabling a unique perspective on events such as climate change. This approach helps us to imagine our actions in the present as connected to a concrete future.

Robinson offers extensive commentary on the periods that have intervened between our present and the novel's present by interspersing the narrative chapters with sections called "Extracts" that provide technological detail of some sort. Some of these explain terraforming possibilities or the long-term effects on human physiology of living under reduced gravity; others provide information about social worldbuilding, such as discussion of interplanetary commerce. Extract 8 summarizes the work of fictional future historian Charlotte Shortback, including her analyses of the period from our present to the emergence of this new society:

> The Dithering: 2005 to 2060. From the end of the postmodern (Charlotte's date derived from the UN announcement of climate change) to the fall into crisis. These were wasted years. The Crisis: 2060 to 2130. Disappearance of Arctic summer ice,

irreversible permafrost melt and methane release, and unavoidable commitment to major sea rise. In these years all the bad trends converged in "perfect storm" fashion, leading to a rise in average global temperature of five K, and sea level rise of five meters—and as a result, in the 2120s, food shortages, mass riots, catastrophic death on all continents, and an immense spike in the extinction rate of other species. Early lunar bases, scientific stations on Mars. (2012, 246)

The narrative names 2312 as a crucial year of change for this new society—that is, three hundred years from our present (the novel's publication year), which is about three hundred years from the historical period in which theorists suggest the Anthropocene was set in motion by the Industrial Revolution. The fact that Robinson's characters are able to stop ecological collapse and restore biodiversity gives us hope that the damage of our last three hundred years can be ameliorated.

After "The Dithering" and "The Crisis" comes "The Turnaround," from 2130 to 2160, when strong AIs, self-replicating factories, the terraforming of Mars, fusion power, and synthetic biology enabled the human diasporic colonization of the solar system, which further enabled "The Accelerando" of 2160–2220. The Accelerando saw the perfection of human longevity technologies, the expansion of more equitable economic rules established for solar colonial trade, and the production of even more technological advances by the strong AIs. The "mutation of values" that enables technological projects to gain momentum is as important to these changes as are the technological innovations themselves (246). In some cases, Robinson describes these technological innovations and even provides detailed scenarios of how they might be accomplished with existing technology. But in others, he simply posits that there will be certain breakthroughs, such as human longevity or self-replicating factories, without offering a blueprint for how to achieve them. When it comes to social change, however, he offers a more precise outline of the steps from here to there, one in which science is among the most significant drivers.

The way the novel's protagonists participate in the consequential changes of 2312 encourages today's readers to think about enacting their own efforts to ameliorate and slow climate change. The narrator tells us, "Although the events right before and after the year 2312 were important and signaled changes latent in the situation at the time, nothing tipped decisively then; there was no portal they passed through saying, 'This is a new period, this is

Cause and Effect?

a new age.' Events set in train were mired and complex, and many took decades more to come to fruition" (551). The novel entwines two potentially pivotal moments: its future and the reader's present, encouraging the reader to think in a time scale beyond the duration of a human lifetime. "Out of this jumbled superimposition of different kinds of temporal models History does in fact emerge," we are told, as "a work of art, like any other work of art, but made by everyone together. And it doesn't stop. Things happen, events, accomplishments; wins and losses; Pyrrhic victories, rearguard actions; and though there can be crucial events, the plot does not end in a year like 2312, but rather several decades later, if that" (551).

The novel includes extensive technical information about how future humans terraform asteroids into various kinds of habitats, giving instructions for everything from how to make soil and control the spin of the asteroid to achieve the desired length of day to how to seed soil with the right mixture of bacteria so that it can later sustain more complex species. These passages are significant in multiple ways: they summarize knowledge from earth and genomic sciences and show how it might be used to redress extinction and other consequences of the Anthropocene, but they also convey the extent of the crisis we face in the present and future if we continue on our current course. For example, we learn that in this future, "19,340 terraria are known to exist in the solar system. Approximately 70 percent of these function as zoo worlds, either dedicated to sustaining an eco-region's suite of animals and plants, or else to creating new combinations of suites, called Ascensions[;] 92 percent of mammal species are now endangered or gone entirely from Earth and live mainly in their off-planet terraria space: the zoo, the inoculant" (211). Although Robinson imagines a terraformed solar system that can support human life in manufactured environments on different planets and moons, he also stresses the limits of this fantasy:[7] "The solar system is our one and only home. Even to reach the nearest star at our best speed would take a human lifetime or more. We say 'four light-years' and those words 'four' and 'years' fool us" (328). This section continues with a detailed explanation of what a "light-year" means and how long it would take to travel to another solar system, sequences that urge us to detach our thinking about space colonization from the sublime promises of Golden Age SF and recognize instead the fragility of Earth and our dependence on its ecosystems.

Robinson uses the time scale of SF and detailed information on terraforming to convey both a sense of love for the diversity of nature and a sense of custodial responsibility for it. The plot of *2312* is mainly focused on other things—the emergence of quantum computing AIs, a political conspiracy, a love story that ends in a marriage—and yet the novel both textually and literally conveys the process of worldbuilding. Near the end of the novel, a metafictional passage addressed to readers of the future observes that texts

> are a kind of time capsule, a speaking to one's descendants. Reading this text, you see back to an older time, when the tumult and disorder may be scarcely believable to you. You may be on the other side of a great divide, your life indefinitely long and headed for the stars. Not so we the living, thrashing around in our little solar system like bacteria filling a new rain puddle. . . . In many ways it's easier to talk to you, generous reader, unborn one. You might live for centuries, this text one tiny part of your education, a glimpse at how it used to be, a little insight into how your world got to be the way it is. Your author however remains stuck in the tail of the balkanization, desperate with hope for the beginning of whatever comes next. (550–51)

The narrative voice seems to collapse into Robinson's own here, lamenting the vicissitudes of the moment in which he finds himself in human history but nonetheless believing—and materializing through the power of his text—that this can be a middle rather than an end, that humanity can change to save itself and with it, the world. The passage also suggests the power of texts to remind us that others have survived through terrible periods while inspiring us to think of readers for whom our present will be history. Fredric Jameson argues that the function of SF is "not to give us 'images' of the future" but rather "to defamiliarize and restructure our experience of our own *present*" (1982, 151) so that we see it in a new way, with new possibilities. This is what Robinson achieves.

Conclusion

For much of the genre's life, fans and critics have argued strenuously over how to define SF and how to differentiate it from fantasy and from other speculative genres. The emergence of the term *hard SF* and its emphasis on scientific plausibility was related to such struggles and especially to a concern with segregating the rigor of SF from the ungrounded speculations of fantasy. Such concerns no longer drive critical discourse, however, and the more inclusive term *speculative fiction* is now often used synonymously with *science fiction*. In the early days of SF, fans emphasized the differences between SF and mainstream literature; they saw themselves as a forward-looking vanguard that recognized the importance of science, to which mainstream literary culture was blind. This division has long since softened, and the SF community regularly awards its most important prizes to works of fiction that the mainstream also claims, from Thomas Pynchon's *Gravity's Rainbow* (1973) to Margaret Atwood's *The Handmaid's Tale* (1989) to Emily St. John Mandel's *Station Eleven* (2014).

The SF genre's engagement with science is ultimately more about visions of a world changed by science, positively and negatively, than it is about the daily practice of science, although the degree of extrapolation and amount of technical detail included has always ranged widely. What is undeniable is that the border between SF and the mainstream has blurred substantially in the last thirty years, especially in the past fifteen, due in large part to shifts in mainstream literary culture. We inescapably live in a world saturated by science; technology now intimately inhabits our homes, our bodies, and our social exchanges. The topics long cherished by SF have become daily realities in most of the industrialized West, and the world is now linked by instantaneous communication, navigable within a day through commercial air travel, and ubiquitously mapped by GPS. Simply to write of the contemporary world, then, compels mainstream novelists to move into topics already charted by SF.

At the same time, the scholarly conversation about SF has shifted significantly. No longer obsessed with taxonomies and structural definitions, scholars have moved away from identifying SF as a set of specific images and icons and toward describing it as a mode of perception, a way of experiencing the world as contingent and open to question. Conceiving of SF as a mode of experiencing and thinking about reality captures the ubiquity of technology in twenty-first-century life and the hegemony of science in contemporary understandings of knowledge and value. The genre's long history of interrogating the kinds of ethical and political questions that now shape our quotidian experience make it an important vernacular theory for the twenty-first century.

Notes

1. There are many arguments about how to define SF and thus when it began. The name dates from the 1920s but was applied retroactively to works published earlier. I find most compelling Roger Luckhurst's argument that something we can reliably call "science fiction" emerged in the late nineteenth century. For a discussion of a number of conditions he deems necessary for SF to emerge, see Luckhurst (2005, 3–5).
2. Judith Merril (1968), another influential American author and editor of the 1950s and 1960s, used "speculative fiction" to promote politically engaged New Wave writing, expanding its meaning to the wide range of imaginative texts that reflect how the term is used today.
3. As Roxburgh and Clayton explore in chapter 1, recent mainstream fiction has, unsurprisingly, addressed these topics as well.
4. This is an extrapolation from contemporary research on transposons (segments of DNA that can change position within a genome), which were first discovered by the biologist Barbara McClintock in the 1950s but largely ignored for most of her career. Decades later, her results were duplicated by other researchers, and in 1983, she received the Nobel Prize in Physiology or Medicine. For an analysis of McClintock's life and work from the perspective of feminist science studies, see Keller (1983).
5. The posthuman, like other SF themes, is increasingly at the center of humanities scholarship. For useful overviews of the approaches that the humanities have taken to this topic, see Grusin 2015 and Braidotti 2013.
6. Terraforming is the process of changing a planet so that it can support human occupation, for example, by creating an atmosphere, adding nitrogen-fixing bacteria to the soil, and so on.
7. His more recent novel, *Aurora* (2016), refuses even this consolation and suggests it is a dangerous fantasy. The only future humans have, it insists, is one on Earth, if we save it.

References

Bacigalupi, Paolo. 2015. *The Water Knife*. New York: Alfred A. Knopf.

Braidotti, Rosi. 2013. *The Posthuman*. London: Polity.

Garland, Alex, dir. 2014. *Ex Machina*. Film4, DNA Films. Universal City, CA: Universal Pictures International.

Gernsback, Hugo. 1926. "A New Sort of Magazine." *Amazing Stories* 1 (1): 3. https://en.wikisource.org/wiki/Page:Amazing_Stories_Volume_01_Number_01.djvu/5.

Gibson, William. 1984. *Neuromancer*. New York: Ace.

Grusin, Richard, ed. 2015. *The Nonhuman Turn*. Minneapolis: University of Minnesota Press.

Heinlein, Robert A. 2011. "On the Writing of Speculative Fiction." In *The Nonfiction of Robert Heinlein*, 1:221–28. Houston: Virginia Edition.

Jameson, Fredric. 1982. "Progress Versus Utopia; or, Can We Imagine the Future?" *Science Fiction Studies* 9 (2): 147–58.

Jones, Gwyneth. *Life*. 2004. Seattle: Aqueduct Press.

Jonze, Spike, dir. 2013. *Her*. Los Angeles: Annapurna Pictures.

Keller, Evelyn Fox. 1983. *A Feeling for the Organism: The Life and Work of Barbara McClintock*. New York: W. H. Freeman.

Kress, Nancy. 1993. *Beggars in Spain*. New York: Avon Books.

———. 1994. *Beggars and Choosers*. New York: TOR.
———. 1996. *Beggars Ride*. New York: TOR.
———. 2003. *Nothing Human*. Urbana, IL: Golden Gryphon Press. Kindle.
Liu, Ken. (2004) 2013. "The Algorithms for Love." In *Twenty-First Century Science Fiction*, edited by David Hartwell and Patrick Nielsen Hayden, 301–13. New York: TOR. http://kenliu.name/stories/algorithms.
Luckhurst, Roger. 2005. *Science Fiction*. London: Polity.
McCaffery, Larry. 1992. *Storming the Reality Studio: A Casebook of Cyberpunk and Postmodern Fiction*. Durham, NC: Duke University Press.
Merril, Judith. 1968. *England Swings SF: Stories of Speculative Fiction*. New York: Ace.
Robinson, Kim Stanley. 1993. *Red Mars (Mars Trilogy)*. New York: Bantam Spectra.
———. 1994. *Green Mars (Mars Trilogy)*. New York: Bantam Spectra.
———. 1996. *Blue Mars (Mars Trilogy)*. New York: Bantam Spectra.
———. 2004. *Forty Signs of Rain*. New York: Bantam Spectra.
———. 2005. *Fifty Degrees Below*. New York: Bantam Spectra.
———. 2007. *Sixty Days and Counting*. New York: Bantam Spectra.
———. 2012. *2312*. New York: Orbit.
———. 2015. *Aurora*. New York: Orbit.
Stephenson, Neal. 1992. *Snow Crash*. New York: Spectra.
Sterling, Bruce. 1989. *Schismatrix*. New York: Ace.
Swirsky, Rachel. 2013. "Eros, Philia, Agape." In *Twenty-First Century Science Fiction*, edited by David Hartwell and Patrick Nielsen Hayden, 85–109. New York: TOR. http://www.tor.com/2009/03/03/eros-philia-agape.
Wark, McKenzie. 2015. *Molecular Red: Theory for the Anthropocene*. London: Verso. Kindle.

9.

Unruly Creatures, Obstinate Things
Bio-Objects and Scientific Knowledge Production in Contemporary Science Fiction

Karin Hoepker
and Antje Kley

In Frank Schätzing's *The Swarm* (2006), humanity is threatened with extinction by an unknown swarm intelligence. When Norwegian biologist Sigur Johanson, one of the novel's key protagonists, is called to give expert testimony before an international task force of military personnel, politicians, and scientists, he says the following: "You know the classic lines you get in sci-fi? *Whatever it is, it's coming our way,* or *Get me the President on the line*? Well, there's always the one about the enemy being superior, though by the end of the story you mostly feel cheated. This time you won't" (755). This metafictional intertextual reference alludes to scenarios that began to appear in American science fiction (SF) in the post–World War II years and have become entrenched in popular culture. In these scenarios, military and political leaders consult a scientist expert about a global threat from an unidentified phenomenon, such as an obscure, hitherto unknown terrestrial life-form or an alien menace from outer space. Then, the expert is asked to determine the source and extent of the threat, and the potential extinction of humanity seems to hinge on the explanatory power of science and the scientist's ability to gauge and describe the nature of the unknown "thing out there."

SF has often negotiated knowledge production via subject-object relations, with an emphasis on the object: human interactions and processes of knowledge production define an object of study, but the object also defines the roles and self-understanding of the participating actors. A confrontation with a distinctly nonhuman "it" may serve to forge and define a communal human "we" in the face of a global alien threat, but this "we" is by no means as homogenous as one might expect. Utterances such as "Oh my god, it's coming directly towards us!" tend to come from characters portrayed as "men of action" (e.g., pilots, ships' captains, and military personnel) rather than from scientists, thus focusing attention on a division of roles between stakeholders and those engaged in scientific knowledge production. In American post–World War II SF, such a division typically devalued scientists and glorified the "men of action" (Allen 2009). Although scientists were often consulted as experts on threatening "things out there," their Cassandra-like warnings went unheeded and were deemed impracticable or—when an interest in exploration seemed to supersede a sense of responsibility to the common good—suspicious (95–96).[1]

In his influential 1979 monograph *Metamorphoses of Science Fiction*, Darko Suvin introduced the concept of the "novum" as a crucial element of SF narrative, defining it as any novelty—whether concept or object—that is explained but that radically deviates from the reader's empirical experience. The novum has a defamiliarizing effect, marking a paradigmatic difference between the fictional and the real, but it differs from the fantastic because it remains framed within a rhetoric of plausibility and scientific explanation.

A novum can foreground the moments of epistemic shift that occur as technological and scientific developments alter a society's way of living and of understanding itself. As Damien Broderick argues in *Reading by Starlight*, "SF is that species of storytelling native to a culture undergoing epistemic changes implicated in the rise and supersession of technical-industrial modes of production, distribution, consumption and disposal" (1995, 155). The novum (which can be a process, an invention, an idea, or some other marked deviation from the present state) is often manifested as a "thing" that contains an element of threat and is an object of scientific interest and study. Whether it is animate or inanimate, human-made or not, this "thing" serves as a central unknown other that can be used to illustrate the mechanisms of knowledge acquisition as well as the limitations of the familiar. Even though the "thing" is the object of scientific analysis, it displays its own agency and becomes an active agent of the narrative; it impacts the human subjects who are analyzing it, defies scientific categorization, and maintains the opacity of the yet unknown. In the 1979 film *Star Trek: The Motion Picture*, Captain James T. Kirk tells Bones, the chief medical officer of the *Enterprise*, "Bones, there's a thing out there.... Headed this way. I need you. Damn it, Bones, I need you." The physician responds grudgingly, subsuming the entire genre tradition in ironic self-reflection: "Why is any object we don't understand always called a thing?" (Wise 1979, ca. 00:33:40–00:33:50).

The "thing" constitutes a prominent element of the SF genre tradition. It occurs in varying constellations with other elements such as "the scientist," "the assistant," "the lab," "the field," "the struggle against obstacles," and "the discovery," forming part of a grammar of popular narrative that allows audiences to place the technoscientific novum within a framework of the familiar. As sociological studies show, public perception of technoscientific developments, especially in biotechnology and the life sciences, tends to be shaped less by the amount and quality of actual information accessible to the public than by the availability of vocabulary, narratives, and visual representations that are capable of reducing complexity and embedding the new within a familiar frame of reference (see, for example, Braun, Starkbaum, and Dabrock 2015).

The scientific object of study in SF is more than just an indicator of each decade's popular obsession, fad, or fear. It belies the passivity that the default denomination as "it" or "thing" suggests and instead acquires its own form of agency, becoming an active "other" to the scientist subject. It offers a promising archive of the not yet known and is exciting for its exoticness and undiscovered secrets, while its agency as a nonhuman other also makes it threatening. In this chapter, we focus on how these "things" elude scientific grasp and inspire narratives of outbreak and failed containment. We will call them "bio-objects" to signal the deep ambiguity of their status: although they are either produced by the life sciences or turned into objects of study, they are also present, resilient, and dynamic as material objects in their own right (Dabrock et al. 2013). Epistemically, they are produced as "objects," but this Foucauldian notion of production does not imply that they are necessarily human-made; they may also be preexistent phenomena that are "discovered" and defined or categorized as objects by the processes of scientific inquiry. Bio-objects complicate binary categorizations of animate versus inanimate and subject versus object, and they resist treatment as passive things that can be manipulated at will.

We will discuss the use and function of bio-objects in selected SF texts to bring to the fore their depiction of social processes of knowledge production. The bio-objects in these novels acquire an unexpectedly powerful degree of agency, blurring the boundaries between animate and inanimate and prompting a confrontation between the logics of scientific inquiry and the broader knowledge economy. Their "unruliness" questions orders of knowledge and is often closely tied to narratives of crisis, as they obstinately refuse access, elude control, escape the lab, or generally explode the categories of an established scientific paradigm. The bio-object thus signals a moment of change, when an explanatory model becomes unsettled from its state of historical dominance and is replaced by a new order of knowledge.

We now examine three examples from the wide spectrum of popular SF: Michael Crichton's *Jurassic Park* (1990) and *Prey* ([2002] 2008) are bestselling mainstream techno-thrillers, whereas Greg Bear's *Darwin's Radio* ([1999] 2000) has been popular with a narrower SF readership that sees it as a serious, well-informed engagement with the life sciences.[2] The three novels we chose all approach scientific knowledge production via narratives of outbreak and containment that feature the novum of a bio-object that, by displaying agency and a resistant opacity, foregrounds how scientific knowledge and its applications are processual and socially produced. Laboratory-produced dinosaurs in *Jurassic Park*, a swarm of nanobots in *Prey*, and a retrovirus in *Darwin's Radio* all acquire degrees of agency and become or give rise to bio-objects; they cause crises that reveal weaknesses in the mechanisms of knowledge production and demand reconsideration of governance at the cross sections between science and other social sectors, such as politics, the economy, and the media. Their narrative function is to question the depersonalized empirical ontologies—"grounded in trained, collective, cultivated habit" of observation and dissemination—that science depends on to establish what counts as reliable knowledge (Daston 2008, 110).

Bio-objects are fictional markers of crisis within an established order on the brink of change, and as such they render the social processes and parameters of knowledge production visible. They challenge notions of functionally differentiated, clearly separated social subdomains like science, technology, economics, and politics; they also demand a responsible reconsideration of questions of governance at the crossroads of science, social landscapes, and the media.

Our readings employ a three-pronged comparative analytic framework. First, we examine the ways in which the bio-objects generate a crisis or shift in scientific paradigm. Second, we consider the nature and function of the object in relation to the social actors, places, and domains involved in scientific knowledge production (e.g., economics, political administration, and the media). And third, we trace the narrative patterns and aesthetic strategies that are used to present and illuminate that content. Our readings are designed to clarify how the revolt of objects and the unfolding narratives of control and containment work within their aesthetic frameworks to challenge the agency of the inquiring human subject at the heart of science's enlightenment genealogy.

Michael Crichton's science thriller *Jurassic Park* (1990) owes part of its popularity to Steven Spielberg's 1993 film, which used advanced computer animation to successfully stage the novel's cloned dinosaurs. When asked about his perception of the novel in relation to the film, Crichton explained that the two media serve different purposes and that only the novel allowed for reflections on the nature of scientific inquiry (Biodrowski 1993). The novel, like the film, is a cautionary tale—an ambiguous genre that provides the pleasurable thrills of reading about transgression and disaster but also takes the moral high ground and sounds a warning. The novel differs significantly, however, in the complexity of its scientific landscape and plot and, indeed, in its allocation of culpability for the potential disaster. *Jurassic Park* neither resorts to demonizing the effects of scientific research nor conjures scenarios in which "mad scientists" produce "dangerous things," as have so many novels and films since *Frankenstein* and *The Island of Doctor Moreau* were first published. Instead, it warns us against specific forms of hubris and against an instrumentalist approach in biotechnology research. Rather than targeting science and scientists, *Jurassic Park* utilizes the spectacle of cloned dinosaurs to critically reflect on important changes in the socioeconomic practices in which the natural sciences are embedded. It explores how current funding practices and increasing privatization impact scientific knowledge production, and it sketches the hazards that come with the unregulated migration of expensive biomolecular research into a profit-driven private sector.[3]

In the novel, the depiction of scientific practice and its settings profits from the broad spectrum and multifaceted nature of the disciplines described. The narrative integrates different scientific cultures and character types: paleontologists Alan Grant and Ellie Sattler seem happiest digging dinosaur eggs out of rock and dust in Montana; the ambitions of the highly gifted geneticist Henry Wu lead him from university research facilities struggling for funding to the state-of-the-art labs of John Hammond's venture capital firm; and the brilliant, sometimes cynical mathematician Ian Malcolm is one of the originators of the new and controversial chaos theory and enjoys near-rock-star status in the scientific community. The novel uses the generic plot element of assembling a task force to generate a social space that opens up between interacting scientists and specialists from multiple disciplines. The team includes experts in the life sciences, paleontology, and mathematical systems modeling as well as experts in practical matters such as IT administration, surveillance, veterinary medicine, and hunting. Hammond's quasi-visionary project of a Jurassic theme park full of cloned dinosaurs has collapsed, and the team is tasked with containing the ensuing crisis. In the novel, Hammond's failure illustrates the dangerous myopia and hubris of the architects of biotech projects that harness the powers of scientific research and seek to profit from marketing discoveries that are not yet fully understood. The Jurassic Park project disregards the complexities of cloning techniques and of bioforms and their habitats; it is the result of what one of the characters calls the "thintelligence" of a narrow, goal-oriented approach that treats life-forms as something that can be engineered for pure entertainment and profit (Crichton 1990, 284). When the creatures give the lie to Hammond's instrumentalist convictions and his scientists' predictions of the animals' behavior, the resulting scenario illuminates the ways in which stakeholders with a profit incentive may shun societal responsibilities, such as managing risk or insuring the sustainable use of resources.

The dinosaurs in the Jurassic theme park are the products of genetic experimentation and speculative imagination, and they eventually rise up against fantasies of control that, as the novel implies, may come with the ownership of patented life-forms. They are not actual clones of extinct species but hybrids that are created by using contemporary amphibian DNA to repair residual dinosaur DNA—a choice, as we learn, with detrimental consequences. The design of new life-forms for a lucrative, high-end entertainment industry turns out to be riskier and more difficult than Hammond's team had bargained for, as becomes apparent when the "commodities" refuse to remain passive and sufficiently malleable. They quickly shatter their creators' fantasies of control and challenge the assumption that animate nature is predictable. The novel's crisis scenario clearly taps into SF-horror traditions, as the lab-born creatures turn out to be dangerous and, in the case of the velociraptors, highly intelligent (147). The novel does not, however, relegate them to the fantastic or grotesque realm of monstrosity. Rather, it emphasizes the ambiguity of human-made life-forms with their own agency, ability to interact, will to survive, and right to exist.

The bio-objects' escape from their laboratory and commodified theme-park existence is not staged as a singular catastrophe but instead as the systematic result of a series of small events. Unpredictable events are bound to happen, because the scientists, technicians, and investors have ignored the complexity of the life-forms—which are numbered like software versions, according to their stage of development (120)—and not taken into account how they might behave in their habitats outside the laboratory. Malcolm criticizes Hammond harshly for this simplistic, instrumentalist view: "You create new life-forms, about which you know nothing at all. Your Dr. Wu does not even know the names of the things he is creating. . . . You create many of them in a very short time, you never learn anything about them, yet you expect them to do your bidding, because you made them and you therefore think you own them; you forget that they are alive, they have an intelligence of their own, and they may not do your bidding" (305–6). The bio-objects thus function as the nemesis of a highly specialized and selective world view that chooses to overlook the fictionality of its own predictive modeling strategies. The members of Hammond's staff, from biologist to IT nerd, think two-dimensionally in terms of linearity and singular causality, and they assume a systemic closure that allows them to define the life-forms they have created as conveniently passive "things." Predictions of the bio-objects' behavior are thus tainted by a scientific rationale that has itself been instrumentalized by a capitalist economy. Statistical extrapolations assume quantifiable probabilities for all processes, and assessments of risk fail to account for the artificial nature of their own assumptions (i.e., the fiction of fully knowable factors). As Malcolm repeatedly points out, predictive assumptions about the behavior of complex living systems, habitats, and ecosystems need to factor in aspects of nonlinearity in developmental patterns. To omit the chaotic, coincidental, or unlikely in order to produce illusions of security and raise shareholder value may indeed result in detrimental consequences. Malcolm argues that "ever since Newton and Descartes, science has explicitly offered us the vision of total control. Science has claimed the power to eventually control everything, through its understanding of natural laws. But in the twentieth century, that claim has been shattered beyond repair. . . . Chaos theory proves that unpredictability is built into our daily lives. It is as mundane as the rainstorm we cannot predict. And so the grand vision of science, hundreds of years old—the dream of total control—has died, in our century. . . . We are witnessing the end of the scientific era" (350–54).

Cause and Effect?

Jurassic Park not only portrays chaos theory and the systemic nature of the unpredictable as a paradigm shift in its content but also *demonstrates* aspects of nonlinearity by employing them in plot development and text structure. Using the aesthetic potential of literary knowledge production, the novel employs narrative form to make nonlinear complexity tangible. A mosaic pattern of alternating plot sequences, focalization, and settings generates a comprehensive systemic perspective of the fictional world and its unfolding lattice of possibilities. Instead of presenting a linear sequence of cause and effect, the plot develops out of a series of small, seemingly meaningless events—unfortunate coincidences, moments of human irrationality, small technological failures, and habitual but misguided actions. By intertwining content and aesthetic form, the novel creates a discursive dynamic that is visually reinforced by using the unfolding fractal iterations of a so-called dragon curve as chapter heading ornaments.

Ultimately, the novel uses its SF plot and aesthetic modes to comment on an unrecognized crisis in late twentieth-century society's systems of scientific communication and practice. It is not scientific progress or a single, ingenious mad scientist and his lack of ethics that cause the crisis in *Jurassic Park* but rather a failure to think of science in terms of its social, economic, and technological embeddedness. The novel's staging of scientists' confrontations with the bio-objects encourages readers to challenge previous explanatory models and concepts of scientific objectivity and statistical truth. As it turns out, literary knowledge production and Malcolm's theory of complex nonlinear systems may share a crucial feature: they both presuppose a self-reflexive awareness of the fictionality of their virtual models of the world. Aware of their hypothetical character and the devices that provide operational closure, they are open to the realization that the truths, which science and society collaboratively produce, must be contingent.

Prey ([2002] 2008), another of Crichton's popular techno-thrillers, was published more than a decade after *Jurassic Park*. Although *Prey* was somewhat less profitable than *Jurassic Park* and its ensuing franchise,[4] it does exemplify to what extent novelistic form impacts the mediation of content. In *Prey*, Crichton again incorporates a technoscientific novum into a gripping thriller that seeks to communicate an understanding of a large scientific paradigm shift to its broad popular audience.

The novel addresses developments in the fields of nanotechnology, genetic engineering, and Artificial Life research (ALife)[5] through the novum of a swarm intelligence of molecular-scale robotic agents that escapes the laboratory and begins to self-replicate and evolve. As events progress, the reader learns about complex nonlinear systems, emergence phenomena, swarm intelligence, and decentered distributed learning. Like *Jurassic Park*, *Prey* utilizes the patterns of the outbreak narrative and the topos of an experiment out of control. As in *Jurassic Park* and other Crichton novels, *Prey* explicitly frames its speculative narrative with nonfiction material. By including documentary sources, a list of additional reading on the subject matter, quotes from renowned scientists, and an introductory preface about nanotechnology and artificial evolution, the novel seeks to summon the legitimacy and authority associated with nonfictional, fact-based textual forms. Yet it remains a clearly fictional and highly imaginary text—readings that take Crichton's devices literally and rely on the novel for an understanding of nanotechnology and genetic engineering as well as scientists' objections that the novel has the science all "wrong" fail to take its fictionality into account.

Crichton's novel uses the mode of fiction to warn that unmonitored, unregulated profit-driven technoscientific progress will put humanity at risk (2008, ix–xv). Highlighting the urgency of its cautionary tale, *Prey* begins in medias res with a moment of crisis and then shifts back in time. Events are narrated in retrospect by Jack, a stay-at-home dad and software engineer who has lost his job and is trying to regain a professional footing in Silicon Valley's tightly knit IT culture. Early in the novel, a task force of scientists and technicians is assembled in order to solve a yet unspecified problem at Xymos, the nanoparticle factory and research facility where Jack's wife, Julia, works. The reader gradually learns that Xymos, located at an isolated site in the desert, has been experimenting with distributive intelligence and airborne robotic nanoswarms, and one of them has been released into the environment. Hindered by the company's efforts to downplay the problem, the task force seeks to understand the "thing's" possibilities and behavior and to contain it. The bio-object of this outbreak narrative is a rapidly evolving artificial entity of swarm intelligence that acts as a quasi-character in the novel and challenges the protagonists' and the reader's category boundaries and definitions of life. The systemic alienness of the swarm's distributed hive intelligence constitutes a radical departure from human notions of actors and participants in social interaction and thus generates uncertainty. In addition to suggesting altered concepts of active agents, the narrative focuses attention on the nanoscale, generating new ways of perceiving the human body. As Jack observes, "If you want to think of it that way, a human being is actually a giant swarm. Or more precisely, it's a swarm of swarms, because each organ . . . is a separate swarm. What we refer to as 'body' is really a combination of all these organ swarms" (362). The nonhuman agency, potentially superior intelligence, and predatory behavior of the swarm challenge an anthropocentric world view and even call the ontic foundations of human individuality and subjectivity into question.

Although the plot tells the story of a radical shift in scientific thinking that seems deeply critical of anthropocentric instrumental reason, on a social level the novel is profoundly conservative, if not reactionary. Reader identification is tied to Jack, a straight white middle-class male protagonist who seeks to save his nuclear family, which has seemingly been put at risk by his successful but morally questionable wife (later replaced in her role as partner and sidekick by another smart, courageous woman scientist who is apparently more appreciative of the protagonist's masculinity). Featuring a highly educated working mother as an inadequate nurturer and a stay-at-home dad as the heroic savior, the novel's gender ideology depicts the exchange of gender roles in Jack's family as an unfortunate aberration in the supposedly natural biological order. The novel, whose thriller tension is based on unfolding a technoscientific and philosophical paradigm shift toward an erosion of linearity and the anthropocentric, thus paradoxically advocates notions of stability and containment on a social level.

The novel employs the characteristic tension-building elements of the thriller, combining a fast-paced, accelerating plot development with retrospection, as Jack repeatedly shifts to the later time frame of a reflecting, narrating I, commenting on his own dangerous ignorance and misjudgments as an experiencing I.[6] Like *Jurassic Park*, *Prey* is a classic tale of warning: the novel develops a scenario of scientific hubris and, more pronouncedly, of economic greed propelled by the harnessing of technoscientific research to private venture capital interests. Mixing elements of the SF and Gothic horror genres, the novel is structured as a diary with a biblical seven-day time frame for the genesis of intelligent life. *Prey* intertextually connects the topic of swarm behavior and artificial intelligence to the gothic novel's roots—namely, the primordial text of human-made artificial life, Mary Shelley's *Frankenstein*, which also uses epistolary elements. In *Prey*, the first-person narrator-scientist is not the one who creates the novum "on a dreary night of November" and, like Dr. Frankenstein at the beginning of Mary Shelley's famous fifth chapter, beholds "the accomplishment of [his] toils" (Shelley [1818] 1985, 105). Instead, Jack is cast in the joint roles of victim and defender of the nuclear American family against the "thing out there." The narrative provides both an alarmist vision of what might happen if privatized technoscience spins out of control and a neoconservative indictment of its female scientist character, who privileges her career and neglects her role as wife and mother: "It's midnight now. The house is dark. I'm not sure how this will turn out" (Crichton 2008, 1).[7]

Like *Jurassic Park* and many other SF novels, *Prey* centers around an object of scientific study that has been produced in a laboratory setting and acquired animate life. Whereas the bio-objects in *Jurassic Park* were human-made genetically engineered organisms, *Prey* features artificial life that is collectively sentient as a swarm—it interacts with its environment, reproduces, and evolves—but consists of nonorganic, self-propelled robots produced by biomolecular nanoassemblers. In these outbreak narratives, the novum of a bio-object asserts its intelligence and status as alive through its resistance to human containment, and it challenges definitions of life that depend on a connection to ideas of nature. Whereas *Jurassic Park* problematized the reification and commodification of genetically altered life-forms, *Prey* challenges the very notion of life as contingent on nature and organic components, confronting the reader with nanoparticle swarms that functionally satisfy the criteria for "life." As Jack notes in one of the typical segments of explanatory discourse—embedded in the dialogue between scientist protagonists but clearly included for the benefit of lay readers—"What you're telling me is this swarm reproduces, is self-sustaining, learns from experience, has collective intelligence, and can innovate to solve problems.... Which means for all practical purposes, it's alive" (245).

The outbreak defies control, access, and containment by its human makers, and the swarm becomes a dangerously intelligent adversary to the human protagonist. Jack's initial optimism that he will be able to contain the escaped bio-object quickly and "fix" the problem is partially based on an underestimation of his adversaries, with whom he is soon engaged in a bitter struggle that can end only in death for one side or the other. The introduction of the technoscientific novum thus suggests a paradigmatic shift away from an anthropocentric view of the world as inherently knowable, controllable, and instrumental to science, the economy, and other human endeavors. Exposed to an ecosystem in which evolutionary predator-prey relationships have been restructured by the introduction of a new human-made agent, the human protagonists find themselves temporarily confronted with this paradigm shift. In the end, however, they are able to contain the bio-object and confirm the notion of a "natural" human hierarchy that is capable of defying social and technoscientific threats.

Prey clearly strains under its ideological and informational load. It is pedagogically informed by an attempt to steer readers toward a unified, unmistakable reading, which leads to a harsh paring down of the novel's formal possibilities. *Prey*'s monologic tendency reduces the complexity and ambiguity of fiction in order to make the warning clear and unambiguous to the presumed lowest common denominator of readership.

The aesthetic choices in *Prey* do not privilege the novelistic form's dialogic character of multiple plot strands, voices, and perspectives but instead generate a narrative impetus that formally counters the centrifugal forces and behavioral patterns that emerge from complex nonlinearity.[8] Jack and the swarm are set as antagonists in a binary opposition of good and evil, human survival and nonhuman threat, that villainizes the nonhuman "thing out there" and counters the content's topic of complexity with a reduction of complexity in form. The monologic form of the diary underscores the centripetal force of a narrative of containment and control with its single plot strand, narrow chronology, and singular focalization through a first-person narrator. The events unfolding around Julia, who seems personally invested in the development of the swarm, remain tied to Jack's perspective since they are revealed only through retrospective reconstruction by the narrator, which leads to an evaluative filtering effect. Forfeiting the dialogic potential of specifically literary knowledge production, the novelistic form groans under the forced pedagogical disambiguation that seeks to harness the literary into the instrumental (Kley 2016).

Like *Jurassic Park* and *Prey*, Greg Bear's *Darwin's Radio* ([1999] 2000)—winner of the 2000 Nebula Award for best SF novel—uses a catastrophic moment to foreground the dynamics of a paradigm shift. The novum in *Darwin's Radio* challenges contemporary models of human evolution and effectively ousts *Homo sapiens* from its self-assigned position at the top of an evolutionary pyramid. Even more so than Crichton's novels, *Darwin's Radio* focuses on the social sphere of scientific practice and highlights issues of public and private funding, economic interests in intellectual property, and the potential profits of biotechnical applicability. It shows how research is deeply embedded in social and political processes and is intricately connected to governmental and nongovernmental administrative structures. The novel negotiates conflicts arising from cultural differences and institutional protocols within the dense web of public and private systems of communication and interaction that influence the production of scientific knowledge. It illustrates what paleontologist and science writer Stephen Jay Gould called "the myth that science itself is an objective enterprise," done properly only when scientists can step outside of their cultures to view the world as it really is: "Science, since people must do it, is a socially embedded activity. It progresses by hunch, vision, and intuition. Much of its change through time does not record a closer approach to absolute truth, but the alteration of cultural contexts that influence it so strongly" (1981, 21–22).

All three novels discussed here adhere to generic patterns of life-science fiction. But *Darwin's Radio* further explores the contemporary thriller's technique of multiple narrative strands. Plotlines interweave and alternate, and the reader follows the changing perspectives of a core set of focalizing protagonists who are presented by a relatively disinterested, heterodiegetic narrator.[9] The novel's engagement with the sociology of scientific knowledge production impacts the plot and the ways that scientists and their objects of study are conceptualized. A fictional tale about how scientific truth is socially coproduced, *Darwin's Radio* might be seen as a literary counterpart to *Laboratory Life* (1979), Latour and Woolgar's endeavor to develop an anthropological gaze on science.

In *Darwin's Radio* the "thing out there" is a pandemic that causes miscarriages and the birth of genetically altered babies. The cause of the initial epidemic turns out to be a retrovirus that has been endogenous to human DNA since early humanoid evolution. The novel's unruly bio-object, SHEVA (Scattered Human Endogenous retro Virus Activation), is a novum in the sense that it defies the explanatory power of dominant models of evolution and requires their theoretical revision. The retrovirus activates previously unexpressed and seemingly redundant sequences of DNA, and what appeared to be an externally contracted infectious disease turns out to be the first step in an evolutionary leap and the birth of a new, posthuman species.

The novel employs the plot pattern of a classical outbreak narrative but references the genre with conscious, self-reflexive intertextuality. As the pandemic progresses, government agencies sponsor media campaigns to manage the public crisis. In a TV spot, Dustin Hoffman calls for calm and attempts to lend himself credibility by referring to his starring role in Wolfgang Petersen's pandemic blockbuster *Outbreak* (1995): "You might remember I played a scientist fighting a deadly disease in a movie called *Outbreak*. I've been talking to the scientists at the National Institutes of Health and the Centers for Disease Control and Prevention, and they're working as hard as they can, every day, to fight SHEVA and stop our children from dying" (Bear 2000, 378). Ironically, Michael Crichton is also part of the media campaign.

The narrative dynamic in *Darwin's Radio* avoids the logic of escalation and catastrophe that more conventional SF thrillers employ. Instead, it uses its novum, SHEVA, to foreground the complex ways in which scientific processes of knowledge production are socially embedded. All the main characters are scientists who risk their positions and reputations by proposing hypotheses that challenge an established paradigm, and the novel's literary structure and narrative perspective tie reader sympathies to them. Their research findings are not narratively framed as "discoveries" like they would be in a conventional science thriller, in which scientific facts tend to come into the world abruptly, in some sort of eureka moment, after which they are irrefutable and self-evident. In *Darwin's Radio*, explanatory hypotheses enter a slow process of testing and peer-group questioning. Before new explanatory models can emerge from scientific dispute and be accepted by the scientific community, the researchers must prove that their hypotheses explain phenomena better than previous hypotheses.

Anthropologist Mitch Rafelson, one of the three main protagonists, compares the shaping of a new scientific truth with "quorum sensing," the mechanism by which single-cell cultures of bacteria or slime mold collectively establish the presence of a critical mass for a change in the state of the whole population (288–89). The scientists, as they consider whether a new theory on SHEVA and human evolution is plausible, display a similar pattern. They wait, linger, and feel out their colleagues about their thinking on the subject until a critical mass is obtained and the risky thinking of an unorthodox hypothesis is converted into the consensus Foucault considered "être dans le vrai" (to be within the true) (1972, 224).[10] In both form and content, the novel emphasizes the discursive and institutional nature of knowledge production as it occurs within a specialist community and within the broader "process of coproduction" in which scientific knowledge and social authority intersect

(Jasanoff 2004). The collective nature of this process calls attention to issues of agency, intentionality, and control. The scientist protagonists try to negotiate the transfer of their findings to the domains of regulatory administration and policy-making, but at times they can only watch helplessly as their results are used and interpreted in unintended ways. When the retrovirus is misclassified as a contagious public health threat called "Herod's Flu," widespread panic and public unrest follow. The reader witnesses the fundamental resistance encountered by scientists proposing reclassification of established taxonomies and dominant explanatory models—in this case, a rewriting of "how we came to be human" (Bear 2000, 423). We see how expert discourses and administrative agendas intersect, how policy-making selectively uses scientific knowledge to fuel public authority, and how "science" can be manipulated into a rhetoric of reason and control that justifies controversial biopolitical measures of containment on behalf of "public health."

Unlike conventional tales of outbreak, the narrative dynamic in *Darwin's Radio* and its 2003 sequel, *Darwin's Children*, has readers rooting for scientists who are marginalized in their scientific communities, for the bio-object SHEVA, and for the new posthuman organisms. When the plot veers away from the thriller's singular catastrophic event—extinction of the human species—and presents us with evolutionary succession, the novel breaks its pattern of contagion and threat. As events reveal, *Homo sapiens* itself had come into being via an earlier bout of the same SHEVA-epidemic that humanity is now so determined to eradicate.

Ultimately, Bear's two novels depict the quarantining policies and bouts of collective violence against the SHEVA-affected in a manner that leads us to question the concept of evolutionary exceptionalism that feeds into humanity's speciesist[11] perspective. By sensitizing us to the contingency of our current truths, the novels alert us to the fact that the necessity of epidemiological measures taken in the story are in fact a violent case of human "genesis amnesia."[12]

The novels *Darwin's Radio*, *Jurassic Park*, and *Prey* generate fictional worlds as laboratories for cultural exploration; more specifically, they invite the reader to consider the preconditions and possible effects of biotechnology research and production from different perspectives. They employ popular topoi of science fiction, such as the "thing out there," to narrate states of emergency and impending disaster in which accepted anthropocentric world views may be questioned and established paradigms overturned. They focus on moments of crisis in order to depict the deeply historic, potentially contingent social processes involved in scientific knowledge production. And they call attention to how complex socioeconomic factors and power struggles codetermine which scientific findings are considered to be "in the true" within a given epistemic frame.

While most SF novels struggle to convey the necessary scientific information and tend to reduce conceptual complexity for the popular genre's broad readership, they vary widely in their aesthetics and particularly in the ways they exploit the distinct possibilities of literary knowledge production. Judgments on the aesthetic quality of a novel are, of course, partially subjective as well as culturally and historically specific. And yet novels that exploit the full potential of the literary to convey multiple voices, ambiguity, and complexity give readers more room to form their own opinions and interpretations about the novel's themes and subject. We would argue that the literary genre of the novel is, by virtue of its historical genesis, length, and potential for narrative complexity, particularly ill-suited to single-stranded and monologic information distribution and, one might add, direct unadulterated ideological indoctrination; after all, monologic form gives away what we regard as the particular potential of literary knowledge production—namely, to elicit what Jürgen Link calls the reader's "generative intelligence" (2003, 22–23).[13]

To illustrate, *Jurassic Park* profits from a self-conscious engagement with aesthetic means of knowledge production. The dinosaurs, as unruly scientific objects, reflect the larger paradigm shift toward chaos theory and link the novel's form—plot strands spinning into complexity, fractals as chapter ornaments, and fragmented information distribution—with the issues of knowledge and predictability in complex, nonlinear systems discussed on the level of content. In *Prey*, form and content relate in a different way, using a monologic form to transport an ideological bias. Whereas the diegetic world offers potentially interesting insights into swarm behavior, learning processes of evolutionary algorithms, and phenomena of emergence that evade conventional notions of linear causality, the narrative form stays linear and monofocal and conveys an ideologically conservative tale, warning of the dangers of technological progress and women who pursue careers. Bear's *Darwin's Radio*, on the other hand, does not resolve the differences of perspective and world view that result from its intersecting plot strands and multiperspectivity. It neither provides a clear framing to mediate the scientific content of the thought experiment nor prescribes a preferred stance for the reader through authorial commentary that would resolve the questions arising from the bio-object's posthuman trajectory. The novel demands a more dynamic engagement of the reader, who has to come to terms with fundamental questions regarding scientific knowledge production and its entanglement in biopolitical agendas of social order and control.

The novels discussed here stage the production of scientific knowledge by human and nonhuman actors operating within multidimensional disciplinary, economic, social, and communicative parameters in different ways. Using bio-objects as functional protagonists and employing themes of outbreak and containment to shape their narrative patterns, the novels portray the process of coproducing scientific knowledge and social authority as it occurs in particular social spaces, with their respective expert personnel and discourses (Jasanoff 2004). They articulate the insight that biotechnology generates socially relevant problems that cannot be addressed by the sciences alone or be translated directly into public policy. The novels show how alternative fictional modes of knowledge production can be used to reflect on the mechanisms that come into play when authorizing a truth, as such, and they generate awareness of what may be at stake when we abandon systematic reflection on those mechanisms. They articulate the need for a wider social and political discussion that is part and parcel of—rather than an obstacle to—scientific progress, lending support to philosopher Sandra Harding's call for a more democratic ethic of discursive participation in science matters: "Science appropriates to itself as merely technical matters decisions that are actually social and political ones. However, a democratic ethic requires that everyone affected should participate in such decisions about how we will live and die—about which groups will flourish and which will lead nasty and short lives" (2008, 25). While the sciences provide some of our most important techniques for exploring, explaining, and shaping the world we live in, they cannot help us decide what to do with that world or how to live in it. We may use scientific knowledge and technology to build a nuclear reactor or to foresee the potential consequences and scenarios that may follow from such an action, but science has neither the tools nor the space for systematic reflection on whether we should indeed build one.

As interdiscursive textual productions, these novels thus allow readers to tap into, absorb, and question culturally relevant bodies of disciplinary knowledge, demanding and generating alternative forms of understanding;

the active, generative intelligence of the reader; and an open engagement with ethical issues. They offer a space for reflection on the social conditions of changing constellations of knowledge and foreground the epistemological powers and social relevance of literary aesthetics.

Notes

1. A marked exception to the generic tradition of post–World War II and Cold War science fiction is Robert Wise's *The Day the Earth Stood Still* (Blaustein 1951), in which overzealous military action almost leads to human extinction. Wise's movie anticipates later ecocritical narratives.

2. Other examples of such engagement include Richard Powers's *Generosity* (2009), Margaret Atwood's Maddaddam trilogy (2003–13), Michel Houellebecq's *Possibilité d'une île* (2005), and Kazuo Ishiguro's *Never Let Me Go* (2005). See, for example, Hoepker (2012, 2014), and Hoepker and Kley (2015).

3. See chapter 7 for further discussion of fictional explorations of the economization of science.

4. For a discussion of the marketing of *Jurassic Park*, see Ken Gelder's *Popular Fiction: The Logics and Practices of a Literary Field* (2004, 111–12), and http://www.publishersweekly.com/pw/print/20021216/34120-crichton-sales-are-up.html.

5. In his preface to *Artificial Life II*, a volume of proceedings of the Santa Fe Institute in the Sciences of Complexity (an avant-garde think tank for complexity and ALife research), Langton stresses, "In addition to providing new ways to study the biological phenomena associated with life here on earth, life-as-we-know-it, Artificial Life allows us to extend our studies to the larger domain of 'bio-logic' of possible life, life-as-it-could-be" (1992, xiii).

6. Retrospective sequences are employed in particular in the "Desert" segment, which explores swarm agency and problem solving (see, for example, 210, 228, or 325).

7. If one follows the novel's narrative dynamic and steering of readers' sympathies through the first-person narrator and focalizer, *Prey* implies a strongly antifeminist and neoconservative backlash rhetoric. A different and more detailed reading of the novel might focus on how the ALife of the swarm is coupled with the female protagonist and leads to a blurring of the threat identified.

8. See Bakhtin ([1934–35] 1981, 272–73) for his reflections on the centrifugal and centripetal forces of language.

9. Structuralist narratology calls third-person narrators or narrative voices that are not part of the narrated world ("diegesis") "heterodiegetic."

10. Drawing on the work of Georges Canguilhem, Foucault (1972) uses the example of Mendel's observations on heredity laws—which long remained outside the boundaries of accepted disciplinary discourse—to illustrate the process.

11. Princeton philosopher Peter Singer first introduced this term in *Animal Liberation*, his 1975 book about the ethics of human interspecies discrimination.

12. The term "genesis amnesia" was introduced by Pierre Bourdieu in his *Outline of a Theory of Practice* ([1977] 1995) but has here been adapted to signify a broader, more literal sense of phylogenetic erasure in which humanity chooses to eradicate its memory of its own origins.

13. The reader's "generative intelligence" may be translated as her or his drive to create informed connections between different types of information. Referring to both Michel Foucault and Antonio Gramsci, Jürgen Link has introduced and continues to work with the idea of literature, art, and popular culture as interdiscourses that may

participate in, and selectively connect, other more specialized discursive formations. In doing so they rely and build on general categories (such as freedom, equality, or progress), collective symbols (such as machine, organism, train, or computer), and myths and elementary narratives (e.g., of rise and fall). Interdiscourses serve to accentuate, discuss, and subjectivize dominant knowledges in relation to specialized discourses. The awareness created in interdiscursive communication and reception processes for the operative moment of various kinds of knowledge production feeds these processes' "generative intelligence," that is, their drive for new interlinkings.

References

Allen, Glen Scott. 2009. *Master Mechanics and Wicked Wizards: Images of the American Scientist as Hero and Villain from Colonial Times to the Present.* Amherst: University of Massachusetts Press.

Atwood, Margaret. (2003–13) 2014. *The MaddAddam Trilogy.* New York: Anchor.

Bakhtin, M. M. (1934–35) 1981. "Discourse in the Novel." In *The Dialogic Imagination: Four Essays*, 259–422. Translated by Caryl Emerson and Michael Holquist. Austin: University of Texas Press.

Bear, Greg. [1999] 2000. *Darwin's Radio.* New York: Ballantine Books.

———. 2003. *Darwin's Children.* New York: Ballantine Books.

Biodrowski, Steve. 1993. "Jurassic Park: Michael Crichton on Adapting His Novel to the Screen." *Cinefanastique* 24 (2): 12. http://cinefantastiqueonline.com/1993/08/jurassic-park-michael-crichton-on-adapting-his-novel-to-the-screen.

Bourdieu, Pierre. (1977) 1995. *Outline of a Theory of Practice.* Translated by Richard Nice. Cambridge, UK: Cambridge University Press.

Braun, Matthias, Johannes Starkbaum, and Peter Dabrock. 2015. "Safe and Sound? Scientists' Understandings of Public Engagement in Emerging Biotechnologies." *PLoS ONE* 10 (12): e0145033. https://doi.org/10.1371/journal.pone.0145033.

Broderick, Damien. 1995. *Reading by Starlight: Postmodern Science Fiction.* New York: Routledge.

Crichton, Michael. 1990. *Jurassic Park.* New York: Ballantine Books.

———. (2002) 2008. *Prey.* New York: HarperCollins.

Dabrock, P., M. Braun, J. Ried, and U. Sonnewald. 2013. "A Primer to 'Bio-Objects': New Challenges at the Interface of Science, Technology and Society." *Systems and Synthetic Biology* 7 (1): 1–6. https://doi.org/10.1007/s11693-013-9104-8.

Daston, Lorraine. 2008. "On Scientific Observation." *Isis* 99 (1): 97–110.

Foucault, Michel. 1972. *The Archaeology of Knowledge and the Discourse on Language.* Translated by A. M. Sheridan-Smith. New York: Pantheon.

Gelder, Ken. 2004. *Popular Fiction: The Logics and Practices of a Literary Field.* New York: Routledge.

Gould, Stephen J. 1981. *The Mismeasure of Man.* New York: Norton.

Harding, Sandra. 2008. *Sciences from Below: Feminisms, Postcolonialities, and Modernities.* Durham, NC: Duke University Press.

Hoepker, Karin. 2012. "Happiness in Distress—Richard Powers' *Generosity* and Narratives of the Biomedical Self." In *Ideas of Order: Narrative Patterns in the Novels of Richard Powers*, edited by Antje Kley and Jan Kucharzewski, 285–312. Heidelberg, DE: Winter.

———. 2014. "A Sense of an Ending—Risk, Catastrophe and Precarious Humanity in Margaret Atwood's *Oryx and Crake*." In *The Anticipation of Disaster: Imagining Environmental Risk in North American Literature and Culture*, edited by Sylvia Mayer and Alexa Weik von Mossner, 161–80. Heidelberg, DE: Winter.

Hoepker, Karin, and Antje Kley. 2015. "Literatur und Wissen: *Life Science* und *The Pursuit of Happiness* in Richard Powers' *Das größere Glück*." In *Quarks and Letters: Naturwissenschaften in Literatur und Kultur der Gegenwart*, edited by Aura Heydenreich and Klaus Mecke, 273–93. Berlin: Walter de Gruyter.

Houellebecq, Michel. 2005. *Possibilité d'une île*. Paris: Fayard.

Ishiguro, Kazuo. 2005. *Never Let Me Go*. New York: Random House.

Jasanoff, Sheila. 2004. "Ordering Knowledge, Ordering Society." In *States of Knowledge: The Co-Production of Science and the Social Order*, edited by Sheila Jasanoff, 13–45. New York: Routledge.

Kley, Antje. 2016. "Literary Knowledge Production and the Natural Sciences in the US." In *Knowledge Landscapes North America*, edited by Simone Knewitz, Christian Klöckner, and Sabine Sielke, 143–77. Heidelberg, DE: Winter.

Langton, Christopher G. 1992. Preface to *Artificial Life II: Proceedings of the Workshop on Artificial Life Held February, 1990 in Santa Fe, New Mexico*, edited by C. G. Langton, C. Taylor, J. D. Farmer, and S. Rasmussen, 13–18. Redwood City, CA: Addison-Wesley.

Latour, Bruno, and Steve Woolgar. 1979. *Laboratory Life: The Construction of Scientific Facts*. Beverly Hills, CA: Sage.

Link, Jürgen. 2003. "Kulturwissenschaft, Interdiskurs, Kulturrevolution." *Kulturrevolution* 45 (46): 10–23.

Petersen, Wolfgang, dir. 1995. *Outbreak*. Burbank, CA: Warner Bros. Pictures.

Powers, Richard. 2009. *Generosity*. New York: Farrar, Straus and Giroux.

Schätzing, Frank. 2006. *The Swarm*. Translated by Sally-Ann Spencer. London: Hodder and Stoughton.

Shelley, Mary. (1818) 1985. *Frankenstein; or, The Modern Prometheus*. New York: Penguin.

Singer, Peter. 1975. *Animal Liberation: A New Ethics for Our Treatment of Animals*. New York: New York Review.

Suvin, Darko. 1979. *Metamorphoses of Science Fiction: On the Poetics and History of a Literary Genre*. New Haven, CT: Yale University Press.

Wise, Robert, dir. 1979. *Star Trek: The Motion Picture*. Hollywood: Paramount Pictures.

———. 1951. *The Day the Earth Stood Still*. Produced by Julian Blaustein. Los Angeles: 20th Century Fox.

10.
A Fictional Risk Narrative and Its Potential for Social Resonance
Reception of Barbara Kingsolver's *Flight Behavior* in Reviews and Reading Groups

Sonja Fücker,
Anna Auguscik,
Anton Kirchhofer,
and Uwe Schimank

Barbara Kingsolver's *Flight Behavior* is one of the most prominent examples in the "currently emerging genre of the climate change novel" (Mayer 2014, 24; see also Trexler and Johns-Putra 2011). Published in 2012, it offers a complex comment on contemporary US-American risk discourses about climate change. Science, as represented in the novel, figures as a detector of ecological risks. At the same time, scientists are shown to lack the capacity for effectively communicating this knowledge to the general public. By representing science and scientists in this way, the novel may itself be read as taking on the task of informing society about the risks of climate change.

Human-made climate change occurs on temporal and geographic scales that place it beyond ordinary human perception (see Trexler 2014, 209, for references). Knowledge of climate change and its anthropogenic nature comes from scientific studies, but this knowledge needs to be communicated effectively to the wider society before it can give rise to activities to counter the associated risks. Using the reception of *Flight Behavior* as a case study, we examine the potential social resonance of this fictional form of risk communication. We adopt the term *resonance* from Niklas Luhmann (1986, 40–43) to emphasize that communication is not a simple, straightforward transmission of information from sender to receiver but rather a highly demanding social process. Luhmann suggests that an act of communication is no more than a tentative stimulus whose effects cannot be predicted with any accuracy. Although we shouldn't discount the possibility that some communicative acts successfully produce well-targeted effects on others, it is more appropriate to speak of the resonance of communication rather than the transmission of information because doing so allows for a broader spectrum of potential communicative outcomes. In addition, the reframing of a communication's meaning by the receiver should not automatically be categorized as a failure of communication or as a misunderstanding. Instead, conceiving of reception as resonance opens up the potential for a rich array of understandings of a communication that go beyond its intended meaning.

We start out with an account of the novel's thematic structure, combining concepts and approaches from sociology and literary studies. This allows us to identify the major aspects of climate change, science, and science communication addressed in the novel, which will serve as a backdrop for our analysis. We then examine to what degree and in what ways these issues are discussed, developed, debunked, or propagated in the reception of the novel, which we view from several angles. We look at reviews in general news and literary review media, science journals, and online sources as well as at reading group discussions in groups of readers with and without professional backgrounds in the natural sciences. The resulting spectrum of responses—what emerges from the correlation between the communicative outcomes, on one hand, and the spectrum of recipients' positions (general readers versus reviewers, readers and reviewers with a science background versus those without), on the other—constitutes the social resonance of *Flight Behavior* as a fictional work of risk communication.

Thematic Structure

Set between November 2010 and March 2011, *Flight Behavior* offers an account of the recent state of the climate change debate in the United States. The novel can be read in two ways: (1) as an analysis of the factors that are responsible for this state and (2) as a meditation on possible suggestions for changing and improving the situation. More specifically, while the novel shows scientists as detectors of the societal risks of climate change, it also shows that they are unsuccessful in effectively communicating these risks to the general public and that other societal actors also fail in this respect. It raises the question of whether alternative channels of communication might be successful, at least on a small scale, where established media and institutions have failed.

The plot is constructed around a fictional scenario in which a change in the migratory patterns of monarch butterflies causes them to hibernate in the Appalachians instead of in the Mexican Sierra Nevada and places the survival and perpetuation of the species at risk. The reader learns of this event—which stands as an ominous sign of the threats that climate change poses for humankind—through encounters between the novel's protagonist and focalizer, Dellarobia Turnbow, who is the wife of a poor Appalachian farmer, and the novel's main scientist character, Ovid Byron, who is a passionate lepidopterist.

The gap between scientific risk knowledge, on one hand, and public awareness of that risk, on the other hand, is staged repeatedly in dialogues between Ovid, Dellarobia, and other characters. Referring to his previous experiences, Ovid criticizes the public expectation that scientists "should be physicians, or some kind of superheroes saving the patient with special powers. That's what people want" (Kingsolver 2012, 228). He rejects the public's demand that science provide a certain diagnosis and a foolproof therapy as unrealistic and articulates serious doubt about his ability to strengthen public consciousness of environmental risks by means of his scientific expertise. The novel consistently shows how he has withdrawn into his role as a detector of risk who has no responsibility to communicate warnings to the public at large. "We are scientists. Our job here is only to describe what exists" (148), he says. Later he repeats himself: "Science doesn't tell us what we should do. It only tells us what *is*" (320). In its analysis of the factors responsible for the current state of the climate change debate in the United States, however, *Flight Behavior* is far from laying the blame at the door of science alone. Instead, it shows a combination of factors contributing to the failure to effectively communicate scientific knowledge to the public about the risk of climate change. In fact, the novel reveals a comprehensive spectrum of causes, ranging from the inadequacy of major players in the public discussion (the mainstream media and misguided moralistic environmental activists) to institutional failures (a partly dysfunctional school system) and socioeconomic injustices (the underprivileged, poorly educated rural population). By showing how all relevant players—journalists, schools, and environmental activists—fail as communicators of risk knowledge, *Flight Behavior* portrays a society that is in danger precisely because of its inadequate risk discourses.

The failure of the highly commercialized mainstream media, as portrayed in Kingsolver's novel, is due to its journalistic focus on human-interest stories. This leads to neglect of the ostensibly boring, extensive, and complicated factual information that substantive reporting on topics related to climate change requires. Instead of transmitting scientific information, journalistic accounts exploit science for ulterior motives. "Every environmental impact story has to be made into something else. Sex it up if possible. . . . It's what sells" (230), says Ovid, while his postdoctoral assistant denounces the media's ostensible goal "to shore up the prevailing view of their audience and sponsors" (230). The novel demonstrates this through Dellarobia's own experience with the news media. Although the journalist interviewing her promises confidentiality, it is precisely the personal, off-the-record part of her account that makes the news, while the scientific reasons for the enigmatic appearance of the butterflies are ignored (see 209). With its exploitative focus on her human-interest story, the news team reveals its cynical fixation on sensational or scandalous material rather than on natural phenomena or scientific knowledge.

The novel also illustrates in a drastic manner how schools fail as mediators of scientific knowledge. When Ovid wonders why he cannot find volunteers for his butterfly project among the local high school students (see 221), Dellarobia tells him about her own school experience: "Our science teacher was the basketball coach, if you want to know. Coach Bishop. He hated biology about twenty percent more than the kids did. He'd leave the girls doing study sheets while he took the boys to the gym to shoot hoops" (222).

The environmental activists' failure to understand the target group they seek to reform sheds light on an underlying problem: if the underprivileged, poorly educated rural population—the social milieu to which Dellarobia and her family belong—fails to be responsive to the communication of scientific knowledge about risk, that is ultimately an effect of socioeconomic deprivation. The environmental activists' campaigns are addressed to the middle-class bad conscience but fail to speak to the impoverished rural milieu of Feathertown, where the novel is set. The "Sustainability Pledge" proposed by one activist is made up of recommendations such as "bring . . .

Tupperware to a restaurant," "reduce the intake of red meat," and "fly less" (327–29)—but Dellarobia cannot afford to eat out or cook much more than macaroni and cheese, and she has never even been on a plane. The sheer irrelevance of the recommendations in the Sustainability Pledge shows how absurdly unfamiliar middle-class activists are with the circumstances of other social groups.

Much of the novel's social realism appears designed to correct such middle-class bias by pointing to social stratification as an important determinant of environmental consciousness and emphasizing the role that poverty and economic factors may play. Dellarobia and her family buy plastic toys from China and waste nonrenewable energy by driving old gas-guzzlers because these are the cheapest alternatives and they can't afford to do otherwise. "Worries like that," Dellarobia's husband remarks about climate change issues, "are not for people like us. . . . We have enough of our own" (172). At the same time, they may in fact have a lower carbon footprint and more sustainable lifestyle than the environmentally conscious middle class, as Dellarobia's difficulty with the Sustainability Pledge shows. They practice sustainability by repairing damaged clothes and buying secondhand, by replacing the broken motor instead of buying a new car, and by breeding sheep to cover their own consumption. In sociological terms, these kinds of sustainable behavior, which do not result from environmental consciousness, are collateral benefits of the economic limitations of consumption.

A similar perspective is linked to a traditional, religion-based understanding of nature as God's creation. Dellarobia's mother-in-law, Hester, exhibits all kinds of backwardness, mental narrowness, and reactionary attitudes. In a conversation with Dellarobia she maintains that the weather is in God's hands, and to Dellarobia's question about the end of the hard rains she replies simply, "Know that the Lord God is mighty" (20). Still, her unshaken religious belief includes a certain respect for a natural environment whose complex interdependencies are beyond human comprehension and should not be tampered with. In order to protect the butterflies, Hester enlists the support of the local pastor to persuade her husband not to sell the Turnbow family land to loggers (see 402–4), and she uses religious arguments to speak against economic profit and for the sustainable treatment of nature. In seeking to convince her husband, Hester appeals to "the laws the Lord God made for this world" and claims that "that land was bestowed on us for a purpose . . . , [a]nd I don't think it was to end up looking like a pile of trash" (403). In other words, the novel shows how in the absence of accurate scientific knowledge, a traditional, religion-based understanding of nature as God's creation may have a positive, or at least an ambiguous, relationship to ecological sustainability.

The novel's presentation of possibilities for changing and improving ecological consciousness does not, however, chiefly rely on the collateral effects of social injustice or traditional religion; instead *Flight Behavior* counters the ostensible insufficiency of established media, schools, and environmental activism as agents of science communication and the limited responsiveness to their efforts among certain social milieus with alternatives that are local, situational, or individual in character. For example, to counter the schools' failure in science education, the novel shows how social resonance for scientific knowledge could be generated among children by portraying an episode in which, at Dellarobia's suggestion, Ovid visits a kindergarten class (see 355–59). The idea that exposing children to an experience of real science from the earliest stages of education will help them relate to abstract scientific facts as they mature is further exemplified in the relationship between Ovid and Preston, Dellarobia's young son. For example, Ovid guides Preston through a logical series of questions about his observations of the butterflies toward an understanding of the process of scientific inquiry (see 118–19).

A successful form of media communication of scientific knowledge about climate change emerges out of a TV interview that initially seems to go wrong. In an attempt to get Ovid to finally speak to the media, Dellarobia has invited a news team to his lab, but communication between the scientist and the journalist proves difficult. When Ovid loses his temper and denounces the inadequacies of public coverage of climate change, the commercial media are not interested and turn off their cameras. But a video of the outburst that Dellarobia's friend Dovey records on her mobile phone goes viral on YouTube and generates the kind of public attention the news media have failed to produce (see 374–75). It remains an open question, to be sure, to what extent such cases can really serve as a bottom-up counterforce against the hegemony of a far more influential commercialized professional journalism.

As a positive counterexample to the inadequate middle-class-oriented Sustainability Pledge, the novel shows how the activists in the 350.org environmental group provide on-site help to the researchers. The "Three-Fifty guys" accept even "strange assignment[s] without question" and are "earnest" about their tasks and "mindless of their jeans, which would never recover" (271). What is more, Ovid shows not only concern for their well-being ("They exist on political commitment and gorp") but also respect for the kind of attention-raising activism they practice (see 277).

While these positive exceptions to the prevalent failure to successfully negotiate the societal risks posed by climate change remain largely episodic, the development that Dellarobia undergoes after the surprise arrival of the monarch butterflies in her world is a central focus of the novel's plot and structure. Dellarobia's individual emancipation through education can itself be seen as a positive counterexample to the general deprivation characteristic of her social milieu. Whereas most of her family and community conform to preconfigured roles and constellations, mutually supervising and sanctioning established mores and ways of living, Dellarobia gradually distances herself from her assigned role. From the novel's outset, she has been characterized as a "marginal person"[1] who maintains an inner distance from many of her community's values and ways of thinking. But she is also unable to translate her reflections into action because she, like everybody else, is constrained by her social milieu's strong pressure to conform. That she is ultimately able to free herself from this pressure is the result of her encounter with Ovid Byron and her direct experience of scientific work related to the consequences of climate change for the butterflies. Learning about climate change is thus the initial vehicle for her personal emancipation.

One example of such a moment of cognitive breakthrough is depicted when Ovid explains the difference between cause and correlation, and Dellarobia draws an analogy with a familiar experience: "I get that. Like, crows flying over the field will cause it to snow tomorrow. My mother-in-law always says that, and I'm thinking, no way. Maybe it's a storm front or something that makes both things happen, but the crows move first" (243). Linking scientific knowledge to her everyday knowledge, she begins to construct for herself a connection between the arrival of the butterflies, which she herself discovered, and abstract scientific concepts of natural disaster. To the extent that her emancipation process is a collateral benefit of Ovid's efforts to advance her understanding of science and climate change, these efforts are shown by the novel to be the most promising way of translating scientific knowledge into the everyday knowledge of ordinary people.

In structural terms, the novel follows the generic model of the bildungsroman (see Mayer 2014, 30; Goodbody 2014, 46–48).[2] In Dellarobia's development, we can distinguish the three characteristic stages through which the *Bildungsheldin* passes. Focusing on a "problematic individual" (Lukács 1971, 78; see also Kirchhofer and Roxburgh 2016, 149) who is ill at ease in her native social context (stage one), the novel sends its protagonist on an outward journey that is simultaneously an inner "journey towards [her]self" (Lukács 1971, 80)—a process of personal, intellectual, and emotional development (stage two)[3] that eventually culminates in her reintegration into a new social situation appropriate to her abilities and desires (stage three).

In the bildungsroman, the individual and society are "realities which mutually determine one another" (78) but do not necessarily evolve in harmony with one another. This has led Franco Moretti to describe it as the "symbolic form of modernity" (2000, 5), not merely portraying but also promoting "modern socialization" and managing the tensions between the two dynamics. Moretti adds, "In our world socialization itself consists first of all in the interiorization of contradiction. The next step being not to 'solve' the contradiction, but rather to learn to live with it, and even transform it into a tool for survival" (10). The bildungsroman is thus a literary genre whose "problematic individual" corresponds to society's "marginal person" and is waiting for the opportunity—which may never occur—to develop and be transformed into an integrated member of society. The marginal person is one who lives in "two societies and in two, not merely different but antagonistic cultures" (Stonequist [1937] 1965, xiv). Robert E. Park gives as examples the immigrant and the person who moves up or down in socioeconomic strata. Such individuals live in "conflict of 'the divided self,' the old self and the new" (1928, 892).[4] The characterization of Dellarobia corresponds to the "marginal person" in the sense that she comes from a family with a "better," more educated background than that of the family she married into. She has experienced downward mobility partly as a result of her father's ill health and economic failure and partly because of her teenage pregnancy and shotgun marriage, which leave her ambition to go to college unrealized.

Dellarobia's favorite mode of identity maintenance involves detached reflections on her former life in high school and with her parents and on her current life with her husband's family and her children. Torn between these two different milieus, she gets support from her best friend, Dovey, who has had a similar trajectory. In other words, despite experiencing themselves as trapped in the rigid role model dictated by their present milieu, both women maintain their self-respect as autonomous individuals via a mental and conversational detachment that provides them with a kind of inner freedom. With the arrival of Ovid as the representative of the world of science—which is even further from her past and current milieus than those milieus are from each other—Dellarobia's marginality intensifies to a critical level. She experiences facets of a self-development based on creativity[5] and approaches "a wider horizon, the keener intelligence, the more detached and rational viewpoint" (Park, in Stonequist [1937] 1965, xvii–xviii). Cognitively, she has transcended both of her social milieus but socially she remains locked in until the end of the novel, when she plans to separate from her husband, take a job, and find a place to live in town with her children so that she can attend night school and resume the education she had given up at the beginning of her marriage.

The novel shows, on one hand, how awareness of environmental risks can emerge on the individual level as part of an overall process of *Bildung*, which is understood as an all-embracing individual self-development. On the other hand, the novel leaves open whether Dellarobia will successfully complete this process of development. In contrast to Axel Goodbody, who speaks of "the uplifting end of the book" (2014, 48), we follow Sylvia Mayer's understanding that "the ending of the novel . . . can be ambiguously read" (2014, 31). In support of Mayer's "ambiguous" reading, two aspects can be pointed out that strengthen the dysphoric element of the conclusion. The first aspect is intertextual: the potential drowning of Dellarobia in a flood that threatens to sweep away her entire village is a clear intertextual reference to the ending of George Eliot's *The Mill on the Floss*—one of the canonical accounts of the dilemmas faced by women with intellectual capacities who transcend the limits of their social situation (and incidentally also a problematic bildungsroman)—whose protagonist Maggie Tulliver proves unable to escape those social limitations and perishes in just such a flood. The second aspect is both structural and topical: the novel's main action begins in the fall of 2010 and ends on March 11, 2011—the date of the Fukushima disaster and tsunami (one of the most spectacular failures of risk anticipation in the recent past), an event about which Dellarobia hears the earliest reports in the morning before she leaves her house.

Like the decidedly incidental nature of the aforementioned positive counterexamples to the general failure of societal risk discourses, the open and most probably tragic individual ending might suggest that we should not console or delude ourselves by thinking that individual efforts alone can effectively prevent large-scale catastrophes resulting from climate change.

Individual consciousness raising is a necessary but certainly not sufficient condition for successfully communicating scientific risk knowledge relating to societal risks, such as human-made climate change.

To sum up, the novel invites us to reflect on the role of science and the communication of scientific knowledge about societal risks in three respects. First, it shows science at work in the detection of societal risks; second, it shows a widespread failure in communication of this risk knowledge on the part of science as well as of other institutions of modern society; and third, it experiments with successful alternatives that arise from the situational creativity of individuals while leaving these institutional failures unaddressed. To read the novel in this way is to emphasize its highly *self-reflexive* dimension: the novel is science communication about the failure of science communication. Without giving a conclusive answer, it raises the question of whether this failure is inevitable or whether it could be overcome, and if so, how. As we turn to the reception of *Flight Behavior*, we will see how reviewers and readers have dealt with this invitation to debate.

Angles of Reception

In the following, we trace the reception of the novel in reviews by literary critics, journalists, and scientists, as well as among members of five exemplary book clubs composed of scientists and general readers of literary fiction. We compare their various readings against the sociological and literary analysis presented here, determining which of the several aspects of scientific risk knowledge different audiences focus on and how they discuss them. Our particular focus is on how specific interests, backgrounds, and levels of scientific education and experience affect the ways that science-related aspects of the novel are debated.

Reviewers

One specific and exceptional feature of "science novels" such as *Flight Behavior* is their potential to have a distinctive "dual impact." These science novels—as we loosely classify novels in which major characters are scientists; the plot hinges on scientific problems, concepts, and practices; and the narration and focalization invite readers of all backgrounds to experience and engage with these—can command two distinct contexts of reception: they are often reviewed in general or specialist science journals as well as in the regular review media for literary or mainstream fiction. In examining these reviews, we focus on the ways in which these novels are credited with the power to affect not only the perception of science among the general reading public but also scientists' self-reflection and their awareness of and interaction with external viewpoints.

We will not take the reviews as prescriptions or as simple mirror images of what actual scientific, general, or "literary expert" readers think of these novels. Instead, we consider the different target audiences for each type of media: the "scientists and the wider public" addressed by *Nature*, the scientists from specific disciplines addressed by monodisciplinary science journals, the socially and politically aware followers of thematic or activist blogs, the "intelligent and affluent readers" of literary magazines such as the *Times Literary Supplement*, and the "affluent and well educated global audience" envisaged by *The Guardian*.[6] We also consider the background expertise of individual reviewers and, most important, the different priorities and patterns of perception that are characteristic for each journal and type of medium. Literary reviewers mainly prioritize the literary quality and topical relevance of the novel (with respect to the author's standing as well as to the novel's matching of plots, characters, narrative voice, and themes). In review articles in science journals, the emphasis tends to be on the accuracy of scientific content and the "realism" of the scientist characters—including, at times, the question of whether the characters are based on past or living real-life scientists—as well as on the relevance of the novel's fictional representation to actual issues and situations within science or in the relationship between science and the wider society. In the following, we describe how the reviews of *Flight Behavior* respond to the elements of the thematic structure described in the first section, discuss how the background factors for each of the various review media shape these individual responses, and, finally, look at how those responses help us gauge the potential for social resonance of this particular fictional risk narrative.

The reviews in science journals tend to explicitly endorse the novel's representation of scientists as well as its use of scientific concepts. They treat the novel and its most important scientist character as reliable sources of information, both about the factors that produce climate change (i.e., as a risk detector) and about the obstacles that stand in the way of effectively communicating this scientific knowledge about risk to society. With regard to accuracy and reliability, it is worth noting that none of the reviewers take issue with any scientific statements made by Ovid and other scientists about climate change or the butterflies, and none are critical of the fact that the novel represents global warming and climate change as established, uncontroversial scientific facts. On the contrary, they emphasize that "[Kingsolver's] portrayal of the scientific team is accurate" (Baldwin Frech 2014) and that "there does not appear to be a single error in the book" (Mattoni 2013). They invoke Kingsolver's own scientific training—the biologist reviewer in the *Journal of the Lepidopterists' Society* describes her as a "biologist-turned-novelist" (Shapiro 2013), and his entomologist colleague in *The Journal of Research on the Lepidoptera* refers to her "education and work experience in Biology"—and stress that she was advised by eminent experts in the field: Kingsolver had "input from Lincoln Brower and other players in both butterfly biology and contemporary conservation" (Mattoni 2013). The novel's scientist protagonist, Ovid Byron, is characterized by another reviewer as "a Lincoln Brower-esque figure" (Shapiro 2013).

The general and literary reviewers tend to pay relatively little attention to the scientist characters as detectors of risk. If Ovid is mentioned in this capacity, it is in the context of making Dellarobia and her circle aware of climate change and its consequences and of Dellarobia's process of coming into knowledge. "The arrival of a team of entomologists led by Ovid Byron . . . delivers the life change [Dellarobia] has craved," reports one reviewer (Jensen 2012); "Ovid enlarges Dellarobia's world," states another (Browning 2012). Regardless of background and site of publication, practically all of these reviewers recognize that the novel contains diagnoses of the failure to effectively communicate scientific knowledge, although they generally single out just one of the causes. They variously note that Kingsolver depicts the failure of the established media—for example, one reviewer wrote that "some of the sharpest scenes in the book critique the way journalists distort and neuter scientific discourse to satisfy what they imagine are their audience's limitations" (Charles 2012); the failure of middle-class eco-activists—for example, as another reviewer commented, "Kingsolver has a sharp eye, too, for the unwitting condescension of the ecocampaigners who set up camp on the mountain" (Jensen 2012); and the failure of scientists—for example, the same reviewer said that "Kingsolver's evocation of TV's contempt for its audiences also includes the observation that scientists are too hamstrung by their own objectivity to transmit their message effectively" (2012), and yet another wrote, "Her field of inquiry is climate change denial. . . . She lays part of the blame on the scientists" (Hore 2012). Only *The Sunday Times* comes close to reviewing the full range and variety of obstacles to effective science communication presented in the novel, listing factors ranging "from the power of modern media to warp important messages, to the need for rural educational reform, and the emotional and social complexities of community, church, extended family, gender politics and marriage" (Atkins 2012). Again, as with the discussion of science as a detector of risk, in the general and literary review media these insights are subordinated to the story of Dellarobia's development and perspective: the novel is mainly about "engag[ing] the reader in the quotidian details of Dellarobia's life," even while it "insist[s] that we never forget the crumbling world beneath her, and our, feet" (Jones 2012).

When science journal reviews single out factors that prevent effective communication of scientific knowledge about risk, they are more likely to turn that deficit into a general complaint: "This lack of communication seems the ultimate cause of the coming environmental collapse by global warming. . . . Nobody wants to hear this. Monsanto does not wish to lose its Roundup profits, etc." (Mattoni 2013). Science blogs tend to be even more emphatic in subjecting the individual obstacles to effective communication to a detailed analysis. The *Climate and Capitalism* blogger concentrates on the economic context (specifically, on class): "Dellarobia and millions like her are not causing climate change: they are victims of forces outside their control, and a green movement that doesn't realize that [it] is surely doomed" (Angus 2012). The American Geophysical Union website singles out the failures of the school system: "These decent, flawed folks (like anyone, anywhere) have been victimized by their schools, where 'science' class is taught by a disinterested basketball coach" (Bentley 2013). And the science journalist Kate Prengaman focuses on the miscommunication by established media in the novel that she reads as "a serious critique of how 'balanced' journalism has mishandled climate change" (2013).

The improvised solutions and microlevel alternatives to traditional science communication that we described in our analysis of the novel's thematic structure are just barely touched on by reviewers. Whatever attention they receive among general reviewers tends to highlight the accidental quality of the purported solution. A *USA Today* review, for instance, places its hope in "[Dellarobia's] sweet 5-year-old son Preston, who might just grow up to be the kind of scientist who can save our natural world" (McClurg 2012); *The Observer* caricatures how "Kingsolver makes her message clear. If only a few more scientists started screaming on TV and radio then we might have a chance to avoid the worst of the calamities that lie ahead" (McKie 2013). Scientific reviewers tend to bypass these situational solutions altogether. When it comes to discussing possible remedies to the failures diagnosed in the novel, scientific reviewers instead tend to share the pessimism voiced by the novel's scientist characters. The obstacles, such as "the woefully inadequate knowledge of science and nature among Americans" (Weber 2013) and the immense lobbying power of companies such as Monsanto (see Mattoni 2013), are often seen as overwhelming.

Although the novel's "situational" solutions receive hardly any attention from reviewers, the question of potential remedies for the current deplorable situation presents itself in a different form: Could the novel itself successfully perform the function of effectively communicating scientific knowledge about societal risks? The spectrum of assessments of this question again reflects the specific priorities and patterns of perception characteristic of the different review media as well as the range of possible responses and viewpoints that combine to form the novel's social resonance.

Among scientific reviewers it is the more activist voices in science-related blogs that tend to formulate the expectation that the novel may have a positive impact (see especially Prengaman 2013; Bentley 2013; Waffle 2013), whereas reviewers in science journals tend to limit themselves to echoing the pessimistic assessment of the situation given by the novel's scientist characters (e.g., "I found it eminently believable, given the woefully inadequate knowledge of science and nature among Americans, that such a cataclysmic manifestation of ecological distress could be dismissed, minimized, glorified, or misinterpreted" [Weber 2013]; see also Mattoni's reference to the lobbyist power of Monsanto and others as well as his statement on the status of possible debate: "Nobody wants to hear this" [2013]). These responses are all in keeping with the patterns of perception characteristic of scientific reviewers: given a novel that provides what they perceive as an accurate representation of scientific concepts and practices as well as credible scientist characters, they treat the novel as an ally and endorse its insights and conclusions—what it presumably conveys to the public about science, on one hand, and its portrayal of the obstacles to effective science communication, on the other hand.

Among literary reviewers the issue of the novel as a successful form of communicating scientific risk knowledge comes up in two different guises: the question of its didacticism and the assessment of the protagonist's outlook and development. Literary reviewers, as it turns out, can acknowledge the novel's communication of scientific risk knowledge as successful only to the degree that it is compatible with the fundamental analytical criteria to which they adhere and specifically their concern with aesthetic credibility.

In one respect, this means that the uplifting perspective is tied to the customary focus on credibility of characters and plots, which, in the case of *Flight Behavior*, translates into reading the novel and the fate of its protagonist as an appeal to recognize the social significance of processes connected with climate change. Correspondingly, Dellarobia's development, her limited mobility and options for breaking out of the status quo, and "the story of Dellarobia's political and personal awakening" (Atkins 2012) form the major focus of most reviews in the general and literary media. In this reading, the significance of the butterfly catastrophe—and the accompanying tourists, environmentalists, media, and scientists—lies in the way it changes Dellarobia's life (e.g., "The arrival of the monarchs transforms her life" [Charles 2012]). The butterflies and, less often, the farm's sheep provide the images through which Dellarobia and her "metamorphosis" (Jensen 2012) are understood. It is "the vagaries of human behaviour" (Clark 2012) and the "fine subtleties of human behaviour" (Hore 2012) that stay at the center of interest. At the same time, reviewers recognize that the individual stories told in the novel have implications for our contemporary society, "the crumbling world beneath [our] feet" (Jones 2012).

In another respect, the concern with aesthetic credibility relates to the fundamental assumption shared by literary reviewers with regard to overt didacticism in a novel, which is seen as, in principle, a fault. In recognizing that the novel seeks to make a point about climate change and global warming and that doing so involves a variety of "science communication," they have to negotiate a characteristic difficulty: How skillfully is the "message" integrated into the artistic structure of the work? And what concessions might be made regarding aesthetic quality, given the social importance of the issue? Practically all reviewers feel the need to address these questions. The spectrum of their responses shows a remarkable range and variety of positions. Some praise Kingsolver for her decision to take on the topic: "Urgent issues demand important art. *Flight Behaviour* rises—with conscience and majesty—to the occasion of its time" (Jensen 2012; see also Clark 2012). Others, however, see the novel's status as an "environmentalist parable" (Tobar 2012) as a major flaw: "Somewhere in its telling, *Flight Behaviour* swerves off the road of literary perfection and gets lost in the fog of a sprawling story which has at its heart a global warming message delivered with a heavy, heavy hand" (Akbar 2012). The most frequent approach, however, is to praise the novel *despite* a perceived didactic tendency: "Kingsolver is a former scientist and, at times, the novel lurches toward the scientific sermon. But her keen grasp of delicate ecosystems—both social and natural—keeps the story convincing and compelling" (*New Yorker* 2012; see also Lipman 2012; Hore 2012; McClurg 2012).

Critics who praise Kingsolver's novel as a literary achievement adopt an ideal of "socially engaged fiction" as the benchmark for success—an ideal that Kingsolver herself aspires to and promotes, as is evident in the interviews she gave around the publication of the novel (see Hoby 2012; Kappala-Ramsamy 2013) and in her establishment of the Bellwether Prize for Socially Engaged Fiction, which she founded to support such work. These critics assert that in describing how the protagonist comes to encounter and experience the scientific evidence for climate change, Kingsolver achieves the integration of her message into the aesthetic structure of her novel. "The monarchs' survival comes to mean as much to us, the reader, as it does to Dellarobia, who finds them by accident, and in doing so, spreads her wings and finds herself," says one reviewer (McClurg 2012), while another finds that "the monarchs open [Dellarobia's] heart to a crazy wanting to protect something larger, nothing less than this gorgeous endangered world of ours" (Browning 2012). This is all, in the opinion of a third reviewer, a welcome exception to similar attempts: "*Flight Behavior* isn't trying to reform recalcitrant consumers or make good liberals feel even more pious about carpooling—so often the purview of environmental fiction—it's just trying to illuminate the mysterious interplay of the natural world and our own conflicted hearts" (Charles 2012).

In general, our analysis of reviewers' responses indicates that *Flight Behavior* contributes in several ways to the social resonance of scientific risk knowledge concerning climate change. The novel received substantial attention in review media addressing a general educated readership as well as in scientific media that focus on one of the aspects of science it touches on. In the scientific media, the scientific content of the novel is recognized as valid, as is its representation of the difficulties of gaining public attention for scientific insights; the question of the novel's potential social resonance is also widely addressed, although predictions of the quality and extent of that resonance differ significantly. In keeping with their primary focus, scientific media tend to treat the central scientist character, Ovid Byron, as a second protagonist. By contrast, many of the reviews in the general and literary media overlook Ovid Byron, focusing instead on the development of the novel's problematic heroine and on its social and economic themes. Although the positive responses to the book as a whole outnumber the negative ones, the responses of literary reviewers remain ambivalent, mostly based on the perceived effectiveness with which the story integrates its environmental message. Among scientific reviewers, the predominant interest in the scientific aspects of the novel results in a widespread sense of recognition of how these aspects are represented, leading to an alignment with the more resigned or critical viewpoints that may variously be associated with the text.

The potential for social resonance is not, of course, contingent on a positive evaluation of the novel by reviewers. This resonance instead comprises the discussion about the themes and the quality of the story as well as the communication about the fictional rendering of scientific facts and about the representation of the factors that make it difficult for these facts to have an effect in public debates as well as on the lives of individuals. Social resonance unfolds in the many forms in which it is discursively recognized that the scientific, personal, and societal dimensions of climate-change-related risk knowledge require continued communicative action.

Reading Groups

Reading groups—also known as book clubs or, in earlier times, literary salons—in which members meet regularly to discuss novels they have all read are a cultural phenomenon that dates back to the bourgeois milieus of early modernity, when they were particularly popular with women (Swann, Pope, and Carter 2011). In reception research there is broad consensus that reading groups can be understood as "interpretive communities" (Fish 1982, 54) in which individual readers' interpretations of a novel can be brought into the group discussion and influence it, while conversely the group discussion may reshape individual interpretations (Childress and Friedkin 2012; Bleich 1986). The outcomes of the group discussion, whether consensual or contested, thus transcend multiple subjective experiences to produce an intersubjectively shared understanding.

In the following, we present findings from discussions of *Flight Behavior* in five reading groups. Members of all groups share a basic literary interest in the novels discussed, and their main reading motivation is to enjoy an interesting piece of literature. Three of these groups consist of general readers (GR) with no professional science background, and two groups consist mostly of scientist readers (SR) who have backgrounds in a variety of fields such as oceanography, biology, zoology, engineering, chemistry, genetics, and geochemistry. In all reading groups, the members share a high level of general education and affinity for middle-class values; and, as voluntary associations, the groups are characterized by a strong homophily (McPherson, Smith-Lovin, and Cook 2001). The groups are based in Germany but international in their composition, with members coming from various countries and cultural backgrounds. Their book choices and discussions are all in English, and they are either native speakers or highly proficient in the language. This small sample of reading groups allows us to make a careful exploratory interpretation, although it does not, of course, provide any statistically representative conclusions.

Each individual reader of a novel, and a reading group as a collective, selects more or less narrow or one-sided aspects of a novel and neglects others, sometimes the most important ones, entirely. Swann and Allington note that "readers' interpretational activity is contingent upon aspects of the contexts in which they read, and that what they say about their reading is closely embedded within sets of social and interpersonal relations" (2009, 250; see also Griswold 1987). In other words, readers and reading groups are not impartial mirrors of what they read but rather interpret it according to their culturally, subculturally, biographically, and situationally formed expectations and attitudes. Bearing this in mind, we assume that novels in general, and science novels in particular, present specific thematic offerings to their readers. In terms of sociological role theory, we then ask how these thematic offerings are used, whether as opportunities for affirmation of roles that readers play in their everyday lives or as opportunities for role distance (Goffman [1961] 1973; Dreitzel 1968; Krappmann 1969; Schimank 1981). The latter possibility is of special interest here, because it means that a novel does not just reinforce existing individual and collective self-understandings but also functions as a stimulus for thinking about experiences and practices that have not heretofore received much reflection or explicit attention. By practicing role distancing, group members cease to automatically conform to their established roles, and they develop a certain detachment without either openly or secretly deviating from their roles. Typically, when role distance is established, an individual still obeys role expectations in situations in which there are pressures to do so but mentally takes one step aside to observe her- or himself from a different angle and think about what she or he is doing by playing this role. This critical self-reflection can go even further in situations in which there is no immediate pressure to act—in particular, while reading a novel and discussing it with others. For nonscientist members of the reading groups, reading a science novel such as *Flight Behavior* offers an opportunity to contextualize and reflect on their own everyday role behavior—for instance, as consumers or car drivers—with regard to its scientification. That is, it is an opportunity to reflect on what it is to live in a knowledge society that is strongly shaped by the application of scientific findings to all spheres of life. Scientists in the reading groups can distance themselves from their occupational roles as scientists by picking up the same thematic offerings and thinking about "doing science" in the larger societal context, with attention to societal influences on science and the uses, misuses, and unintended consequences of scientific knowledge in various spheres of life.

So how much role distancing did we see during the reading group discussions, and which of the thematic offerings described in our first section did the different members pick up? Beginning with discussions of Ovid Byron as the novel's main scientist character, our first group of general readers (GR1) digressed into a discussion of the scientist's popular image in former centuries[7] and of the contemporary image of the scientist as a "prophet of doom" who must inform the public and tell us "how to mend our ways" (GR1). Linking these general observations to their reading of the novel, group members saw Ovid's role as that of a mentor "who tells us what's happening" and whose task is "to convince us maybe to change our lives" (GR1). At the same time, they recognized how unrealistic such a normative expectation of the scientist's prophetic mission is: "The only thing they [the scientists] see is exactly what they're doing and . . . those people aren't necessarily the best persons to interpret and to draw conclusions to bring it across so that we can understand" (GR1). This is a case of role distancing: members of the group realized that they, in their roles as users of scientifically based technologies as well as citizens affected by the negative effects of those technologies, make naive demands of scientists, who are not able to live up to them. Reaching this insight is a precondition for more realistic thinking about what scientists can and cannot do in regard to handling the risks of climate change.

Sharing the first group's view of scientists as highly specialized, sometimes eccentric individuals, our second group of general readers (GR2) emphasized that scientists needed to make a special effort to communicate to the general public: "If you [as a scientist] want to reach the big community you have to be able to explain something complicated in easy, simple words. So that's very important, otherwise you . . . keep on living in your own world" (GR2). The group members further elaborated on this point with regard to Ovid Byron, emphasizing that "he could explain if he wanted to, . . . to the little children, but he just couldn't explain it to the journalist" (GR2). They concluded that "he was a good teacher" (GR2) but not a good public communicator of scientific knowledge. Again, this differentiated assessment by group members expresses a role distance that has been stimulated by the novel.

The first scientist reading group (SR1) began with a controversial discussion about Ovid's passionate concern for the butterflies, which they assessed as implausibly romantic. Their view of the typical scientist was in keeping with Parsons's characterization of the scientific habitus as governed by strict "affective neutrality" (1951, 435). More realistic to them was the novel's treatment of Ovid Byron as a "teaching scientist" who likes to talk about his work, knowledge, and discoveries when he encounters genuinely interested laypersons: "That's very realistic for a scientist. . . . If someone asks me a question about the oceans, you know, like how the tides work . . . , I start to lecture" (SR1). The group members thus recognized themselves as scientists in the character of Ovid. The last statement might seem to be a case of role conformity, with that member reaffirming an expected role, but it is actually a form of self-criticism: a "lecture," in the context of this statement, is a prototypical scientific communication format that is typically considered boring, incomprehensible, and so on. Thus, the statement is a manifestation of role distancing, expressing the view that scientists—the speaker included—should use other ways to communicate their findings to the concerned public.

In sum, both general and scientist readers focused some of their attention on the scientist character, and role distancing in both kinds of groups seemed to have narrowed any gap in their perspectives. General readers recognized that they should not expect too much of scientists, and scientist readers became conscious of their weakness of falling back into inappropriate forms of communication with laypersons. A common middle ground of adjusted role expectations with regard to scientists is thus in sight.

Unlike reviewers, the readers in the reading groups did not pay much attention either to the specific institutional failures of risk communication or to the alternatives the novel describes. With regard to these second and third thematic strands of our textual analysis, the reading group discussions concentrated instead on a more fundamental issue: the cognitive incompatibility of the kind of information provided by science with the kind of information that the public wants.

From the general readers' perspective, scientists present a "little mosaic piece" (GR1), whereas the general public expects to be given the whole picture: "People want answers, and the scientist can't answer them because he's never sure. . . . He can only say, 'We are tending in this direction'" (GR1). These readers recognized the inherent contradiction when they reiterated that "people in general want certainty, whereas a scientist can never deliver certainty" (GR1). According to these readers, the public's expectations of science are unrealistic and cannot be fulfilled: scientists "are just counting the square meter of how many dead butterflies," and "everyday people are looking at this and say[ing], 'They are nuts'" (GR1). The reading group members acknowledged that laypersons are missing an awareness—due to a lack of basic understanding of scientific theories and methods—of why such strange behavior might make sense and that since people do not understand, they dismiss the conclusions as nonsense: "Their [the scientists'] job is to be objective and to just bring together the evidence, and . . . it's all, you know, expressed in numbers and, you know, it's not something that normal people relate to. So, who believes it, right?" (GR1). With this realistic assessment, the readers not only distanced themselves from a naive public's expectations of what science can provide but also sought to explain to themselves why science communication largely fails.

Like the general readers, the scientist readers also came to question their own roles, in this case as professional scientists. Unlike the scientific reviewers (Mattoni 2013), they focused on scientific language and methods as the main obstacle to the communication of scientific risk knowledge on climate change: "And this main thing about global warming: Who can explain it? Scientists have a problem. They say, 'Maybe, maybe not.' The politicians, they, they have a different way of talking about that" (SR2). Also in contrast to the scientific reviewers, the reading group scientists spent some time discussing whether *Flight Behavior* is an accurate portrayal of the risks of climate change. One reader with a degree in zoology said she found the fictional scientific plot implausible; she maintained that Kingsolver "should have chosen a place that would be ecologically realistic" (SR1) and that "the butterflies would have done something else" (SR1). From that reading, the group concluded that fictional narratives might give readers a false understanding of scientific facts and theories: "You see, and if people come and there are a hundred novels that describe fictional settings, the minds of people will be set into the wrong direction" (SR1). But some group members saw the novel's plot as an aesthetic tool for making science accessible; they highlighted its potential to "get the message across much better with something beautiful than with something ugly" (SR1).[8] They maintained that in *Flight Behavior* the useful information about science outweighs any harm to scientific truth that might come from its fictionalization, as was noted by another speaker: "But I think you learn more about science or biology by reading the book than getting a wrong impression of anything" (SR1). Overall, the scientist reading groups found the novel to be both dangerous and effective as a tool for communicating the risks of global warming. Whereas the former assessment expresses role conformity, the latter is a second-sight concession originating from role distance.

In both sets of reading groups, milieu-based perceptions of the risks of climate change were a strong focus of readers' attention. The novel's representation of the poor rural population as being risk indifferent was perceived as correct, and discussions about Dellarobia centered on her place in this milieu. None of the reading group members had direct experience with this social milieu, which surely had something to do with the amount of highly selective attention it received in one of the groups of general readers, who emphasized their distance from it. The absence of risk perception in the novel's lower-class milieu was explained by the terse comment that "only educated people do this [practice sustainable lifestyles], because the others don't care" (GR1).[9] The readers in that group identified themselves as the author's target group—that is, people who should be made aware of how people in this lower-class milieu live: "We don't know anything about them.... They are not people we want to have lunch with" (GR1). This snobbish qualification, although expressed in a self-ironic tone, revealed the need to maintain a strict distance from "these people." Still, it is exactly this styling of the described social milieu as a "constitutive outside" (Laclau 1990; Laclau and Mouffe 1985) that then provokes a self-critical turn in which group members ask whether "we" and "our" way of dealing with climate change and other ecological problems is not as inadequate, although in a different manner, as "theirs."

Although the group members did not go into details about the possible economic, educational, and religious reasons for the deficient and distorted awareness of human-made climate change in the milieu that the novel portrays, the "wrong" conduct of a different social group stimulated critical thinking about their own handling of human-made climate change—another significant example of role distance. They became aware of the possibility that while the lower classes are simply ignorant, the educated middle classes deliberately suppress their knowledge of human-made climate change to avoid having to change their way of life: "But if we were really to be environmental wouldn't we have to do that? Wouldn't we really have to stop buying things and reuse everything?" (GR3). In line with the literary reviewers' conclusions about Kingsolver's ability to sensitize the reader (Charles 2012), these readers experienced mental dissonance between their clear insight about what they *should* do and their willingness to act accordingly: "It's very, very hard to be consistent with that [ideals of sustainability]" (GR3) because "it doesn't really touch you here and now" (GR2).

This expression of the difficulties of ecologically responsible behavior resonates with a robust finding from sociological studies known as the "volunteer's dilemma" (Diekmann 1985):[10]

- Behaving in an ecologically responsible manner has added costs, in terms of money, time, effort, coordination with others, or acceptance of quality reductions.
- The impact of my ecological behavior depends on how many others do the same.
- If it is doubtful how many others will or actually do behave ecologically, I will do so only if my costs are very low.

As one reader stated, "I ride my bike whenever I can and leave the car in the garage. But then again, I do other things. I have a swimming pool, which has to be heated, although only in summer" (GR3). In considering this general dilemma, another group member observed that "we would have to change everything. . . . It is kind of self-defense, to say, keep those scientists away from us because if we really follow what they are saying we would have to turn our lives over" (GR1). Another reader then asked rhetorically, "And who is prepared to do this with thousands of others at the same time?" (GR1). That is, with thousands of others whose behavior is doubtful! And of course, if everybody follows this reasoning, nobody will start acting ecologically—even if ecological awareness and concern is the norm. Everybody prefers to be a free rider, profiting if enough others come together to produce ecological improvement as a collective good and, if this does not happen, having no additional costs of behaving ecologically without any impact.[11]

By alluding to these dilemmas, reading group members expressed a strong sense of guilt: "We don't have to read this book to learn that species are dying. . . . The people who read these books are aware of the risks and scientific evidence of climate change. . . . We know these things about nature, we are informed about this, and we pick up a Barbara Kingsolver book because she writes this literature. . . . And we feel clubbed over the head with it because we know" (GR1).[12] This attitude shows that these group members experienced a strong distancing from their roles as consumers, car drivers, tourists, and so forth.

Unlike the general readers, with their focus on class-based identity distinctions, the scientist readers used the novel's portrayal of the lower classes as an occasion to question the perception that scientific literacy is essential for an ecologically sustainable lifestyle. In cognitive terms, scientific knowledge was relativized: "But what I can imagine is that these people might not be educated, but in some cases, they know more about the biology than the scientists coming in" (SR1). Group members questioned the value of Ovid Byron's—and their own—scientific expertise, which they realized is esoteric, specialized, analytic, and generally removed from everyday life. Furthermore, in terms of practices, the scientists also argued that the knowledge Dellarobia and her family have about lambs, wool production, and local plants serves as a valuable resource in handling the risks of global warming, although without reflection. Unlike members of the well-educated middle class, which the scientists themselves belong to, Dellarobia is, as one reader said, the "lowest possible emitter of carbon in the United States" (SR2). At the same time, one group also commented on how the novel portrays the negative side effects of economic constraints, as when Dellarobia's father-in-law wants to sell part of his woodland to a logging company: "There is always this interest on one hand about logging, and they need money, and on the other hand the climate is changing" (SR1).

The analysis of the reception of *Flight Behavior* in groups of general and scientist readers has shown that several of the novel's themes were picked up by both kinds of readers as opportunities for role distancing. But the discussions also included longer statements that were sure expressions of role conformity. This was the case whenever scientists were preoccupied with discussing the scientific accuracy of the novel. There were several phases of such discussions in both scientist reading groups that lasted a total of twenty minutes, for 16 percent of the overall discussion time (SR1), and twenty-six minutes, for 25 percent of the overall discussion time (SR2). The general readers remained stuck in conformity with their everyday life roles when, as happened frequently, they neglected the novel's scientific issues and talked only about the human-interest parts of the story, such as Dellarobia's life situation or social milieu. They dedicated sixteen (GR1), nineteen (GR2), and seventeen (GR3) minutes of their discussion time to these aspects, representing 13, 21, and 17 percent, respectively, of the total discussion time. The novel's thematic structure allows for both kinds of reception, role conformity and role distance. In order to explore the novel's potential for enlightening readers—in the sense of helping them view customary roles from a different perspective—we have put the emphasis on role distancing, but reaffirmation of one's established role and behavior is certainly also an important function of novel reading. Presumably, a novel is most satisfying to a reader when its thematic structure offers a balance of opportunities for both role conformity and role distancing.

Conclusion

Comparing the novel's thematic structure, its reception by the two kinds of reviewers, and its reception by the two kinds of readers, we arrive at some interesting conclusions. Our use of social resonance as a sensitizing analytical concept has proven quite productive. Responses to the novel from all four groups range from affirmation of certain perspectives—either because the novel confirms preexisting views or persuades effectively with its espoused views—to critical reflection on specific themes and total disregard of others. Furthermore, the patterns of response across our various categories of study participants differ substantially in most but not all respects—we find four distinct but overlapping readings of the novel, each shaped by a particular combination of science background and venue.

For the reviewers with science backgrounds, the overall finding is that the novel's depiction of scientists made them feel well understood. As they read the novel, it portrays their world and worldview accurately. This agreement between lived experience and reading experience is much less pronounced for the natural scientists in the reading groups. They were more ambivalent. On one hand, they used the novel as an opportunity to take a step back from their daily lives as scientists and look at themselves and their roles from a different angle, projecting scientific work into its larger societal context. On the other hand, they repeatedly fell back into their circumscribed roles when they discussed whether particular scientific facts were presented accurately by the novel, and they worried about general readers reading the fiction as fact. The outstanding finding among the general reviewers was their critical characterization of *Flight Behavior* as a novel suffering from a didactic delivery of its message. Considering literary criticism's tradition of valuing the autonomy of works of art in preference to any societal concerns, including moral or political messages, this critique is hardly surprising. But it is exactly this violation of the conventions of literary criticism that may have supported ordinary readers in distancing from their roles as scientists, consumers, and so on. Thus, a novel that is judged as deficient according to artistic criteria works well as an opportunity structure for its readers' role distance.

Flight Behavior is a special science novel with regard to science communication because its central topic is the failure of science communication, a reflexivity that sits well with readers who themselves feel a sense of personal failure when it comes to doing something about the ecological risks of contemporary society. Among scientists, the novel speaks particularly to those who are genuinely concerned about climate change and have tried to warn the general public and politicians against its dangerous consequences. They can identify with Ovid Byron's resigned attitude, and at the same time they are shown potential alternative ways of creating a societal awareness of these ecological risks. General readers from the economically saturated, well-educated, and ecologically aware upper middle class feel that the novel speaks to them too. Their reading experience stimulated expressions of resigned admission to an all-too-frequent discrepancy between talk and action (Brunsson 1989), not only in their roles as consumers but in their lives in general. They felt they had been caught in the act of not doing what they know they should do as ecologically concerned persons. The fact that the novel holds a mirror up to them with its portrait of a social milieu that very much differs from their own, however, allowed them to draw their own conclusions about changing their lifestyle. With these two venues of reception and categories of readers, the novel occupies a distinct niche of social resonance within the larger group of climate change novels.

Notes

1. To adopt Robert Park's (1928) well-known sociological concept of "marginal man."

2. On the genre tradition of the *Bildungsroman* in general, see Hirsch 1979 and Moretti 2000; on the "green" *Bildungsroman*, see Niven 1997.

3. In *Flight Behavior*, stage two does not involve the heroine's physical departure but rather her encounters with the outsiders who follow the butterflies into her world.

4. Stonequist likewise notes that "the individual who through migration, education, marriage, or some other influence leaves one social group or culture without making a satisfactory adjustment to another finds himself on the margin of each but a member of neither" ([1937] 1965, 2–3).

5. Péter Hanák (1998) emphasizes social marginality as a potential origin of creativity.

6. See "About Nature," http://www.nature.com/nature/about/index.html; "How to Advertise," https://www.the-tls.co.uk/how-to-advertise; and "Audience," https://www.theguardian.com/advertising/2014/oct/07/audience.

7. They discussed the scientific "hero" in the eighteenth century, the "mad scientist" of the nineteenth century, and the "Nazi scientist" in the middle of the twentieth century.

8. This assumption is confirmed by a nonscientist member of one of the other groups who stated, "But would we have liked the book without the topic of the Monarchs?" (GR2).

9. Mary Douglas and Aaron Wildavsky outline the view that education promotes social and ecological consciousness (1982, 1993).

10. This is a variant of the well-known "prisoner's dilemma," a model of self-contradictory ecological behavior (Moser and Dilling 2007; Bulkely 2000; Leiserowitz 2005; Norgaard 2011).

11. Results of a survey on public awareness of the need for behavioral change required by climate change indicate, similar to the reading group discussions, that personal responsibility is delegated to general actions of the local community (Bulkely 2000, 319).

12. Another illustrative example of this phenomenon is given in an interview sequence in Norgaard's ethnographic study on the societal impacts of weather changes in Norway when a proband comments, "We live in one way, and we think in another" (2011, 5).

References

Akbar, Arifa. 2012. Review of *Flight Behaviour*, by Barbara Kingsolver. *Independent*, November 17, 2012. http://www.independent.co.uk/arts-entertainment/books/reviews/flight-behaviour-by-barbara-kingsolver-8320461.html.

Angus, Ian. 2012. "*Flight Behavior*: Climate Change, Poverty and Butterflies." *Climate and Capitalism*, December 3, 2012. http://climateandcapitalism.com/2012/12/03/flight-behavior.

Atkins, Lucy. 2012. Review of *Flight Behaviour*, by Barbara Kingsolver. *Sunday Times*, October 28, 2012. https://www.thetimes.co.uk/article/flight-behaviour-by-barbara-kingsolver-nkkwhhphov5.

Baldwin Frech, Cheryl. 2014. "Book and Media Recommendations: Our Changing Planet and the Impact of Words: *Flight Behavior*." *Journal of Chemical Education* 91:951–53.

Bentley, Callan. 2013. Review of *Flight Behavior*, by Barbara Kingsolver. AGU Blogosphere, February 19, 2013. http://blogs.agu.org/mountainbeltway/2013/02/19/flight-behavior-by-barbara-kingsolver.

Bleich, David. 1986. "Intersubjective Reading." *New Literary History* 17 (3): 401–21.

Browning, Dominique. 2012. "The Butterfly Effect." Review of *Flight Behavior*, by Barbara Kingsolver. *New York Times*, November 9, 2012. http://www.nytimes.com/2012/11/11/books/review/flight-behavior-by-barbara-kingsolver.html.

Brunsson, Nils. 1989. *The Organization of Hypocrisy: Talk, Decisions, and Actions in Organizations*. Chichester, UK: Wiley.

Bulkely, Harriet. 2000. "Common Knowledge? Public Understanding of Climate Change in Newcastle, Australia." *Public Understanding of Science* 9 (3): 313–33.

Charles, Ron. 2012. "Barbara Kingsolver's Novel Approach in 'Flight Behavior.'" *Washington Post*, October 30, 2012. https://www.washingtonpost.com/entertainment/books/book-world-barbara-kingsolvers-novel-approach-in-flight-behavior/2012/10/30/4722523e-1d14-11e2-9cd5-b55c38388962story.html?utmterm=.ef6575bed5a5.

Childress, Clayton C., and Noah E. Friedkin. 2012. "Cultural Reception and Production: The Social Construction of Meaning in Book Clubs." *American Sociological Review* 77 (1): 45–68.

Clark, Alex. 2012. "Amber Warning." *Times Literary Supplement*, November 30, 2012.

Diekmann, Andreas. 1985. "Volunteer's Dilemma." *Journal of Conflict Resolution* 29 (4): 605–10.

Douglas, Mary, and Aaron Wildavsky. 1982. *Risk and Culture. An Essay on the Selection of Technological and Environmental Dangers*. Berkeley: University of California Press.

———. 1993. "Risiko und Kultur: Können wir wissen, welchen Risiken wir gegenüberstehen?" In *Riskante Technologien: Reflexion und Regulation; Einführung in die sozialwissenschaftliche Risikoforschung*, edited by Wolfgang Krohn and Georg Krücken, 113–37. Frankfurt am Main: Suhrkamp.

Dreitzel, Hans P. 1968. *Die gesellschaftlichen Leiden und das Leiden an der Gesellschaft: Vorstudien zu einer Pathologie des Rollenverhaltens*. Stuttgart: Enke.

Fish, Stanley. 1982. *Is There a Text in This Class? The Authority of Interpretive Communities*. Cambridge, MA: Harvard University Press.

Goffman, Erving. (1961) 1973. "Role Distance." In *Encounters: Two Essays on the Sociology of Interaction*, 75–135. Indianapolis: Bobbs-Merrill.

Goodbody, Axel. 2014. "Risk, Denial and Narrative Form in Climate Change Fiction: Barbara Kingsolver's *Flight Behavior* and Ilija Trojanow's *Melting Ice*." In *The Anticipation of*

Catastrophe: Environmental Risk in North American Literature and Culture, edited by Sylvia Mayer, 39–58. Heidelberg, DE: Winter.

Griswold, Wendy. 1987. "The Fabrication of Meaning: Literary Interpretation in the United States, Great Britain, and the West Indies." *American Journal of Sociology* 92 (5): 1077–1117.

Hanák, Péter. 1998. "Social Marginality and Cultural Creativity in Vienna and Budapest, 1890–1914." In *The Garden and the Workshop: Essays on the Cultural History of Vienna and Budapest*, edited by Péter Hanák, 147–77. Princeton, NJ: Princeton University Press.

Hirsch, Marianne. 1979. "The Novel of Formation as Genre: Between Great Expectations and Lost Illusions." *Genre* 12 (3): 293–311.

Hoby, Hermione. 2012. "Barbara Kingsolver: Interview." *Telegraph*, October 22, 2012. http://www.telegraph.co.uk/culture/books/bookreviews/9618239/Barbara-Kingsolver-Interview.html.

Hore, Rachel. 2012. Review of *Flight Behaviour*, by Barbara Kingsolver. *Independent*, November 4, 2012. http://www.independent.co.uk/arts-entertainment/books/reviews/flight-behaviour-by-barbara-kingsolver-8280364.html.

Jensen, Liz. 2012. Review of *Flight Behaviour*, by Barbara Kingsolver. *Guardian*, November 2, 2012. https://www.theguardian.com/books/2012/nov/02/flight-behaviour-barbara-kingsolver-review.

Jones, Beth. 2012. Review of *Flight Behaviour*, by Barbara Kingsolver. *Telegraph*, November 1, 2012. http://www.telegraph.co.uk/culture/books/fictionreviews/9635964/Flight-Behaviour-by-Barbara-Kingsolver-review.html.

Kappala-Ramsamy, Gemma. 2013. "Barbara Kingsolver: 'Motherhood Is So Sentimentalised in Our Culture.'" *Guardian*, May 11, 2013. http://www.theguardian.com/books/2013/may/11/barbara-kingsolver-interview-flight-behaviour.

Kingsolver, Barbara. 2012. *Flight Behavior*. New York: HarperCollins.

Kirchhofer, Anton, and Natalie Roxburgh. 2016. "The Scientist as 'Problematic Individual' in Contemporary Anglophone Fiction." *Zeitschrift für Anglistik und Amerikanistik* 64 (2): 149–68.

Krappmann, Lothar. 1969. *Soziologische Dimensionen der Identität: Strukturelle Bedingungen für die Teilnahme an Interaktionsprozessen*. Stuttgart: Kohlhammer.

Laclau, Ernesto. 1990. *New Reflections on the Revolution of Our Time*. London: Verso.

Laclau, Ernesto, and Chantal Mouffe. 1985. *Hegemony and Socialist Strategy: Towards a Radical Democratic Politics*. London: Verso.

Leiserowitz, Anthony A. 2005. "American Risk Perceptions: Is Climate Change Dangerous?" *Risk Analysis: An Official Publication of the Society for Risk Analysis* 25 (6): 1433–42.

Lipman, Elinor. 2012. "A Visitation of Butterflies to a Town and to a Life." *New York Times*, November 18, 2012. http://www.nytimes.com/2012/11/19/books/barbara-kingsolvers-flight-behavior.html.

Luhmann, Niklas. 1986. *Ökologische Kommunikation: Kann die moderne Gesellschaft sich auf ökologische Gefährdungen einstellen?* Opladen, DE: Westdeutscher Verlag.

Lukács, Georg. 1971. *The Theory of the Novel*. Translated by Anna Bostock. London: Merlin Press. Originally published in German in 1920.

Mattoni, Rudi. 2013. Review of *Flight Behavior*, by Barbara Kingsolver. *Journal of Research on the Lepidoptera* 46:23.

Mayer, Sylvia. 2014. "Explorations of the Controversially Real: Risk, the Climate Change Novel, and the Narrative of Anticipation." In *The Anticipation of Catastrophe: Environmental Risk in North American Literature and Culture*, edited by Sylvia Mayer, 21–38. Heidelberg, DE: Winter.

McClurg, Jocelyn. 2012. "Kingsolver Finds Heroine in 'Flight Behavior'" *USA Today*, November 13, 2012. https://www.usatoday.com/story/life/books/2013/06/28/kingsolver-finds-heroine-in-flight-behavior/2470659.

McKie, Robin. 2013. Review of *Flight Behaviour*, by Barbara Kingsolver. *Observer*, November 11, 2013. https://www.theguardian.com/books/2012/nov/11/flight-behaviour-barbara-kingsolver-review.

McPherson, Miller, Lynn Smith-Lovin, and James M. Cook. 2001. "Birds of a Feather: Homophily in Social Networks." *Annual Review of Sociology* 27 (1): 415–44.

Moretti, Franco. 2000. "The Bildungsroman as Symbolic Form." In *The Way of the World: The Bildungsroman in European Culture*, 3–13. London: Verso.

Moser, Susanna C., and Lisa Dilling. 2007. *Creating a Climate for Change: Communicating Climate Change and Facilitating Social Change*. Cambridge, UK: Cambridge University Press.

New Yorker. 2012. Review of *Flight Behavior*, by Barbara Kingsolver. December 24, 2012. https://www.newyorker.com/magazine/2012/12/24/flight-behavior.

Niven, Bill. 1997. "The Green *Bildungsroman*." In *Green Thought in German Culture: Historical and Contemporary Perspectives*, edited by Colin Riordan, 198–209. Cardiff: University of Wales Press.

Norgaard, Kari M. 2011. *Living in Denial: Climate Change, Emotions, and Everyday Life*. Cambridge, MA: MIT Press.

Park, Robert E. 1928. "Human Migration and the Marginal Man." *American Journal of Sociology* 33 (6): 881–93.

Parsons, Talcott. 1951. *The Social System*. Glencoe, IL: The Free Press.

Prengaman, Kate. 2013. "*Flight Behavior*: A Critique on the Climate Change Conversation?" *Xylem: An Ecology and Environment Blog*, March 4, 2013. https://web.archive.org/web/20130314202337/http://kateprengaman.com/flight-behavior-a-critique-on-the-climate-conversation/.

Schimank, Uwe. 1981. *Identitätsbehauptung in Arbeitsorganisationen: Individualität in der Formalstruktur*. Frankfurt am Main: Campus.

Shapiro, Arthur. 2013. Review of *Flight Behavior*, by Barbara Kingsolver. *Journal of the Lepidopterists' Society* 67 (1): 70.

Stonequist, Everett V. (1937) 1965. *The Marginal Man: A Study in Personality and Culture Conflict*. New York: Russell and Russell.

Swann, Joan, and Daniel Allington. 2009. "Reading Groups and the Language of Literary Texts: A Case Study in Social Reading." *Language and Literature* 18 (3): 247–64.

Swann, Joan, Robert Pope, and Ronald Carter. 2011. "How Reading Groups Talk About Books: A Study of Literary Reception." In *Creativity in Language and Literature: The State of the Art*, edited by Joan Swann, 217–30. Basingstoke, UK: Palgrave Macmillan.

Tobar, Hector. 2012. "Barbara Kingsolver's Got the Red State Blues in 'Flight Behavior.'" *Los Angeles Times*, November 2, 2012. http://articles.latimes.com/2012/nov/04/entertainment/la-ca-jc-barbara-kingsolver-20121104.

Trexler, Adam. 2014. "Mediating Climate Change: Ecocriticism, Science Studies, and the Hungry Tide." In *The Oxford Handbook of Ecocriticism*, edited by Greg Garrad, 205–24. Oxford, UK: Oxford University Press.

Trexler, Adam, and Adeline Johns-Putra. 2011. "Climate Change in Literature and Literary Criticism." *Wiley Interdisciplinary Reviews: Climate Change* 2 (2): 185–200.

Waffle, Van. 2013. "Flight or Flow: Where Will It Take Us?" *Speed River Journal: An Urban Naturalist's Progress*, June 22, 2013. http://www.vanwaffle.com/2013/06/22/flight-or-flow-where-will-it-take-us/#sthash.SieDov11.dpbs.

Weber, Donald C. 2013. "Entomology in Recent Fiction: *Flight Behavior*." *American Entomologist* 59 (2): 123.

Contributors

Anna Auguscik lectures at the University of Oldenburg and is a member of the Fiction Meets Science research group. She is the author of *Prizing Debate: The Fourth Decade of the Booker Prize and the Contemporary Novel in the UK*, a study of literary prizes and the waves of critical and public reactions.

Jay Clayton is William R. Kenan, Jr. Professor of English and director of the Curb Center for Art, Enterprise, and Public Policy at Vanderbilt University. He is author of a number of books about literature, science, and technology and is currently leading an NIH-funded study on the impact of culture on public attitudes toward genetic privacy.

Carol Colatrella is a professor in the School of Literature, Media, and Communication at the Georgia Institute of Technology, as well as the executive director of the Society for Literature, Science, and the Arts. Her books discuss evolutionary theory in novels, Herman Melville's fiction, and narrative representations of women engaging with science and technology.

Sina Farzin is a professor of sociology at Universität der Bundeswehr München. Her research interests include theories of society, social inclusion and exclusion, and the sociology of culture and literature.

Sonja Fücker is a researcher at the University of Hanover with a PhD in sociology from the Free University Berlin. Her interests include cultural sociology and the sociology of knowledge. In her research she focuses on the reception and effects of science communication. She is interested in how people acquire scientific knowledge in their everyday lives and the role of narrative and participatory approaches of knowledge transfer.

Susan M. Gaines is author of the science novels *Accidentals* and *Carbon Dreams* and of the nonfiction book *Echoes of Life: What Fossil Molecules Reveal About Earth History*. She has degrees in chemistry and oceanography, and is a writer in residence and initiator of the Fiction Meets Science program at the University of Bremen.

Raymond Haynes was a senior principal research scientist with the Australia Telescope National Facility and an active observational astronomer for thirty years. A fellow of the Astronomical

Society of Australia, he has coauthored a history of Australian astronomy and published 380 scientific papers. His current interests include science and scientists in film.

Roslynn D. Haynes is an associate professor at the University of New South Wales, a fellow of the Australian Academy of the Humanities, and a Fiction Meets Science fellow. She has published nine books (most recently *Desert: Nature and Culture* and *From Madman to Crime Fighter: The Scientist in Western Culture*), book chapters, and journal articles.

Luz María Hernández Nieto is a researcher and lecturer at the Autonomous University of San Luis Potosí in Mexico. She holds a master's degree in interdisciplinary media studies from Bielefeld University, where she also obtained her doctoral degree with a thesis on the representation of science in animated series for children.

Emanuel Herold holds degrees in philosophy, English studies, and social theory. He completed his PhD in sociology at the University of Hamburg and published his thesis, "Utopien in utopienfernen Zeiten," in 2020. He is now working for the Green Party of Germany on European affairs and economic policy.

Karin Hoepker is an associate professor of North American studies at Friedrich-Alexander-Universität, Erlangen-Nürnberg, Germany. Her research focuses on literature and the life sciences, science fiction, and the narrative form of the novel. Her current project investigates the emergence of risk and the function of fiction in US antebellum literature.

Anton Kirchhofer is a professor of English literature at Oldenburg University and a founding director of Fiction Meets Science. He specializes in Anglophone narrative fiction, including the media and the cultural settings and discursive environments of literature. Recent publications include the coedited *Precarious Alliances: Cultures of Participation in Print and Other Media* (2016).

Antje Kley is a professor of American literary studies at FAU Erlangen-Nürnberg. Her research focuses on the history and cultural functions of the US-American narrative; literature and knowledge; ethics and aesthetics; media theory; autobiography and confessional culture; and narratives of the end of life. Recent publications include *What Literature Knows: Forays into Literary Knowledge Production* (with Kai Merten).

Natalie Roxburgh is a lecturer in the Department of English and American Studies at the University of Hamburg in Germany. She researches Anglophone literature at the interstices of science and economics, and her current book project rethinks aesthetic disinterestedness in the nineteenth century.

Uwe Schimank is a professor of sociological theory at the University of Bremen. His research interests include theories of modern society, organizational studies, science, and higher education studies.

Sherryl Vint is a professor of media, cultural studies, and English at the University of California, Riverside, directing Speculative Fictions and Cultures of Science. She has published *Bodies of Tomorrow, Animal Alterity, The Wire*, and *Science Fiction: A Guide to the Perplexed*. She is an editor of *Science Fiction Studies, Science Fiction Film and Television*, and *Science and Popular Culture*.

Peter Weingart is professor emeritus of sociology and science policy at the University of Bielefeld, Germany, and a cofounder of the Fiction Meets Science research collaborative. He is a research fellow at CREST at Stellenbosch University (South Africa) and a member of the Berlin-Brandenburg Academy of Sciences as well as the Academy of Engineering Sciences (acatech).

Index

alchemists, 37–40, 56, 63, 68, 71, 77
Aleutian trilogy (Jones), 185
"Algorithms for Love, The" (Liu), 182–83
alien species, 186–88
All Over Creation (Ozeki), 22
Altmann, Jeanne, 132
Amazing Stories (magazine), 175–76
Anderson, Kurt, *Turn of the Century*, 26
Anil's Ghost (Ondaatje), 81
Ann Veronica (Wells), 4
Anthropocene, 10, 32, 179, 190, 191
artificial intelligence (AI), 22, 26–28, 179–83
Asimov, Isaac, 7
Astounding Science Fiction (magazine), 176
Attenborough, David, 10
Atwood, Margaret
  Handmaid's Tale, The, 105, 108–9, 195
  MaddAddam, 23, 102, 107, 109, 110, 168
  In Other Worlds, 107, 109
  speculative fiction, views on, 101–2, 104–7, 178
  Year of the Flood, The, 31, 102, 107, 109
  See also *Oryx and Crake* (Atwood)
Auburn, David, *Proof*, 90
Aurora (Robinson), 196n7

Bacigalupi, Paolo
  Water Knife, The, 189–90
  Windup Girl, The, 29
Bacon, Francis, 2, 37–39
Ballard, J. G., 7, 29, 177
Barrett, Andrea, *Ship Fever*, 24
Bear, Greg
  Darwin's Children, 212
  Darwin's Radio, 201, 209–14
Beautiful Mind, A (Nasar), 90
Beggars trilogy (Kress), 184

Big Bang Theory, The (television sitcom), 69–70
"big science," 46–47
bildungsroman, 224–26
bio-objects 200–14
  in *Darwin's Radio* (Bear), 210–12
  defined, 200–1
  in *Jurassic Park* (Crichton), 204–6, 208, 212–13
  in *Prey* (Crichton), 201, 208–9, 212–13
biotechnology, 162, 165–66, 200, 202, 203, 210, 212, 214. See also *Oryx and Crake* (Atwood)
book clubs. *See* reception of science novels
Born in Exile (Gissing), 4
Bourdieu, Pierre, 12
Boyd, William. See *Brazzaville Beach* (Boyd)
Boyle, Robert, 38–39
Brave New World (Huxley), 108
Brazzaville Beach (Boyd)
  gender issues, 127, 131–34, 142, 144
  risks to scientists, 78, 80–81, 87, 90, 94
  stereotypes of scientists, 60, 66–68
Broderick, Damien, *Reading by Starlight*, 199
Bug, The (Ullman), 27
Bush, Vannevar, 45
Butler, Octavia, 7, 29
Byatt, A. S., *A Whistling Woman*, 127, 129–31, 142
Byers, Michael, *Long for This World*, 24, 88–89

Campbell, John W., 176
Canin, Ethan, *A Doubter's Almanac*, 95–96
Cantor's Dilemma (Djerassi), 60
capitalism, 32, 109–10, 116, 119, 157–58, 204. *See also* economization of science

Carbon Dreams (Gaines)
  climate change, 29–33, 159
  gender issues, 127, 134–37, 142, 144
  news media and scientists, 30, 135
  research funding, 148, 151, 158–59, 167
Carson, Rachel, 9
Cavendish, Margaret, 2–3, 128
chaos theory, 94, 204–5, 213. *See also* mathematicians in fiction
ChickieNobs, 102, 108, 112–17
Circle, The (Eggers), 27–29
Clarke, Arthur C., 7
cli-fi. *See* climate fiction
climate change
  news media coverage, 9–10
  societal risk and, 10, 48–49 230
  See also climate fiction
climate fiction, 22, 29–34
  economization in, 151–60, 164–65, 167–69
  and science fiction (SF), 29, 119, 188–94
  societal risk and, 29–32, 186–87
  terraforming in, 190–93
  See also Carbon Dreams (Gaines); *Flight Behavior* (Kingsolver); *Science in the Capital* trilogy (Robinson); *State of Fear* (Crichton)
Cloud Atlas (Mitchell), 23
communalism, 161
Conrad, Joseph, 6, 139
consilience, 34
Cosmos (Humboldt), 79
Cosmos (television documentary), 9
Country Doctor, A (Orne), 127
Crichton, Michael
  Jurassic Park, 201–9, 212–13
  Next, 23, 24–25, 26
  Prey, 201, 205–9, 212–13, 215n7
  State of Fear, 29, 60–62, 67
Crick, Francis, 128
Cryptonomicon (Stephenson), 26
Curie, Marie, 128
Curie, Pierre, 128
cyberspace, 178

Darwin, Charles, *On the Origin of Species*, 4
Darwin's Children (Bear), 212
Darwin's Radio (Bear), 201, 209–14
Davy, Humphry, 4
Description of a New World, Called the Blazing World, The (Cavendish), 2–3

Dickens, Charles, *The Mudfog Papers*, 3
Disappearing Number, A (McBurney), 94
disciplines, scientific, 5, 40–43
Djerassi, Carl, *Cantor's Dilemma*, 60
Don Juan, or The Love of Geometry (Frisch), 91
Doubter's Almanac, A (Canin), 95–96
Doxiadis, Apostolos, *Uncle Petros and Goldbach's Conjecture*, 90
Dr. Breen's Practice (Howell), 127
Dr. Zay (Phelps), 127
Dudman, Clare, *Wegener's Jigsaw*, 78–80
dystopia, 101, 104–5, 120n6. *See also Oryx and Crake* (Atwood)

Echo Maker, The (Powers), 88
ecology. *See* climate fiction; environmental issues
economization of science, 63–64, 77, 148–72
  academic capitalism, 149, 160–63
  business interests, 149, 157–60
  competition, 149, 153–57, 163
  defined, 47–48, 148
  facets of, overview, 149
  homo academicus-oeconomicus, 149, 163–67
  societal risk and, 63–64
  underfinancing, 149–53
  See also Oryx and Crake (Atwood)
Eggers, David, *The Circle*, 27–29
Einsamkeit und Freiheit (Humboldt), 50
Einstein, Albert, 44
Ein tiefer Fall (Kegel), 148, 152, 157, 167
Eliot, George, 4, 226
Entanglement (Singh), 32–34
environmental issues
  and Anthropocene, 179
  and economization, 158
  in *Oryx and Crake*, 116, 119
  in SF, 186–94
  and societal risk, 49
  See also climate fiction
"Eros, Philia, Agape" (Swirsky), 180–83
Ethics in/of science, 63–65, 68, 78, 83–89, 97–98.
  Atwood, Margaret on, 106, 118
  economization and, 157, 162–67
  gender and, 139–40
  genomics and, 24, 26, 116–18

history, 3, 8, 44–45
  and SF, 187–88, 190, 195, 205, 215
  ethos of science, 152, 161–62, 166, 167
eugenics, 25–26, 64–65, 83
Eugenides, Jeffrey, *Middlesex*, 24
evolution, 3, 4, 6, 22, 28, 69, 129, 209–12
Ex Machina (film), 180
Experimental Heart (Rohn), 82, 85–86

Fable of the Bees (Mandeville), 165
Falling Sky, The (Goldschmidt), 90, 148, 151, 167
Faulkner, W., 144
Faust (Goethe), 127
Felski, Rita, 12, 97
Female Man, The (Russ), 177
feminist science studies, 126–27, 141, 144–45.
  See also gender; women scientists
Feynman, Richard, 10
Fifty Degrees Below (Robinson), 30, 148, 168
films, science in, 66–67, 94, 180, 202
First Class Man, A (Freeman), 94
Flaubert, Gustave, 11
Flight Behavior (Kingsolver), 11, 29, 218–47
  Brower, Lincoln, 229
  climate change in, 218–27
  reviews, 227–34
  science communication and, 218–27, 228, 230–32, 233–34, 242–44
  social resonance of, 218–19, 233–34, 242–44
  See also reception of science novels
Flood, The (Gee), 31
Forty Signs of Rain (Robinson), 30, 148, 153, 159–61
Foucault, Michel, 211
Fowler, Karen Joy, *We Are All Completely Beside Ourselves*, 11
Frankenstein (Shelley), 3, 207–8
Frankenstein as archetype, 58, 63, 64, 66, 79, 89, 127, 202
Franklin, Rosalind, 128
fraud, 60, 83–85, 142, 152–53, 155–56
Freeman, David, *A First Class Man*, 94
French Mathematician, The (Petsinis), 90–91
Frisch, Max, *Don Juan, or The Love of Geometry*, 91

Gaines, Susan M. See *Carbon Dreams* (Gaines)
Galatea 2.2 (Powers), 26, 27–28

Galois, Évariste, 91
Garland, Alex, *Ex Machina* (film), 180
Gaskell, Elizabeth, *Wives and Daughters*, 4
Gee, Maggie, *The Flood*, 31
gender
  of artificial intelligence (AI), 179–83
  and genomics, 184–87
  mad scientist stereotype and, 89
  and scientific knowledge, 143–44
  See also feminist science studies; women scientists
Generosity (Powers), 22, 24, 148, 162, 165–67
genesis amnesia, 212
genomics, 21–26, 65, 83–89, 165–66, 179, 184–88
  in *Oryx and Crake* (Atwood), 102–4, 108–9, 111, 113–17, 119
  See also eugenics
Gernsback, Hugo, 175–76
Ghosh, Amitav, *The Hungry Tide*, 78, 81–82
Gibson, William, *Neuromancer*, 178
Gilbert, Elizabeth, *The Signature of All Things*, 127, 128–29, 141
Gissing, George, *Born in Exile*, 4
global warming. See climate change
Godwin, Francis, *The Man in the Moone*, 2
Goethe, *Faust*, 127
Gold Bug Variations, The (Powers), 21, 24, 25
Goldschmidt, Pippa, *The Falling Sky*, 90, 148, 151, 167
Goldstein, Rebecca
  Mind-Body Problem, The, 90, 94–95
  Properties of Light, 66–68, 90, 92–93
Goodall, Jane, 80–81, 132
Goodman, Allegra. See *Intuition* (Goodman)
Gould, Stephen Jay, 10, 210
Gravity's Rainbow (Pynchon), 195
Great Bay, The (Pendell), 30
Gulliver's Travels (Swift), 3

Haber, Fritz, 44
Hahn, Otto, 44
Handmaid's Tale, The (Atwood), 105, 108–9, 195
Haraway, Donna, 144
Harding, Sandra, 141, 214
hard SF, 177, 194–95. *See also* science fiction (SF)
Hardy, Thomas, *Two on a Tower*, 4

Index

Hauptman, Ira, *Partition*, 94
Heart of Darkness (Conrad), 139
Heinlein, Robert A., 104, 176
Heisenberg, Werner, 93
Her (film), 180
Herschel, Caroline, 128
homo academicus-oeconomicus, 149, 163–67
Honest Look, The (Rohn), 60, 86–87, 148, 152, 162, 167
Howell, William Dean, *Dr. Breen's Practice*, 127
Humboldt, Alexander von, 78, 79
Humboldt, Wilhelm von, 41, 50
Hungry Tide, The (Ghosh), 78, 81
Hunt, Timothy, 127
Hutchins, Scott, *A Working Theory of Love*, 27, 28
Huxley, Aldous, *Brave New World*, 108

Indian Clerk, The (Leavitt), 94
information technology (IT). *See* artificial intelligence (AI)
In Other Worlds (Atwood), 107, 109
Intuition (Goodman)
   economization of science, 148, 150–52, 154–56, 161, 164, 167
   ethical risks for scientists, 84–85
   gender issues, 127, 136–39, 142
   stereotypes of scientists, 59–60
Ishiguro, Kazuo, *Never Let Me Go*, 23
Island of Doctor Moreau, The, 202

James, Henry, 6
Jewett, Sarah Orne, *A Country Doctor*, 127
Jones, Gwyneth, 184–86, 188
Jurassic Park (Crichton), 201–9, 212–13
Jurassic Park (film), 202

Kapur, Jagat Narain, *Ramanujan's Miracles*, 94
Kegel, Bernhard, *Ein tiefer Fall*, 148, 152, 157, 167
Kehlmann, Daniel, *Measuring the World*, 78, 79
Keller, Evelyn Fox, 143–44
Kepler, Johannes, 2
Kim Possible (television series), 68–69
Kingsolver, Barbara, 1, 97, 229, 233. *See also Flight Behavior* (Kingsolver)
Kirby, David A., 54–55

Klass, Perri, *Recombinations*, 22
knowledge society, 50, 236
Kress, Nancy
   Beggars trilogy, 184
   Nothing Human, 186–88

lab lit, 11
Laboratory Life (Latour and Woolgar), 10, 85, 210
Langton, Christophe G., 215n5
Large Hadron Collider, 51n6
Latour, Bruno, 85, 210
Lawrence, D. H., 6
Leavitt, David, *The Indian Clerk*, 94
Le Guin, Ursula K., 7, 29, 105, 106
Liebig, Justus, 41–42
Life (Jones), 184–86, 188
Life and Adventures of Peter Wilkins (Paltock), 3
Linnaeus, *Systema Naturae*, 40
Lippmann, Walter, 57, 58
Liu, Ken, "The Algorithms for Love," 182–83
Long for This World (Byers), 24, 88–89
Lorenz, Edward, 94
Love and Mr Lewisham (Wells), 4
Luhmann, Niklas, 57–59, 70–71, 218–19
Lyell, Charles, 4, 129

Machines Like Me (McEwan), 27
MaddAddam (Atwood), 23, 102, 109, 110, 168
"mad scientist." *See* stereotypes
Mandel, Emily St. John, *Station Eleven*, 195
Mandeville, Bernard, *Fable of the Bees*, 165
Manhattan Project, 44–45, 46
Man in the Moone, The (Godwin), 2
Man Who Knew Infinity, The (film), 94
marketization of science. *See* economization of science
Mars Trilogy (Robinson), 190, 191
Marsupilami (television series), 68
mathematicians in fiction, 90–96. See also *Brazzaville Beach* (Boyd); *Jurassic Park* (Crichton)
Matilda effect, 137
Matthew effect, 87
Mawer, Simon, *Mendel's Dwarf*, 11, 23, 25–26, 65, 67, 83
McBurney, Simon, *A Disappearing Number*, 94

McCaffery, Larry, *Storming the Reality Studio*, 177
McClintock, Barbara, 128, 196n4
McEuen, Paul L., 110
McEwan, Ian
  Machines Like Me, 27
  Saturday, 24
  Solar, 22, 29, 55, 87–88, 148, 164–65, 167, 169
McMahon, Thomas, *Principles of American Nuclear Chemistry*, 22
Measuring the World (Kehlmann), 78, 79
media. *See* films; news; popular science; reception of science novels; television
Mendel, Gregor, 25, 26
Mendel's Dwarf (Mawer), 11, 23, 25–26, 65, 67, 83
Metamorphoses of Science Fiction (Suvin), 199
Middlemarch (Eliot), 4
Middlesex (Eugenides), 24
Miéville, China, 105
Mill on the Floss, The (Eliot), 226
Mind-Body Problem, The (Goldstein), 90, 94–95
Mitchell, David, *Cloud Atlas*, 23
Mitchell, Maria, 128
Moore v. Regents of the University of California (1990), 24
morality. *See* ethics in/of science
Moylan, Tom, 170
Mudfog Papers, The (Dickens), 3

Nasar, Sylvia, *A Beautiful Mind*, 90
Nash, John Forbes, 90
National Institutes of Health, 43, 46, 153. *See also Intuition* (Goodman)
National Science Foundation (NSF), 45, 126. *See also Forty Signs of Rain* (Robinson)
Neuromancer (Gibson), 178
Never Let Me Go (Ishiguro), 23
New Atlantis, The (Bacon), 2, 39
New Public Management (NPM), 154–57, 163
news media, science coverage, 42, 48, 49–50. *See also Flight Behavior* (Kingsolver)
Newton, Isaac, 39
Next (Crichton), 23, 24–25
1984 (Orwell), 105, 176–77
Nothing Human (Kress), 186–88
novum, 199–200. *See also* bio-object

Novum Organon (Bacon), 39
nuclear science, 8, 10, 22, 44–45, 48–49, 176, 179. *See also* Manhattan Project

Observations upon Experimental Philosophy (Cavendish), 2, 3
Odds Against Tomorrow (Rich), 29, 31
Oldenburg, Henry, 39
Ondaatje, Michael, *Anil's Ghost*, 81
On the Origin of Species (Darwin), 4
Oppenheimer, Robert, 44, 45
Organisation for Economic Co-operation and Development (OECD), 46, 57
Orwell, George, 105, 176–77
Oryx and Crake (Atwood), 101–25
  ChickieNobs, 102, 108, 112–17
  dystopian science and, 102–4
  economization of science in, 63–64, 148, 162–63, 166–68
  as speculative fiction, 101–2, 104–7
  stereotypes of scientists, 62–65, 67
  See also reception of science novels
Overstory, The (Powers), 29
Ozeki, Ruth, *All Over Creation*, 22

Paltock, Robert, *Life and Adventures of Peter Wilkins*, 3
Park, Robert E., 225
Partition (Hauptman), 94
Patchett, Ann, *State of Wonder*, 11, 127, 139–41, 142, 148, 159
patents, 39, 148, 160
Pendell, Dale, *The Great Bay*, 30
Perfect Life (Pollack), 11
Peter, Lothar, 149, 163
Petsinis, Tom, *The French Mathematician*, 90–91
Phelps, Elizabeth Stuart, *Dr. Zay*, 127
physical danger. *See* scientists at risk
Physical Society of London, 42
Physics, 5, 23, 44, 46–47, 48
  in *Big Bang Theory, The*, 69
  gender and, 126, 127, 143–44
  in *Properties of Light*, 66, 92–93
Pinker, Steven, 97
plagiarism, 83–94, 87–88, 128
Plowing the Dark (Powers), 26
policy, science, 10, 43–46, 48–49, 62, 65, 168, 212, 214
Pollack, Eileen, *Perfect Life*, 11

Index

popular science, 1, 4, 5, 9, 42–43. *See also* science communication
posthuman embodiment, 186–88
post-modern fiction, 11–12, 177
Powerbook, The (Winterson), 26–27
Powers, Richard
　Echo Maker, The, 88, 96–97
　Galatea 2.2, 26, 27–28
　Generosity, 22, 24, 148, 162, 165–67
　Gold Bug Variations, The, 21, 24, 25
　Overstory, The, 29
　Plowing the Dark, 26
Prey (Crichton), 201, 205–9, 212–13
　swarm intelligence, 206, 208
　See also bio-objects
Principles of American Nuclear Chemistry (McMahon), 22
Principles of Geology (Lyell), 4
"projective realism," 170
Proof (Auburn), 90
Properties of Light (Goldstein), 66–68, 90, 92–93
public engagement with science, 10–11, 47–50, 161. *See also* economization of science; popular science; reception of science novels; science communication
Pynchon, Thomas, *Gravity's Rainbow*, 195

Quantum Leap (television series), 55

Ramanujan, Srinivasa, 93
Ramanujan (film), 94
Ramanujan's Miracles (Kapur), 94
Reading by Starlight (Broderick), 199
reception of science novels, 218–19
　Flight Behavior (Kingsolver), 227–44
　Oryx and Crake (Atwood), 102, 105–19
　in reading groups, 234–44
　in science journals, 107, 110, 112–13, 115, 228–29
　in social media, 27, 50, 58, 102, 108, 111, 127
Recombinations (Klass), 22
Rich, Nathaniel, *Odds Against Tomorrow*, 29, 31
risk. *See also* scientists at risk; societal and social risk
　narrative, 30, 110, 228
　society, 10, 29, 78
Robinson, Kim Stanley, 105, 167
　Aurora, 196n7
　ecological themes of, 179, 189

Fifty Degrees Below, 30, 148, 168
Forty Signs of Rain, 30, 148, 153, 159–61
Mars Trilogy, 190, 191
　Science in the Capital trilogy, 29, 30–32, 33, 160, 168–70, 190–91
　Sixty Days and Counting, 30, 148, 168 2312, 191–94
robotics. *See* artificial intelligence
Rohn, Jennifer L.
　Experimental Heart, 82, 85–86
　Honest Look, The, 60, 86–87, 148, 152, 162, 167
role distancing, 235–38, 240, 242
Roosevelt, Franklin Delano, 44
Rose, Hilary, 134
Royal Society (Britain), 2–3, 38–39
Russ, Joanna, *The Female Man*, 177

Sacks, Oliver, *The Man Who Mistook His Wife for a Hat*, 88
Sagan, Carl, *Contact*, 127
Salvage the Bones (Ward), 29
Saturday (McEwan), 24
Schätzing, Frank, *The Swarm*, 198
schemata, stereotypes as, 57–59, 70–71. *See also* stereotypes
Schiebinger, Londa, 132
Schismatrix (Sterling), 186
science communication, 70, 205, 210. *See also Flight Behavior* (Kingsolver); popular science
science fiction (SF)
　artificial intelligence (AI) and robotics, 22, 26–28, 179–83
　climate change, 22–23, 29–34, 188–94
　definitions of, 101–2, 105–6, 175–79, 195, 213
　elements of, 200
　genomics and genetic engineering, 21–26, 184–88
　hard SF, 177, 194–95
　history of, 7–8, 11, 175–79
　novum concept, 199
　speculative fiction and, 102, 104–6, 176, 195
　subject-object relations, 198–200
　worldbuilding, 7, 178–79, 185–86, 188, 191, 194
　See also bio-objects; *specific titles*
Science in the Capital trilogy (Robinson), 29, 30–32, 33, 160, 168–70, 190–91
science journals, 5, 42. *See also* reception of science novels

Index

science, organization of, 37–50
scientific associations, 39, 42. *See also* National Science Foundation (NSF)
scientific community, professionalization of, 39–40, 59
scientific literacy, 1, 9, 176, 241. *See also* public engagement with science
scientific misconduct, 83–86, 157, 162
scientific revolution, 37–38
scientists at risk, 77–100, 167–70, 211
  academic capitalism and, 157–63
  competition and, 153–57
  ethical challenges and, 78, 83–89
  gender and, 126–45
  homo academicus-oeconomicus and, 149, 163–67
  mental health and, 78, 89–97
  physical danger and, 78–82
  research funding and, 149–53, 157–60
Sea Around Us, The (Carson), 9
Search, The (Snow), 83
Shadwell, Thomas, *The Virtuoso*, 3
Shelley, Mary, *Frankenstein*, 3, 127, 202, 207–8
Ship Fever (Barrett), 24
Shteyngart, Gary, *Super Sad True Love Story*, 27
Signature of All Things, The (Gilbert), 127–29, 141
Silent Spring (Carson), 9
Singh, Vandana, *Entanglement*, 32–34
Sixty Days and Counting (Robinson), 30, 148, 168
Slonczewski, Joan, 178
Smith, Zadie, *White Teeth*, 22
Snow, C. P.
  Search, The, 83
  "two cultures," 7, 176
Snow Crash (Stephenson), 178
social class. *See Flight Behavior* (Kingsolver)
social contract for science, 47–49
societal and social risk, 10, 12, 48–49
  in science novels 22–32, 63, 110
  scientists and, 58, 77–78
  in SF, 168, 186–87, 203–4, 206
  See also Flight Behavior (Kingsolver); risk society
Solar (McEwan), 22, 29, 55, 87–88, 148, 164–65, 167, 169
Somnium (Kepler), 2

speculative fiction, 101–25
  Atwood on, 104–7
  defined, 101–2
  Heinlein on, 176
  science fiction and, 102, 104–6, 176, 195
  See also Oryx and Crake (Atwood)
Star Trek (film), 199–200
State of Fear (Crichton), 29, 60–62, 67
State of Wonder (Patchett), 11, 127, 139–42, 148, 159
Station Eleven (Mandel), 195
Stephenson, Neal, 26, 178
stereotypes
  and complex representations of science, 56–57, 70–71
  definition and cognitive role, 57–58
  "mad scientist," 38, 54–57, 64, 65, 66, 68, 71, 89–90, 92, 202, 205
  media genres and, 56, 58–59
  as schemata, 57–59, 70–71
  in science novels, 59–69, 77–78
  of scientists, gender and, 80, 87, 126–27, 143
  of scientists, history of, 7, 23, 37, 51, 54–56
  of scientists in TV series, 57–62, 68–70
Sterling, Bruce, *Schismatrix*, 186
Stewart, Abigail, 143
Stone Gods, The (Winterson), 29, 105
Storming the Reality Studio (McCaffery), 177
Strassmann, Fritz, 44
Suvin, Darko, *Metamorphoses of Science Fiction*, 199
Swarm, The (Schätzing), 198
Swift, Jonathan, *Gulliver's Travels*, 3
Swirsky, Rachel, "Eros, Philia, Agape," 180–83
Systema Naturae (Linnaeus), 40
Szilard, Leo, 44

Tagore, Rabindranath, 93
technology transfer, 48, 158–59
television, science on, 9, 55, 57–62, 68–72. *See also individual names of shows*
Teller, Edward, 45
Three Mile Island, 48
Time Machine, The (Wells), 189
Tono-Bungay (Wells), 4
Traweek, Sharon, 144
Truman, Harry S., 45
Turing, Alan, 26, 27
Turn of the Century (Anderson), 26
2312 (Robinson), 191–94

"two cultures," 7, 34, 176
Two on a Tower (Hardy), 4

Ullman, Ellen, *The Bug*, 27
Uncle Petros and Goldbach's Conjecture (Doxiadis), 90
utopia, 105, 120n6, 168–70. *See also* dystopia

Vermillion Sands (Ballard), 177
Verne, Jules, 3, 7, 79, 106, 175
Virtuoso, The (Shadwell), 3
volunteer's dilemma, 240

Ward, Jesmyn, *Salvage the Bones*, 29
Water Knife, The (Bacigalupi), 189–90
Watson, James, 128
Watts, Peter, 178
We Are All Completely Beside Ourselves (Fowler), 11
Wegener, Alfred, 79–80
Wegener's Jigsaw (Dudman), 79–80
Wells, H. G., 3, 7, 175
  Ann Veronica, 4
  Love and Mr Lewisham, 4
  Time Machine, The, 189
  Tono-Bungay, 4
Whale, John, 64
Whistling Woman, A (Byatt), 127, 129–31, 142
White Teeth (Smith), 22
Wilkins, Maurice, 128
Wilson, E. O., 34

Windup Girl, The (Bacigalupi), 29
Winterson, Jeanette
  Powerbook, The, 26–27
  Stone Gods, The, 29, 105
Wise, Robert, *The Day the Earth Stood Still*, 215n1
Wives and Daughters (Gaskell), 4
women scientists, 126–47
  in *Brazzaville Beach* (Boyd), 131–34, 142, 144
  in *Carbon Dreams* (Gaines), 134–37, 142, 144
  in *Intuition* (Goodman), 137–39, 142
  mentoring and, 128, 131, 134, 135, 137–38, 143
  risk and, 80–82, 87, 96
  in *Signature of All Things, The* (Gilbert), 127–29, 141
  in *State of Wonder* (Patchett), 139–42
  stereotypes and, 80, 87, 126–27
  in *Whistling Woman, A* (Byatt), 127, 129–31, 142
  See also feminist science studies; gender
Woolf, Virginia, 6
Woolgar, Steve, 85, 210
Working Theory of Love, A (Hutchins), 27, 28
worldbuilding, 7, 178–79, 185–86, 188, 191, 194

Year of the Flood, The (Atwood), 31, 102, 107, 109

Zola, Émile, 3